Gasc Le Brun

The Translator, English into French

Salzwasser

Gasc Le Brun

The Translator, English into French

1. Auflage | ISBN: 978-3-84604-934-1

Erscheinungsort: Frankfurt, Deutschland

Erscheinungsjahr: 2020

Salzwasser Verlag GmbH

THE

TRANSLATOR,

ENGLISH INTO FRENCH.

SELECTIONS FROM THE

BEST ENGLISH PROSE WRITERS,

WITH PRINCIPLES OF TRANSLATION, IDIOMATIC PHRASES, AND NOTES.

BY

PROFS. GASC, LE BRUN, ETC. ETC.

PRINCIPLES OF TRANSLATION.

As it is necessary, in order to translate well, not only to render every word with exactness, but at the same time to preserve its value and order in a sentence, while paying due regard to the grammar, perspicuity, and harmony of the language, we shall proceed to make some suggestions upon Expression — Construction — Accuracy — Grammatical correctness — and Clearness ; and we shall conclude by offering a series of *English idiomatic phrases,* with their French translation.

I.—OF EXPRESSION.

§ 1. As each word has its peculiar import, a careful writer must be supposed not to select without a reason one word in preference to another for the embodiment of the thought which he desires to convey. It is, therefore, the true meaning and value of the expression which must be studied, in order to reproduce it with the greatest exactness.

§ 2. It often happens that the same word has different acceptations. We need not observe that we must never, like some careless students, be too hasty in adopting the first word that occurs to us, without proving that it bears on the general sense.   This would expose us to the possibility of writing phrases such as these :—

1. Bring me my horse.
   Apportez-moi mon cheval,—instead of
   Amenez-moi mon cheval.

2. She has *light* hair.
   Elle a des cheveux *légers*,—instead of
   Elle a des cheveux *blonds*.

3. Where *do you live?*
   Où *vivez-vous?*—instead of
   Où *demeurez-vous?*

4. I *know* that lady. .
   Je *sais* cette dame,—instead of
   Je *connais* cette dame.

5. *Take* that child to school.
   Prenez cet enfant à l'école,—instead of
   Menez cet enfant à l'école.
   Take this letter to the post.
   Portez cette lettre à la poste.

6. His purse is well *lined.*
   Sa bourse est bien *doublée*,—instead of
   Sa bourse est bien *garnie*.

§ 3. One English word may often externally be identical with another French word, without presenting in the least the same signification.   If the translator allows himself to be deceived by such resemblance, which occurs most frequently in words derived from the Latin, he will fall into the grossest errors, and connect incompatible words conveying no meaning in French.

For example, do not translate, *He* DETERMINED *to go*, by *Il* DÉTERMINA *d'*ALLER ; nor, *I* HEARD *of that* GENTLEMAN, by *J'*ENTENDIS *de ce* GENTILHOMME ; but say, *Il* RÉSOLUT *de* S'EN ALLER, and *J'*ENTENDIS PARLER *de ce* MONSIEUR.

As these faults occur very frequently, we shall point out some of them :—

1. They *will return* from the country, must not be translated thus, —Ils *retourneront* de la *contrée*; but, Ils *reviendront* de la *campagne*.

2. My old father is now very *altered*, must not be translated,—Mon vieux père est maintenant très-*altéré*; but, Mon vieux père est maintenant très-*changé*.

3. Have you *paid* a visit to his brother? must not be translated,—Avez-vous *payé* une visite à son frère? but, Avez-vous *rendu* une visite à son frère?

4. My *grandson* is *industrious*, must not be translated,—Mon *grand fils* est *industrieux*; but, Mon *petit-fils* est *laborieux*.

5. The history of Joseph *continued*, must not be translated,—L'histoire de Joseph *continuée*; but, *Suite* de l'histoire de Joseph.

6. I *was* born in Paris, must not be translated,—J'*étais* né à Paris; but Je *suis* né à Paris.

7. He has *married* my sister, must not be translated,—Il a *marié* ma sœur; but, Il a *épousé* ma sœur.

8. We employed twenty *laborers*, must not be translated,—Nous avons employé vingt *laboureurs*; but, Nous avons employé vingt *journaliers*.

9. She *supported* her *parents*, must not be translated,—Elle *supporta* ses *parents*; but, Elle *soutint son père et sa mère*.

10. Tell me the *time*, must not be translated,—Dites-moi le *temps*; but, Dites-moi *l'heure*.

11. She deserves your *confidence*, must not be translated,—Elle mérite votre *confidence*; but, Elle mérite votre *confiance*.

12. I will *subscribe* to that *paper*, must not be translated,—Je *souscrirai* à ce *papier*; but, Je *m'abonnerai* à ce *journal*.

13. I must make *apologies* to your grandmother, must not be translated,—Je dois faire des *apologies* à votre grand'mère; but, Je dois faire des *excuses* à votre grand'mère.

14. We heard the bells in the *distance*, must not be translated,—Nous entendîmes les cloches dans la *distance*; but, Nous entendîmes les cloches dans le *lointain*.

15. He *used* my pen, must not be translated,—Il *usa* ma plume; but, Il *se servit* de ma plume.

16. The traveller was obliged to *retrace* his steps, must not be translated,—Le voyageur fut obligé de *retracer* ses pas; but, Le voyageur fut obligé de *revenir sur* ses pas.

17. Do you know the latest *intelligence?* must not be translated,—

Connaissez-vous la dernière *intelligence?* but, Connaissez-vous les dernières *nouvelles?*

18. I bought two beautiful *copies* of Milton, must not be translated, —J'ai acheté deux belles *copies* de Milton; but, J'ai acheté deux beaux *exemplaires* de Milton.

II.—OF CONSTRUCTION.

§ 4. We call construction the order in which the words composing a sentence are arranged. This order, which is determined by the desire to place a certain idea before another, and more especially to present the cause before the effect, gives to each phrase a form which corresponds with the thought of the writer, and represents it with fidelity. To change the construction would always disturb the sentence, and often alter its character so completely as to render its true meaning unintelligible. For example :

Goldsmith, in speaking of the youth of Catherine I. of Russia, introduces her to us employed in the humblest occupations, for the support of her mother, and he adds : " While Catherine spun, the old woman would sit by and read some book of devotion."

If we translate — " La vieille femme s'asseyait près d'elle et lisait quelque livre de dévotion, *pendant que Catherine filait,*" we change Goldsmith's idea, who is writing the history of Catherine and not that of her mother. He wishes, therefore, to speak of her occupations in the first place, and if he adds those of the old mother, it is only to fill up the picture.

We must, therefore, translate—" *Pendant que Catherine filait,* la vieille femme était assise près d'elle et lisait quelque livre de dévotion."

§ 5. In order to aid the inexperienced in this task, we shall give a few examples of translation, embracing the most important cases :—

1. That illness proceeds *from your not eating.*
   Cette maladie vient *de ce que vous ne mangez pas.*
2. I insist *upon your going* to the sea-side.
   J'insiste *pour que vous alliez* au bord·de la mer.
3. I remember it *without your telling.*
   Je m'en souviens *sans que vous me le disiez.*
4. He laughs *at my not being able* to speak French.
   Il se moque *de ce que je ne puis* parler français.
5. *The learning* anything speedily *requires* great application.
   Pour apprendre quelque chose promptement, *il faut* une grande application.
6. Greater virtue *is required to bear* good fortune than bad.
   Il faut une plus grande vertu *pour supporter* la bonne fortune que la mauvaise.
7. *From idleness arises* neither pleasure nor advantage.
   La paresse ne produit ni plaisir ni avantage.
8. *Had he been* more prudent, he would have been more fortunate.
   S'il eût été plus prudent, il aurait *été* plus heureux.
9. *Let* all your thoughts, words, and actions be tinctured with modesty.
   Que toutes vos pensées, vos paroles et vos actions soient empreintes de modestie.
10. Those *only* are truly great who are really good.
    Ceux-là *seuls* sont vraiment grands qui sont vraiment bons ; or,
    Il n'y a de vraiment grands *que* ceux qui sont vraiment bons.
11. *These* two things cannot be disjoined : a good life and a happy death.
    Voici deux choses qu'on ne peut séparer : une bonne vie et une heureuse mort.
12. . . . . Fling away ambition ;
    By that sin fell the angels.—(Shakspeare, Henry VIII.)
    Repousse l'ambition ; *c'est* par ce péché *que* sont tombés les anges.
13. *The more* difficult a thing is, *the more* honorable.
    Plus une chose est difficile, *plus* elle est honorable.
14. *How wonderful are* the works of God !
    Que les ouvrages de Dieu *sont admirables!*

15. *It is with* the diseases of the heart *as with* those of the body.
 Il en est des maladies du cœur *comme de* celles du corps.
16. *Should that happen,* what would you do ?
 Si cela arrivait, que feriez-vous ?

§ 6. In many cases, where the English language employs the passive form, the French prefers the active, preceded by the indefinite pronoun *on.*

EXAMPLES:

1. *It is believed* that the queen will arrive next week.
 On croit que la reine arrivera la semaine prochaine.
2. *We have been told* that your father is in London.
 On nous a dit que votre père est à Londres.

§ 7. If the sentence is more precise and the subject personal, the French, instead of the passive, makes use of the reflective verb.

EXAMPLES:

1. True pleasure *is* only *to be found* in the paths of virtue.
 Le vrai plaisir ne *se trouve* que dans les sentiers de la vertu.
2. Old friends *are preserved* and new ones *are procured* by a grateful disposition.
 Les vieux amis *se conservent* et les nouveaux *s'obtiennent* par l'amabilité du caractére.
3. Great merit *is* often *concealed* under the most unpromising appearances.
 Un grand mérite *se cache souvent* sous les dehors les plus désavantageux.

§ 8. Frequently also the reflective verb is employed in the impersonal.form.

1. Many years *have elapsed.*
 Il s'est passé bien des années.
2. Great preparations *are going forward.*
 Il se fait de grands préparatifs.

III.—OF ACCURACY.

§ **9.** We have urged the necessity of finding the correct expression, and of preserving as rigorously as possible the place occupied by each word, since this is the only way of conveying exactly the writer's thought; for, without accuracy, true translation cannot be said to exist. We should never forget that a literal translation is the best, provided it accord rigorously with the genius of both languages. The text of the writer is a drawing, which ought to be rendered faithfully by reproducing it stroke by stroke; translation ought to be nothing but a faithful copy. All addition or suppression leads the reader into error.

§ **10.** A single example will explain this better than many precepts.

Here follows a passage from Miss Edgeworth, with a translation recently published in Paris:

"It is now so late in the evening, that perhaps the travellers will sleep at Dunstable instead of going on the next stage; and it is likely that whosoever gave you the guinea instead of a halfpenny, has found out their mistake by this time. All you can do is, to go and inquire for the gentleman who was reading in the chaise."

"Comme il est un peu tard, les voyageurs se sont arrêtés au prochain relais, et à cette heure celui qui vous a donné la guinée, s'est sans doute aperçu de sa méprise. Votre premier soin doit être de vous enquérir du voyageur qui lisait dans la voiture."

Il est un peu tard may be said of an hour of the day; here, on the contrary, it is already the end of the day, and this is what the author has intended to express by *in the evening*. It is, therefore, this idea which must be conveyed ; and, moreover, nothing would have been easier than to say, *Comme la soirée est déjà fort avancée.*

The travellers will sleep at Dunstable instead of going on the next stage, means, *Les voyageurs coucheront à Dunstable au lieu d'aller jusqu'au prochain relais.* The translator in writing *Les voyageurs se·sont arrêtés au prochain relais*, says quite another thing, and completely misunderstands the passage ; for the old woman would never send the children to a stage perhaps ten miles off.

The translator should not have displaced *by this time*, which was so easy to retain at the end of the sentence.

Votre premier soin bears no relation to the idea, *All you can do;* and, finally, we do not see why *gentleman* is translated by *voyageur*, and *chaise* by *voiture.*

§ 11. Here is the same extract translated according to the principles we have laid down—

"La soirée est maintenant si avancée, que peut-être les voyageurs coucheront à Dunstable au lieu d'aller jusqu'au prochain relais ; et il est vraisemblable que celui qui vous a donné la guinée au lieu d'un sou, s'est aperçu de sa méprise à l'heure qu'il est. Tout ce que vous pouvez faire, c'est d'aller vous enquérir du monsieur qui lisait dans la chaise."

§ 12. It sometimes happens that we are puzzled by a word which does not permit us to preserve the English construction. In such cases we must have recourse to an expedient which demands a profound knowledge of both languages. We substitute one part of speech for another, and either give an adjective for a noun, or a noun for an adjective. Example : *How I love the fresh green fields and the shady trees !* It would here be impossible to follow the order of the words and to translate literally, *Combien j'aime les* FRAIS VERTS *champs et les* OMBREUX *arbres !*

But by means of the proceeding we have just indicated, we can say correctly, and even elegantly, without making any change in the order of the words : *Combien j'aime la* FRAÎCHE VERDURE *des champs et* L'OMBRE *des arbres !*

IV.—OF GRAMMATICAL CORRECTNESS.

§ 13. It is evident that, if the desire of accuracy ought not to allow the translator to forget the peculiarities and idioms of his own language, still less ought it to permit him to neglect grammatical correctness, from which no one can depart without offending common sense. Yet correctness is the chief stumbling-block in the way of those who practise translation. The habit of speaking their own language induces them to think, at first, that the forms which are so familiar to them are to be found in the syntax of another tongue also ; but this fallacy leads them to serious mistakes. To instance all these errors would demand a summary of the rules of French grammar, which does not come within the plan of these preliminary remarks.

There are certain difficulties which often present themselves, and upon which we feel compelled to dwell a little longer.

We shall class them according to the parts of speech.

PRONOUNS.

§ 14. We cannot make use in French as in English of the ellipsis of the adjective, when the subject and verb are expressed. We must not, therefore, translate, *Our cousins are rich but we are not,* by *Nos cousins sont riches, mais nous ne sommes pas.* It is necessary to recall the notion of the adjective by the invariable pronoun *le*, which answers to the English *it*, and in this case stands nearly for *so.* We must therefore say, *Nos cousins sont riches, mais nous ne* LE *sommes pas.*

§ 15. The pronoun *cela* is never used before an adjective followed by a verb in the infinitive mood. Do not then translate, *We have found* IT *necessary to put off the meeting,* by *Nous avons jugé* CELA *nécessaire de remettre la réunion,* but simply say, *Nous avons jugé nécessaire de remettre la réunion.*

§ 16. At the beginning of a sentence, before the verb *être* followed by an adjective, *it* is translated by *il,* if the adjective is followed by the preposition *de,* or by the conjunction *que.*

EXAMPLES:

IT *is just to pay your debts,*
IL *est juste* DE *payer vos dettes.*
IT *is just that you should pay him.*
IL *est juste* QUE *vous le payiez.*

It would be a great mistake to say, *C'est juste* DE *payer vos dettes;* or, *C'est juste* QUE *vous le payiez.*

But, if the adjective stands alone, then translate *it* by *ce.*

EXAMPLES:

You paid him; IT *was just.*
Vous l'avez payé; C'*etait juste.*

§ 17. If a Cardinal number, an Adverb of quantity, or an Indefinite pronoun, stand by themselves in English, never translate them without preceding the verb in the sentence by the pronoun *en.*

Do not therefore say :

    1. *You have five apples, but* SHE HAS TWENTY.
    Vous avez cinq pommes, mais ELLE A VINGT.

Neither say :

    2. *I received the peaches, but* YOU SENT TOO MANY; *it would have been sufficient to* HAVE SENT A FEW. *J'ai reçu les péches, mais* VOUS AVEZ ENVOYÉ TROP; *il suffsait d'*ENVOYER QUELQUES-UNES.

But translate thus :

    1. *Vous avez cinq pommes, mais elle* EN *a* VINGT.
    2. *J'ai reçu les péches, mais vous* EN *avez envoyé* TROP; *il suffisait d'*EN *envoyer* QUELQUES-UNES.

§ 18. In English, the antecedent of the Relative pronoun is often preceded by the Demonstrative pronoun *that, those.* In French, the Article alone is sufficient.

This passage in Shakspeare, *Cherish* THOSE *hearts that hate thee,* ought not to be translated, *Chéris* CES *cœurs qui te haïssent,* but *Chéris* LES *cœurs qui te haïssent.*

Translate in the same way the following sentence :

    They pray to THESE *idols which can neither hear, nor see, nor give them any help.*
    Ils prient DES *idoles qui ne peuvent ni les entendre, ni les voir, ni leur donner aucun secours.*

§ 19. The suppression of the Demonstrative *ce* before *qui* and *que* is impossible in French. Translate then—*You must do* WHAT *is right,* and *He did* WHAT *I told him,* by *Vous devez faire* CE QUI *est bien;* *Il a fait* CE QUE *je lui ai dit.*

§ 20. Do not say : *A friend of* MINE, *Un ami* DES MIENS; but say, *Un* DE MES AMIS.

Translate in the same way : *A cousin* OF OURS, *Un* DE

NOS COUSINS ; *Two relations* OF YOURS, *Deux* DE VOS PA-
RENTS, etc.

§ 21. In English, an adjective is never used by itself
in the vocative ; it always follows the pronoun. Example :
YE WICKED, *fear the last day.*   In French we cannot say,
VOUS MÉCHANTS, *craignez le dernier jour.*   The pronoun
is always suppressed, as the adjective acquires the power
of a substantive ; and we say, MÉCHANTS, *craignez le dernier jour.*

§ 22. Do not translate, SUCH *a bad man,* by *Un* TEL
méchant homme, because an indefinite adjective cannot
modify an adjective of quality, as that is the office of the
adverb.   Say, therefore, with an adverb, *Un* SI *méchant
homme.*

VERBS.

§ 23. Some verbs which are *active* in English, are
neuter in French.   In such cases it would be a great mistake to translate their passive form literally.

Do not therefore say :

> 1. *I* WAS *very much* PLEASED *with that pupil.*
> *Je* FUS *très-*PLUS *avec cet élève.*

Nor :

> 2. *My letter* HAS *not* BEEN ANSWERED.
> *Ma lettre n'*A *pas* été repondue.

But say :

> 1. *Cet élève m'*A *beaucoup* PLU.
> 2. *On n'*A *pas* répondu *à ma lettre.*

PREPOSITIONS.

§ 24. The prepositions, it will be remembered, serve to
establish a connection between nouns and other words.

But, as these connections are not always considered from the same point of view in all languages, it follows that there exist considerable diversities in the meaning of prepositions. Now, as these little words recur in almost every sentence, it is evident that if we do not take care to employ them correctly, we shall fall into mistakes as frequent as they are strange.

Here are some cases which most commonly mislead students :

For.

§ 25. Do not always translate *For* by *Pour*.

EXAMPLES:

1. They were at Windsor *for* three days.
   Ils ont été à Windsor *pendant* trois jours.
2. I will not come *for* a week.
   Je ne reviendrai pas *d'ici* à huit jours.
3. He inquired *for* you.
   Il a demandé *après* vous.
4. Do it *for* charity.
   Faites cela *par* charité.
5. *For* pity, *For* fear, *For* instance.
   Par pitié, *Par* crainte, *Par* exemple.
6. Champion *for* liberty.
   Champion *de* la liberté.

With.

§ 26. Do not always translate *With* by *Avec*.

EXAMPLES:

1. We must be contented *with* little.
   Nous devons être contents *de* peu.
2. The table was covered *with* plate.
   La table était couverte *d'*argenterie.
3. They fought *with* swords.
   Ils se battirent *à* l'épée.
4. His name begins *with* a P.
   Son nom commence *par* un P.

5. To fill a bottle *with* wine.
Remplir une bouteille *de* vin.
6. To starve *with* hunger.
Mourir *de* faim.
7. I am tired *with* walking.
Je suis fatigué *de* marcher.
8. She is gifted *with* a good memory.
Elle est douée *d'*une bonne mémoire.
9. Do not meddle *with* that affair.
Ne vous mêlez pas *de* cette affaire.
10. His horses cost him, one *with* the other, forty pounds.
Ses chevaux lui coûtent, l'un *dans* l'autre, quarante livres.

In.

§ 27. Do not always translate *In* by *Dans.*

EXAMPLES:

1. Is he arrived *in* time ?
Est-il arrivé *à* temps ?
2. *In* a few minutes.
En quelques instants.
3. *In* the fifteenth century.
Au quinzième siécle.
4. *In* the reign of Tiberius.
Sous le règne de Tibère.
5. He lived *in* the country.
Il demeurait *à* la campagne.
6. My servant participated *in* that plot.
Mon domestique avait pris part *à* ce complot.
7. You must begin *in* that manner.
Vous devez commencer *de* cette manière.
8. You spend all your time *in* talking.
Vous perdez tout votre temps *à* causer.
9. He was five years *in* my service.
Il fut cinq ans *à* mon service.
10. The Spanish hats are much *in* fashion.
Les chapeaux espagnols sont fort *à* la mode.
11. My sister paints *in* oil.
Ma sœur peint *à* l'huile.

12. To be *in* the sun.
    Etre *au* soleil.
13. She was the best spinner *in* the parish.
    C'était la meilleure fileuse *de* la paroisse.
14. It was five *in* the morning.
    Il était cinq heures *du* matin.

By.

§ 28. Do not always translate *By* by *Par.*

EXAMPLES:

1. He works too much *by* candlelight.
   Il travaille trop *à* la chandelle.
2. Sit down *by my side.*
   Asseyez-vous *à côté de moi.*
3. What time is it *by* your watch ?
   Quelle heure est-il *à* votre montre ?
4. I must come back *by* seven o'clock.
   Il faut que je revienne *à* sept heures.
5. You will oblige me *by* writing a note.
   Vous m'obligerez *en* écrivant un petit mot.
6. They began *by* counting.
   Ils commencèrent *à* compter.
7. *By* studying constantly you will improve.
   A force d'étudier vous ferez des progrès.
8. She keeps money *by* herself.
   Elle garde de l'argent *par devers* elle.

To and At.

§ 29. Do not always translate *To* and *At* by *A.*

EXAMPLES:

1. You ought to be civil *to* everybody.
   Vous devez être poli *envers* tout le monde.
2. Will you go *to* your brother's ?
   Irez-vous *chez* votre frère ?
3. I was going *to* Italy.
   J'allais *en* Italie.
4. He was *at* sea.
   Il était *en* mer.

5. Wordsworth lived *to* a very great age.
  Wordsworth vécut *jusqu'à* un âge très-avancé.
6. It is ten chances *to* one that he will succeed.
  Il y a dix chances *contre* une qu'il réussira.
7. They were twenty *to* one.
  Ils étaient vingt *contre* un.
8. They laughed *at* him.
  Il se moquèrent *de* lui.
9. We were *at* the 30th degree of latitude.
  Nous étions *par* 30th degrés de latitude.
10. Heir *to* the crown.
  Héritier *de* la couronne.

Of and From.

§ 30. Do not always translate *Of* and *From* by *De.*

EXAMPLES:

1. I have been sensible *of* your kindness.
  J'ai été sensible *à* vos bontés.
2. I thought *of* your advice.
  Je pensais *à* votre conseil.
3. Take care *of* that mistake.
  Prenez garde *à* cette faute.
4. His property consists *of* three farms.
  Son bien consiste *en* trois fermes.
5. Do not take example *from* him.
  Ne prenez pas exemple *sur* lui.

On and Upon.

§ 31. Do not always translate *On* and *Upon* by *Sur.*

EXAMPLES:

1. *On* these solemn occasions.
  Dans ces occasions solennelles.
2. *On* this condition.
  A cette condition.
3. He lives *upon* bread and milk.
  Il vit *de* pain et *de* lait.
4. It depends *upon* your conduct.
  Cela dépend *de* votre conduite.

5. He plays *upon* the fiute.
   Il joue *de* la ffûte.
6. *On* your return.
   A votre retour.

§ 32.   **About, Out of, Till, Under.**

EXAMPLES:

1. I have no money *about* me.
   Je n'ai pas d'argent *sur* moi.
2. The pupil is *about* her exercises.
   L'élève est *après* ses exercices.
3. His friends were all *about* him.
   Ses amis étaient tous *autour de* lui.
4. I was looking *out of* the window.
   Je regardais *par* la fenêtre.
5. They drank *out of* the bottle.
   Ils burent *à* la bouteille.
6. I will not come *till* Monday.
   Je ne' viendrai pas *avant* lundi.
7. *Under* such circumstances.
   Dans de pareilles circonstances.

1st OBSERVATION.

§ 33. There are other cases where the English preposition is not to be translated at all.

EXAMPLES:

1. Listen *to* your master.
   Ecoutez votre maitre.
2. Wait *for* your sister.
   Attendez votre sœur.
3. We asked *for* the bill.
   Nous avons demandé la note.
4. They looked *at* the flowers.
   Ils regardèrent les fleurs.
5. I met *with* your father.
   J'ai rencontré votre père.
6. We arrived early *in* the morning.
   Nous sommes arrivés le matin de bonne heure.

   7. I will come *on* Thursday.
      Je viendrai jeudi.
   8. He was born *on* the 9th of March, 1814.
      Il naquit la neuf Mars mil huit cent quatorze.

2nd OBSERVATION.

§ 34. Also, on the contrary, there are cases in which a preposition must be employed in French though there is none in English.

EXAMPLES:

   1. They enjoy all the comforts of this life.
      Ils jouissent *de* tous les plaisirs de la vie.
   2. We were approaching the cottage.
      Nous approchions *de* la chaumière.
   3. He does not remember you.
      Il ne se souvient pas *de* vous.
   4. He forgave his son.
      Il a pardonné *à* son fils.
   5. Obey your parents.
      Obéissez *à* vos parents.
   6. She pleased my mother.
      Elle plut *à* ma mère.
   7. Louis XIV. survived his grandson.
      Louis XIV survécut *à* son petit-fils.
   8. We must repent our errors.
      Nous devons nous repentir *de* nos fautes.
   9. Henry VII. succeeded Richard III.
      Henry VII succéda *à* Richard III.
  10. T. Moore opposed the king.
      T. Moore résista *au* roi.
  11. I asked my sister what it was.
      Je demandai *à* ma sœur ce que c'était.

CONJUNCTIONS.

§ 35. WHEN is not translated by *lorsque*, if preceded by a noun expressing time to which it relates. It would be a great mistake to translate the following phrase, *I was not at home* THE DAY WHEN *he arrived, Je n'étais pas à la maison* LE JOUR LORSQU'*il arriva.* It must be rendered, *Je n'étais pas à la maison* LE JOUR QU'*il arriva.*

§ 36. After the verb *attendre,* TILL must not be translated by *jusqu'à ce que.* *Que* alone is to be used.

EXAMPLES:

Wait TILL *I have finished.*
Attendez QUE *j'aie fini.*

In a negative sentence, do not employ the conjunctive expression, *jusqu'à ce que ;* but make use of the prepositive form *avant de.* Example : *Never sign your name to a paper* TILL *you have read the contents of it.* *Ne signez jamais un papier* AVANT D'*en avoir lu le contenu.* It would not be French here to say, JUSQU'A CE QUE *vous en ayez lu le contenu.*

§ 37. Observe that the conjunctions, *quand, lorsque, aussitôt que* and *dès que,* require the verb which follows to be in the future when the principal verb of the sentence is itself in the future or the imperative.

EXAMPLES:

I will pay you when you LIKE.
Je vous payerai quand vous VOUDREZ.
As soon as you HAVE DONE, *come to me.*
Aussitôt que vous AUREZ FINI, *venez me trouver.*

§ 38. In English, a conjunction may have several verbs depending upon it. Examples :—As *that affair is now public, and you have resolved to speak, I will be a witness to you.* SINCE *he wishes to come, and his father gives him leave, I shall be glad to receive him.* In French, whatever may be the first conjunction, the verbs that follow must always be preceded by *que.* Examples : COMME *cette affaire est maintenant publique, et* QUE *vous avez resolu de parler, je vous servirai de témoin.* PUISQU'*il desire venir, et* QUE *son père lui en donne la permission, je serai heureux de le recevoir.*

§ 39. The conjunction THOUGH has generally as a correspondent the word YET. Example : THOUGH *all men are in arms against truth,* YET *this does not prevent its triumphing.* In French it would be a mistake, in that case, to translate *yet* as it is too often rendered, by *cependant.* You must suppress it and say, QUOIQUE *tous les hommes soient armés contre la vérité, cela ne l'empêche pas de triompher.*

ADVERBS.

§ 40. NEARLY and ALMOST must not be translated indifferently by PRESQUE or PRÈS DE.

PRESQUE is an adverb which modifies an adjective, a participle, or another adverb. Examples : *Elle était* PRESQUE FOLLE, *She was nearly mad.—La maison est* PRESQUE *rebàtie, The house is almost rebuilt.—Ils vivaient* PRESQUE *somptueusement, They lived almost sumptuously.*

PRÈS DE is an adverb of quantity which is only found before a number. Examples : *Il a* PRÈS DE *quinze ans, He is nearly fifteen—J'ai reçu* PRÈS DE *cent livres, I received nearly one hundred pounds.*

It would be wrong to say, *Il a* PRESQUE *quinze ans ; J'ai reçu* PRESQUE *cent livres.*

§ 41. The adverb NOW is frequently found in a sentence the verbs of which are in the past tense. Example : *This reply did not lessen the monarch's surprise, for he* NOW *began to suspect his preceptor of mental derangement.* In French, MAINTENANT is only used with the present tense ; it would be impossible to say, MAINTENANT *il commençait.* In this case we must make use of ALORS, and translate thus: *Cette réponse ne diminua pas la surprise du monarque, car* ALORS *il commençait à soupçonner son précepteur d'avoir l'esprit dérangé.*

V.

The translator must not only conform to the requirements of the syntax, but he must also carefully observe two laws which are paramount in French; I mean *Clearness* and *Euphony.*

OF CLEARNESS.

§ 42. "What is not clear is not French," said Voltaire, and he was right; for clearness is the distinctive quality of the French language.

§ 43. The relative pronoun WHICH permits constructions in English that would be impossible in French, because the pronouns *qui* and *que* refer equally to persons and things, and are at the same time of both genders and both numbers.

If, for example, we translate the following phrase, preserving the order of the construction, *Expect the same filial duty from your children* WHICH *you paid to your parents,* we should have, *Attendez le même respect de vos enfants* QUE *vous aurez eu pour vos parents;* which would be obscure, as *que* may refer as well to *enfants* as to *respect.* We must therefore change the order of the phrase, so as to place immediately before the pronoun *que* the noun which it represents. We should say then:

Attendez de vos enfants le même RESPECT QUE *vous aurez eu pour vos parents.*

§ 44. Sometimes the antecedent of the relative pronoun is followed by words which cannot be displaced. Example : *Il est une autorité bien plus puissante que* CELLE *des hommes,* DONT *la voix commande jusqu'au fond de nos cœurs.* *Dont,* which has *celle* for its antecedent, appears thus to relate rather to *hommes* than to *autorité.* As, in this case, the words *des hommes* cannot be displaced, we must repeat the antecedent substantive itself, and say, *Il est une autorité bien plus puisssante que celle des hommes,* AUTORITÉ DONT. *la voix commande jusqu'au fond de nos cœurs.*

VI.—IDIOMS.

§ 45. To make the subject better understood, we give below some English Idioms with their French translations. The forms, the elements of which often defy all analysis, and against which the translator would struggle in vain, are called *Idioms.*

§ 46. *Some English Idioms with the French translation.*

1. I was by myself.
   J'étais seul.
2. It is all over.
   C'en est fait.
3. I should do it but for hurting him.
   Je le ferais si je ne craignais de le blesser.
4. It happened three years ago.
   Cela est arrivé il y a trois ans.
5. It is five years since.
   Il y a cinq ans de cela.
6. What will become of my children ?
   Que deviendront mes enfants ?
7. He was wet through.
   Il fut mouillé jusqu'aux os.
8. I was looking for you.
   Je vous cherchais.
9. I sent for you.

Je vous ai envoyé chercher.

10. He is in my debt for six pounds.
Il me doit six livres.

11. Put out the candle.
Soufflez la chandelle.

12. The fire is going out.
Le feu va s'éteindre.

13. I must part with you.
Il faut que je vous quitte.

14. She is nine.
Elle a neuf ans.

15. What o'clock is it by your watch?
Quelle heure est-il à votre montre?

16. It is ten minutes past three.
Il est trois heures dix minutes.

17. It is ten minutes to four.
Il est quatre heures moins dix minutes.

18. They are all one with us.
Ils sont tous du même sentiment que nous.

19. He frightened him out of the drawing-room.
Il lui fit quitter le salon en l'effrayant.

20. The rain pours down.
La pluie tombe à verse.

21. At these words, the prisoner turned very pale.
A ces mots, l'accusé devint très-pâle.

22. He has been run over.
Il a été écrasé.

23. The old beggar shook his stick at her.
Le vieux mendiant la menaça de son bâton.

24. How will you meet such an expense?
Comment ferez-vous face à une pareille dépense?

25. What is the matter?
Qu'y a-t-il?

26. What is the matter with you?
Qu'avez-vous?

27. He walked up and down his room.
Il se promenait de long en large dans sa chambre;
Or, Il allait et venait dans sa chambre.

28. It is a matter of course.
Cela va sans dire.

29. To show somebody in.
Faire entrer quelqu'un.

30. He looks very ill.
    Il a l'air très-malade.
31. He pretends to be deaf.
    Il fait semblant d'être sourd ;
Or, Il fait le sourd.
32. She was dressed up.
    Elle était en grande toilette.
33. Are you glad to have a carriage of your own ?
    Êtes-vous content d'avoir une voiture à vous ?
34. He frowned at him.
    Il le regarda de travers.
35. I do not question his honor.
    Je ne doute pas de son honneur ;
Or, Je ne mets pas son honneur en question.
36. She was taken ill.
    Elle tomba malade.
37. The enemies fled for their lives.
    Les ennemis cherchèrent leur salut dans la fuite.
38. You helped me out.
    Vous m'avez tiré d'affaire.
39. He does not know how to read.
    Il ne sait pas lire.
40. Your interest is at stake.
    Il y a va de votre intérêt.
41. Go and call your father.
    Allez appeler votre père.
42. I am hungry, thirsty, cold, &c.
    J'ai faim, soif, froid, &c.
43. His shoes let in water.
    Ses souliers prennent l'eau.
44. They put the inhabitants to the sword.
    Il passerent les habitants au fil de l'épée.

THE TRANSLATOR.

ENGLISH INTO FRENCH.

---

1 THE DERVIS.

A DERVIS, travelling[1] through Tartary, being arrived at the town of Balck, went into the king's palace by mistake, thinking it to be[2] a public inn or caravansary. Having looked about[3] for some time, he entered into[4] a long gallery, where he laid down his wallet and spread his carpet, in order to repose himself upon it,[5] after the manner of the Eastern nations. He had not been long in this position, before he was[6] discovered by some of the guards, who asked him what was his business[7] in that place. The dervis told them he[8] intended to take up his night's lodging[9] in that caravansary. The guards let him know,[10] in a very angry manner,[11] that the house he was in[12] was not a caravansary, but the king's palace. It happened[13] that the king himself passed through the gallery during this debate, and, smiling at[14] the mistake of the dervis, asked him how he could possibly be so dull as not to[15] distinguish a palace from a caravansary. "Sire, give me leave to ask your majesty[16] a question or two. Who were the persons that lodged[17] in this house when it was first built?"[18] The king replied, "My ancestors." "And who," says the dervis, "was the last person who lodged here?"[19] The king replied, "My father." "And who is it," says the dervis, "that lodges here at present?" The king told him that it was he himself.[20] "And who," says the dervis, "will be here after you?" The king answered, "The young prince, my son." "Ah, Sire," said the dervis, "a house that changes its inhabitants so often,[21] and receives such a perpetual succession[22] of guests, is not a palace, but a caravansary."—(ADDISON, *Spectator*.)

A TURKISH TALE.

We are told[1] that the Sultan Mahmoud, by his perpetual wars abroad and his tyranny at home,[2] had filled his dominions with[3] ruin and desolation, and half unpeopled the Persian empire. The vizier to[4] this great sultan (whether a humorist[5] or an enthusiast, we are not informed)[6] pretended to have learnt of a certain dervis to understand the language of birds,[7] so that there was not a bird that could open his mouth but[8] the vizier knew what it was he said.[9] As he was one evening with the sultan, on[10] their return from hunting, they saw a couple of owls,[11] upon a tree that grew near an old wall out of a heap of rubbish. "I would fain know,"[12] says the sultan, "what those two owls are saying to one another ;[13] listen to their discourse, and give me an account of it."[14] The vizier approached the tree, pretending[15] to be very attentive to the two owls.[16] Upon his return to the[17] sultan : "Sir,"[18] says he, "I have heard part[19] of their conversation, but dare not tell you what it is."[20] The sultan would not be satisfied with[21] such an answer, but forced him to repeat, word for word, everything the owls had said. . "You must know[22] then," said the vizier, "that one of these owls has a son and the other a daughter, between whom they are now upon a treaty of marriage.[23] The father of the son said[24] to the father of the daughter, in my hearing,[25] 'Brother, I consent to this marriage, provided you will settle upon your daughter fifty ruined villages for her portion.'[26] To which the father of the daughter replied,[27] 'Instead of fifty, I will give her five hundred, if you please.[28] God grant a long life to Sultan[29] Mahmoud; whilst he reigns over us we shall never want[30] ruined villages.'"

The story says,[31] the sultan was so touched with the fable that he rebuilt the towns and villages which had been destroyed, and from that time forward consulted the good of his people. — (ADDISON, *Spectator*.)

TIT FOR TAT.[1]

A friend of Dean[2] Swift one day sent him a turbot, as a present,[3] by a servant who had frequently been on similar errands,[4] but who had never received the most trifling mark of the dean's generosity. Having gained admission,[5] he opened the door of the study, and, abruptly putting down[6] the fish, cried very rudely, "Master has sent you[7] a turbot." "Young man," said the dean, rising from his easy chair,[8] "is that the way you deliver your message?[9] Let me teach you better manners;[10] sit down in my chair, we will change situations,[11] and I will show you how[12] to behave in future." The boy sat down; and the dean, going to the door, came up to[13] the table with a respectful pace, and making a low[14] bow, said, "Sir, my master presents his kind compliments,[15] hopes you are well,[16] and requests your acceptance of[17] a small present." "Does he?"[18] replied the boy; "return him my best thanks,[19] and there's half-a-crown for yourself."[20] The dean, thus drawn into[21] an act of generosity, laughed heartily, and gave the boy a crown for his wit. — (* * *)

---

4 RABELAIS A TRAITOR.[1]

This celebrated wit[2] was once at a great distance from Paris, and without money to bear his expenses[3] thither. The ingenious author being thus sharp set,[4] got together[5] a convenient quantity of brickdust, and having disposed of it into several papers,[6] wrote upon one, *Poison for Monsieur ;*[7] upon a second, *Poison for the Dauphin ;*[8] and on a third, *Poison for the King.* Having made this provision for[9] the royal family of France, he laid his papers so that the landlord, who was an inquisitive man and a good[10] subject, might get a sight of them.[11] The plot succeeded as he desired ;[12] the host gave immediate intelligence to[13] the secretary of state. The secretary presently sent down[14] a special messenger, who brought up the traitor to court, and provided him, at the king's expense, with proper accommodations on the road.[15] As soon as he appeared, he was known to be[16] the celebrated Rabelais, and his powder, upon[17] examination, being[18] found very innocent, the jest was only laughed at ;[19] for which a less eminent droll would have been sent to the galleys. — (BUDGELL, *Spectator.*)

THE HARE AND THE TORTOISE.

A hare jeered at a tortoise for[1] the slowness of his pace. But he laughed and said that he would run against her and beat her any day she should name.[2] " Come on,"[3] said the hare, "you shall soon see what my feet are made of."[4] So it was agreed that they should start at once.

The tortoise went off jogging along, without a moment's stopping, at his usual steady pace.[5] The hare, treating the whole matter very lightly, said she would first take[6] a little nap, and that she should soon overtake the tortoise. Meanwhile the tortoise plodded on,[7] and the hare, over-sleeping herself, arrived at the goal only to see[8] that the tortoise had got in before her.

Slow and steady wins the race.[9]

(James's *Fables of Æsop.*

MULY MOLUC.

When Don Sebastian, king of Portugal, invaded the territories of Muly Moluc, emperor of Morocco, in order to dethrone him, and set his crown upon the head of his nephew, Moluc was wearing away with[1] a distemper which he himself knew was[2] incurable. However, he prepared for the reception of[3] so formidable an enemy. He was, indeed, so far spent with[4] his sickness that he did not expect to live out the whole day;[5] but, knowing the fatal consequences that would happen to[6] his children and his people, in case he should die before he put an end[7] to that war, he commanded his principal officers, that, if he died during the engagement, they should conceal[8] his death from[9] his army, and that they should ride up to[10] the litter in which his corpse was[11] carried, under pretence of receiving orders as usual.[12] Before the battle[13] began, he was carried through all the ranks of his army in an open litter, as they stood drawn up in array,[14] encouraging them[15] to fight valiantly in[16] defence of their religion and country.[17] Finding[18] afterwards the battle to go[19] against him, though he was very near his last agonies,[20] he threw himself out of his litter, rallied his army, and led them on to the charge, which[21] afterwards ended in a complete victory on the side of the Moors. He had no sooner brought his men[22] to the engagement, but[23] finding himself utterly spent, he was again replaced in his litter, where, laying his finger on his mouth, to enjoin secrecy to his officers who stood about him, he died a few moments after in that posture.—(*Spectator*.)

DESTRUCTION OF THE ALEXANDRIAN LIBRARY.[1]

When Alexandria was taken by the Mahomedans, Amrus, their commander, found there Philoponus,[2] whose conversation highly pleased him, as Amrus was a lover of letters,[3] and Philoponus was a learned man.[4] On a certain day[5] Philoponus said to him : " You have visited all the repositories or public warehouses in Alexandria, and you have sealed up[6] things of every sort that are found there.[7] As to those things that may be useful to you, I presume to say nothing ;[8] but as to things of no service to you,[9] some of them perhaps may be more suitable to me."[10] Amrus said to him : " And what is it you want ? "[11]—" The philosophical books," replied he, " preserved[12] in the royal libraries."—"This," said Amrus, " is a request upon which I cannot decide. You desire a thing where[13] I can issue no orders, till I have leave from Omar, the commander of the faithful." Letters were accordingly written[14] to Omar, informing him of what Philoponus had said ; and an answer was returned by Omar to the following purport :[15] "As to the books of which you have made mention, if there be contained in them what[16] accords with the book of God (meaning[17] the Koran), there is without them,[18] in the book of God, all that is sufficient. · But, if there be any thing in them repugnant[19] to that book, we in no respect want them.[20] Order them therefore to be all destroyed."[21] Amrus upon this ordered them to be dispersed through[22] the baths of Alexandria, and to be there burnt in making the baths warm.[23] After[24] this manner, in the space of six months they were all consumed. Thus ended this noble library ; and thus began, if it did not begin sooner, the age of barbarity and ignorance. — (HARRIS.)

§ THE ART OF PLEASING.

The art of pleasing is a very necessary one to possess, but a very difficult one to acquire.[1] It can hardly be reduced to rules ;[2] and your own good sense and observation will teach you more of it than I can.[3] Do as you would be done by,[4] is the surest method that I know[5] of pleasing : observe carefully what pleases you in others, and probably the same things in you will please others. If you are pleased with[6] the complaisance and attention of others to your humours,[7] your tastes, or your weaknesses, depend upon it,[8] the same complaisance and attention[9] on your part to theirs will equally please them. Take the tone of the company that you are in,[10] and do not pretend to give it ; be serious, gay, or even trifling,[11] as[12] you find the present humour of the company : this is an attention due from every individual to[13] the majority. Do not tell stories in company ; there is nothing[14] more tedious and disagreeable : if by chance you know a very short story, and exceedingly applicable[15] to the present subject of conversation, tell it in as few words as possible ; and even then throw out[16] that you do not love to tell stories, but that the shortness of it[17] tempted you.[18] Of all things, banish egotism[19] out of your conversation, and never think of entertaining people with your personal concerns, or private affairs ; though they are interesting to you, they are tedious and impertinent to everybody else,[20] besides that, one cannot keep one's own private affairs too secret.[21] Whatever you think your own excellencies may be,[22] do not affectedly display them[23] in company ; nor labour, as many people do,[24] to give that turn to the conversation which may supply you with an opportunity of exhibiting them.[25] If they are real, they will infallibly be discovered,[26] without your pointing them out yourself;[27] and with much more advantage. Never maintain an argument with heat and clamour, though you think or know yourself to be in the right,[28] but give your opinion modestly and coolly, which is[29] the only way to convince ; and, if that does not do,[30] try to change the conversation by saying with[31] good humor : " We shall hardly convince one another, nor is it necessary that we should ;[32] so let us talk of something else."[33]

At last, remember that there is a local propriety to be observed[34] in all companies, and that what is extremely proper in one company may be, and often is, highly improper in another.

These are some[35] of the arcana necessary for your initiation in the great society of the world.[36] I wish I had known them better[37] at your age ; I have paid the price of three and fifty years for them, and shall not grudge it[38] if you reap the advantage.   Adieu.— (CHESTERFIELD, *Letters to his Son.*)

DESCRIPTION OF ENGLAND.

Few countries exhibit a greater variety of surface than England, or have been more highly favored by nature.[1] " Although," says Dr. Aikin, " its features are moulded on a comparatively minute scale,[2] they are marked with all the agreeable interchange[3] which constitutes picturesque beauty. In some parts,[4] plains clothed in the richest verdure, watered by copious streams, and pasturing innumerable cattle, extend as far as the eye can reach :[5] in others,[6] gently rising hills[7] and bending vales, fertile in corn, waving with woods,[8] and interspersed with flowery meadows, offer the most delightful landscapes of rural opulence and beauty.[9] Some tracts furnish prospects of the more romantic and impressive kind : lofty mountains, craggy rocks, deep dells, narrow ravines, and tumbling[10] torrents ; nor are there wanting, as a contrast to[11] those scenes in which every variety of nature is a different charm, the vicissitudes of[12] black barren[13] moors and wide inanimated heaths." Such is[14] a vivid description of the general appearance of England. But the beauty and fertility of the country are not the only things to excite[15] admiration. The mildness of the climate, removed alike from the extremes of heat and cold ; the multitude of rivers, their depth, and the facility they afford to internal navigation ; the vast beds of coal and other valuable minerals hid under the surface ;[16] the abundance and excellence of the fish in the rivers and surrounding seas ; the extent of sea-coast ; the number, capaciousness, and safety of the ports and bays, and the favorable situation of the country for commerce, give[17] England advantages that are not enjoyed in an equal degree by any other nation.[18]— (J. R. M'CULLOCH, *Statistical Account of the British Empire.*)

MAHOMET'S MIRACLES.

The votaries of Mahomet are more assured than himself of his miraculous gifts, and their confidence and credulity increase as they are further removed[1] from the time and place[2] of his spiritual exploits. They believe or affirm that trees went forth to meet him;[3] that he was saluted by stones; that water gushed from his fingers; that he fed the hungry and the sick, and raised the dead;[4] that a beam groaned to[5] him; that a camel complained to him;[6] that a shoulder of mutton informed him of its being[7] poisoned; and both animate and inanimate nature[8] were equally subject to this apostle of God. His dream of a nocturnal journey is seriously described as a real and corporeal transaction.[9] A mysterious animal, the Borak, conveyed him from the temple of Mecca[10] to that of Jerusalem; with his companion Gabriel, he successively ascended the seven heavens, and received and repaid the salutations of the patriarchs, the prophets, and the angels, in their respective mansions.[11] Beyond the seventh heaven, Mahomet alone was permitted to proceed;[12] he passed the veil of unity, approached within two bow-shots[13] of the throne, and felt a cold that pierced him to the heart,[14] when his shoulder was touched by the hand of God. After a familiar, though important conversation, he again descended[15] to Jerusalem, remounted the Borak, returned to Mecca, and performed in the tenth part of a night the journey of many thousand years.[16] — (GIBBON, *Decline and Fall of the Roman Empire.*)

COWPER TO MR. SAMUEL ROSE.

(ON THE EMPLOYMENT OF TIME.)

DEAR SIR,

Though it be long since I received your last,[1] I have not yet forgotten the impression it made upon me, nor how sensibly I felt myself obliged[2] by your unreserved and friendly communications.[3] I will not apologize for[4] my silence in the interim, because, apprised as you are of[5] my present occupation, the excuse that I might allege will present itself to you of course, and to dilate upon it would, therefore, be waste of paper.[6]

You are in possession of the best security imaginable for the due improvement[7] of your time, which is a just sense of its value.[8] Had I been,[9] when at your age,[10] as much affected by[11] that important consideration as I am[12] at present, I should not have devoted, as I did,[13] all the earliest parts[14] of my life to amusement only. I am now in the predicament into which the thoughtlessness of youth betrays nine-tenths[15] of mankind, who never discover that the health and good spirits[16] which generally accompany it,[17] are in reality blessings only according to the use we make of them, till advanced years[18] begin to threaten them with[19] the loss of both. How much wiser would thousands have been,[20] than now they ever will be,[21] had[22] a puny constitution, or some occasional infirmity,[23] constrained them to devote those hours to study and reflection, which, for the want of some such check,[24] they have given entirely to dissipation! I, therefore,[25] account you happy, who,[26] young as you are, need not be informed that you cannot always be so,[27] and who already know that the materials upon which age can alone build its comfort,[28] should be brought together at an earlier period.[29] You have, indeed, in losing a father, lost a friend, but you have not lost his instructions. His example was not buried[30] with him, but happily for you (happily because you are desirous of availing yourself of it) still lives[31] in your remembrance, and is cherished in your best affections.[32]

SIR ROGER DE COVERLY.

Having often received an invitation from my friend Sir Roger de Coverly[1] to pass away a month with him in the country, I last week accompanied him thither, and am settled[2] with him for some time at his country-house, where I intend to form several of my ensuing speculations.[3] Sir Roger, who is very well acquainted with[4] my humor, lets me rise and go to bed when I please,[5] dine at his own table or in my chamber, as I think fit,[6] sit still and say nothing without bidding me be merry.[7] When the gentlemen of the country[8] come to see him, he shows me[9] at a distance. As I have been walking in his fields, I have observed them stealing a sight of me[10] over a hedge, and have[11] heard the knight desiring them[12] not to let me see them,[13] for that I hated to be stared at.[14]

I am the more at ease in Sir Roger's family, because it consists[15] of sober, staid persons ; for as the knight is the best master in the[16] world, he seldom changes his servants ;[17] and as he is beloved by all about him, his servants never care for leaving him :[18] by this means his domestics are all in years, and grown old with[19] their master. You would take his valet-de-chambre for his brother; his butler is grey-headed;[20] his groom is one of the gravest men that I have[21] ever seen,[22] and his coachman has the looks[23] of a privy councillor. You see the goodness of the master even[24] in his old house-dog, and in a grey pad that is kept[25] in the stable with great care and tenderness, out of regard to[26] his past services, though he has been useless for[27] several years.

I could not but observe with a great deal[28] of pleasure the joy that appeared in[29] the countenances of these ancient domestics upon[30] my friend's arrival at his country-seat. Some of them could not refrain from tears[31] at the sight of their old master; every one of them pressed forward to do something for him,[32] and seemed discouraged[33] if they were not employed.[34] At the same time the good old knight, with a mixture of the father and the master of the family, tempered the inquiries after his own affairs with[35] several kind questions relating to themselves. This humanity and good-nature[36] engages everybody to him;[37] so that when he is pleasant upon any of them, all his family are in[38] good humor, and none so much as the person whom he diverts himself with:[39] on the contrary, if he coughs, or betrays[40] any infirmity of old age, it is easy for a stander-by to observe a secret concern in the looks of all his servants.[41]

My worthy friend has put me under the particular care[42] of his butler, who is a very prudent man, and, as well as the rest of his fellow-servants, wonderfully desirous of pleasing me,[43] because they have often heard their master talk of me as of his particular friend. — (ADDISON, *Spectator.*)

COWPER TO MR. J. NEWTON.

(ON SOME PLEASURES IN RURAL LIFE.)

MY DEAR FRIEND,

Following your good example, I lay before me a sheet of my largest paper. It was this moment fair and unblemished,[1] but I have begun to blot[2] it, and having begun, am not likely[3] to cease till[4] I have spoiled it.[5] I have sent you many a sheet that in my judgment of it has been very unworthy of your acceptance,[6] but my conscience was in some measure[7] satisfied by reflecting,[8] that if it were good for[9] nothing, at the same time[10] it cost you nothing, except the trouble of reading it. But the case is altered now.[11] You must pay a solid price for frothy matter;[12] and though I do not absolutely pick your pocket,[13] yet you lose your money, and, as the saying is, are never the wiser.[14]

My green-house is never so pleasant as when we are just on the point of being turned out of it. The gentleness of the autumnal suns, and the calmness of this latter season, make it[15] a much more agreeable retreat than we ever find it[16] in the summer; when the winds being generally brisk,[17] we cannot cool it by admitting[18] a sufficient quantity of air, without being at the same time incommoded by it.[19] But now I sit with all the windows and the door wide open,[20] and am[21] regaled with[22] the scent of every flower, in a garden as full of flowers as I have known how to make it.[23] We keep[24] no bees; but if I lived in[25] a hive, I should hardly hear more of their music. All the bees in the[26] neighborhood resort to a bed[27] of mignonette opposite to the window, and pay me for the honey they get out of it,[28] by[29] a hum which, though rather[30] monotonous, is as agreeable to my ear[31] as the whistling of my linnets. All the sounds that Nature utters[32] are delightful, at least in this country. I should not perhaps find the roaring of lions in Africa, or of bears in Russia, very pleasing ;[33] but I know no beast[34] in England whose voice I do not account musical,[35] save and except always the braying of an ass. / The notes of all our birds and fowls[36] please me, without one exception. I should not indeed think[37] of keeping a goose in a cage, that I might[38] hang him up in the parlor for the sake of[39] his melody ; but a goose upon a common,[40] or in a farm-yard, is no bad performer ;[41] and as to[42] insects, if the black beetle, and beetles indeed of all hues, will keep out of my way, I have no objection to any of the rest ;[43] on the contrary, in whatever key they[44] sing, from the gnat's fine treble to[45] the bass of the humble-bee, I admire them all. Seriously, however, it strikes me as a very observable instance of providential kindness to man, that[46] such an exact accord has been contrived[47] between his ear and the sounds with which, at least in a rural situation, it is almost every moment visited.[48] All the world is sensible of[49] the uncomfortable effect that certain sounds have upon the nerves, and consequently upon the spirits ;[50] and if a sinful world[51] had been filled with such as would have curdled[52] the blood, and have made the[53] sense of hearing a perpetual inconvenience, I do not know that[54] we should have a right to complain. But now the fields, the woods, the gardens, have each their concert, and the ear of man is forever[55] regaled by creatures who seem only to please themselves.[56] Even the ears that are deaf to the Gospel are continually entertained, though without knowing it, by sounds for which they are solely indebted to its author.[57] There is, somewhere in infinite space, a world, that does not roll within the precincts of mercy ; and as it is reasonable, and even scriptural,[58] to suppose that there is music in heaven,[59] in those dismal regions perhaps the reverse of it is found ;[60] tones so dismal, as to make[61] woe itself more insupportable, and to acuminate even[62] despair. But my paper admonishes me in good time to draw[63] the reins, and to check the descent of my fancy into deeps, with which she is but too familiar.[64]

———

THE COMPARISON OF WATCHES.

When Griselda thought[1] that her husband had long enough[2] enjoyed his new existence, and that there was danger of his forgetting[3] the taste of sorrow, she changed her tone.[4] One day, when he had not returned home exactly at the appointed minute,[5] she received him with a frown such as[6] would have made even Mars himself recoil,[7] if Mars could have beheld[8] such a frown upon the brow[9] of his Venus.

" Dinner has been kept waiting for you this hour, my dear."[10]

" I am very sorry for it ; but why did you wait, my dear ?[11] I am really very sorry I am so late ;[12] but " (looking at[13] his watch) " it is only half-past six by me."[14]

" It is seven by me."[15]

They presented their watches to each other, he in an apologetical, she in a reproachful attitude.[16]

" I rather think you are too fast,[17] my dear," said the gentleman.

" I am very sure you are too slow,[18] my dear," said the lady.

" My watch never loses a[19] minute in the four and twenty[20] hours," said he.

" Nor mine a second," said she.

" I have reason to believe I am right,[21] my love," said the husband, mildly.

" Reason !"[22] exclaimed the wife, astonished. " What reason can you possibly[23] have to believe you are right, when I tell you I am morally certain you are wrong, my love ? "

" My only reason for doubting it is[24] that I set my watch by the sun[25] to-day."

" The sun must be wrong then,'" cried the lady, hastily. " You need not laugh ;[26] for I know what I am saying : the variation, the declination, must be allowed for in computing it with the clock.[27] Now,[28] you know perfectly well what I mean, though you will not explain it for me, because you are conscious[29] I am in the right."[30]

" Well, my dear, if you are conscious of it, that is sufficient. We will not dispute any more about such a trifle. Are they bringing up dinner ?"[31]

" If they know that you are come in ; but I am sure I cannot tell whether they do or not. Pray,[32] my dear Mrs. Nettleby," cried the lady, turning to a female friend,[33] and still holding her watch in her hand, " What o'clock is it by you? There is nobody in the[34] world hates disputing about trifles so much as I do ;[35] but I own I do love to convince people[36] that I am in the right."

Mrs. Nettleby's watch had stopped :[37] how provoking ![38] Vexed at having no immediate means[39] of convincing people that she was in the right, our heroine consoled herself by proceeding to criminate[40] her husband, not in this particular instance,[41] where he pleaded guilty,[42] but upon the general charge of being always too late for dinner, which he strenuously denied.[43]

There is something[44] in the species of reproach, which advances thus triumphantly from particulars to generals,[45] peculiarly offensive[46] to every reasonable and susceptible mind ;[47] and there is something in the general charge of being always late for dinner which the punctuality of man's nature cannot easily endure,[48] especially if he be hungry. We should humbly advise our female friends [49] to forbear exposing a husband's patience to this trial,[50] or at least to temper it with [51] much fondness, or else mischief will infallibly ensue.[52]—(MISS EDGEWORTH, *Modern Griselda.*)

HEARERS AND DOERS.[1]

The clock has just struck[2] nine. The family are rising from the breakfast-table.[3] A ring at the door-bell![4] The servant enters.

"Sir, a young man, Mr. A.'s clerk,[5] has called, and hopes you will not be offended, but he would feel particularly obliged if you could settle his account.[6] He called[7] twice last week. He would not trouble you if it were not a case of necessity."[8]

"Necessity or no necessity,[9] I have not one minute to spare,"[10] replied the gentleman, with a shrug of[11] his shoulders, whilst giving[12] the last pull to his great-coat, as he was putting it on.[13] "I am going[14] by the next train, so bid him call again."[15]

This gentleman was not upon the whole an unfeeling

man ; but carried on by the spirit of the times,[16] railway speed,[17] he too often did not allow himself[18] time to reflect, or[19] to put himself in[20] the place of his fellow-man.[21] Had he,[22] in this instance, troubled himself to think, he would have seen that he had just a few[23] minutes to spare, and would still have been in time for[24] the train;—but even had it been otherwise, his duty was too plain to be mistaken.[25] A neglected debt had prior claim to the commercial concerns to which he was hastening.[26]

The clerk turned[27] sorrowfully from the house; he knew that on the[28] payment of that money his employer's continuance in business[29] depended; and[30] consequently his own dismissal was involved in this refusal. Mr. A.'s family was large,[31] his receipts were small,[32] and in reliance[33] on this sum he had promised to meet a heavy bill that day;[34] he was now unable to do so.[35] The traveller[36] to whom he owed it was a hasty, harsh-judging man;[37] Mr. A. could expect to find no favor, nor did he.[38] Here, then, was a whole household, besides those in their employ,[39] thrown into distress by that fatal sentence: "I have not a minute to spare." And yet those who caused that distress were not altogether regardless of the forms of religion.[40] They were in the custom of having family prayer,[41] and of reading daily from that word[42] where it is written: "*Owe no man any thing.*" *[43]

This gentleman's wife, an hour after her husband's departure, was[44] stopped, as she was leaving the parlor, by her maid, who said,[45] "There is a poor woman who wishes to speak to you."

"Who is she, what is she?"[46]

---

* Romans xiii. 8.

"I don't know, ma'am, but she particularly wishes to see you."

"Tell her, I can't possibly see her now,[47] I have 'not a minute to spare,' my children are waiting for me in the nursery."[48]

"Alas!" thought the poor woman, "I too have[49] children; it is for my child I want to see her." She went heart-broken[50] from that door.

The next day, that lady heard that the poor woman who had called upon her the day before[51] had lost her child; and that the doctor[52] had said, the child's life to all appearance might have been saved, had she used[53] the means prescribed. That mother could not;[54] she had spent her last shilling, and this was the last application of three calls she had made, and from each house she had been turned away with words to the same effect.[55]

Is it, can it be,[56] that a child must be left to die, and a mother's best feelings to wither,[57] and by one, too, who so far professes the Christian religion, as to read the Bible in her family[58]—that Bible where it is written: "*Say not unto thy neighbour,*[59] *Go, and come again, and to-morrow I will give;*[60] *when thou hast it by thee?*"*[61] This lady had the habit of giving people the trouble to call twice, when once[62] should have sufficed. She would not put herself out of the way[63] in order to meet the convenience of[64] others. In setting too high a value on[65] her own time, she forgot that the time of others was of equal, and often of greater value.[66] Whilst she was finishing a chapter in some interesting book, a pattern in needle-work,[67] or a note[68] she was writing, she would keep a dressmaker waiting,[69] or send away a tradesman's[70] ser-

---

* Proverbs iii. 28.

vant, forgetting that to[71] them "Time is money,"[72] nay their very bread.[73] — (S. CLARENCE, *Not a Minute to Spare.*)

SCENE FROM "THE GOOD-NATURED MAN."

(MR. HONEYWOOD AND JARVIS.)

HON. Well, Jarvis, what messages from[1] my friends this morning?

JAR. You have no friends.

HON. Well; from my acquaintances then?

JAR. [*Pulling out bills.*][2] A few of our usual cards of compliment,[3] that's[4] all. This bill from your tailor; this[5] from your mercer; and this[6] from the little broker in Crooked-lane. He says he has been at a great deal of trouble[7] to get back[8] the money you borrowed.[9]

HON. That I don't know; but I'm sure[10] we were at a great deal of trouble in getting him[11] to lend it.

JAR. He has lost all patience.

HON. Then he has lost a very good thing.

JAR. There's that[12] ten guineas you were sending[13] to the poor gentleman and his children in the Fleet.[14] I believe that would stop his mouth,[15] for a while at least.

HON. Ay,[16] Jarvis, but what will fill their mouths[17] in the meantime? Must I be cruel because he happens to be[18] importunate; and, to relieve his avarice, leave them to insupportable distress?[19]

JAR. S'death![20] sir, the question now is how[21] to relieve yourself. Yourself—haven't I reason[22] to be out of my senses,[23] when I see things going at sixes and sevens?[24]

HON. Whatever reason[25] you may have for being out

of your senses, I hope you'll allow[26] that I'm not quite unreasonable for continuing in mine.[27]

JAR. You're the only man alive,[28] in your present situation,[29] that could do so.—Everything upon the waste.[30] There's Miss Richland and her fine fortune gone[31] already, and upon the point of being given to your rival.

HON. I'm no man's rival.

JAR. Your uncle in Italy preparing to disinherit you; your own fortune almost spent; and nothing[32] but pressing creditors, false friends,[33] and a pack of drunken servants, that your kindness has made unfit for[34] any other family.

HON. Then they have the more occasion for being[35] in mine.

JAR. Soh![36] What will you have done with[37] him that I caught[38] stealing your plate in the pantry? In the fact;[39] I caught him in the fact.

HON. In the fact! If so,[40] I really think that we should pay him his wages, and turn him off.[41]

JAR. He shall be turned off at Tyburn, the dog; we'll hang him, if it be only to frighten the rest of the family.[42]

HON. No, Jarvis; it's enough that we have lost what he has stolen; let us not add to it the loss of a fellow-creature.

JAR. Very fine;[43] well, here was the footman just now,[44] to complain of the butler; he says he does most work, and ought to have most wages.

HON. That's but just; tho' perhaps here comes the butler[45] to complain of the footman.

JAR. Ay, it's the way with them all,[46] from the scullion to the privy councillor. If they have a bad master, they keep quarrelling with him;[47] if they have a good master, they keep quarrelling with one another.[48]

ANECDOTE.

There was a boy in the class, who stood always at the top,[1] nor could I with all my efforts supplant him.[2] Day came after day,[3] and still he kept his place, do what I would;[4] till at length I observed that when a question was asked him,[5] he always fumbled with his fingers at[6] a particular button in the lower part of his waistcoat.[7] To remove it, therefore, became expedient in my eyes; and in an evil moment it was removed with a knife. Great was my anxiety to know the success of my measure; and it succeeded too well. When the boy was again questioned,[8] his fingers sought again for the button, but it was not to be found.[9] In his distress he looked down for it;[10] it was to be seen no more than be felt.[11] He stood confounded, and I took possession of his place; nor did he ever recover it, or ever,[12] I believe, suspect who was the author of his wrong.[13] Often, in after-life, has the sight of him smote me as I passed by him;[14] and often have I resolved to make him some reparation; but it ended in good resolutions.[15] Though I never renewed my[16] acquaintance with him, I often saw[17] him, for he filled some inferior office[18] in one of the courts of law in[19] Edinburgh. Poor fellow![20] I believe he is dead; he took early to drinking.[21] — (W. SCOTT, *Autobiography*.)

A TRAVELLING INCIDENT.[1]

The tendency of mankind when it falls asleep in coaches, is[2] to wake up cross; to find its legs in the way; and its corns an aggravation.[3] Mr. Pecksniff not being exempt from the common lot of humanity, found himself, at the end of his nap, so decidedly[4] the victim of these infirmities, that he had an irresistible inclination[5] to visit them upon his daughters ; which he had already begun to do in[6] the shape of divers random kicks,[7] and other unexpected motions[8] of his shoes, when the coach stopped, and, after a short delay, the door was opened.[9]

"Now mind,"[10] said a thin sharp voice[11] in the dark. "I and my son go inside,[12] because the roof is full,[13] but you agree to charge us outside prices.[14] It's quite understood that we won't pay more. Is it?"[15]

"All right,[16] Sir," replied the guard.

"Is there anybody inside now?" inquired the voice.

"Three passengers,"[17] returned the guard.

"Then I ask the three passengers to witness this bargain, if they will be so good," said the voice. "My boy, I think we may safely get in."[18]

In pursuance of which[19] opinion, two people took their seats[20] in the vehicle,[21] which was solemnly licensed by Act of Parliament to carry any six persons who could be got in at the door.[22]

"That was lucky!"[23] whispered the old man, when they moved on again.[24] "And a great stroke of policy in you[25] to observe it. He, he, he![26] We couldn't have gone[27] outside. I should have died[28] of the rheumatism!"

Whether it occurred[29] to the dutiful son that he had in some degree overreached himself,[30] by contributing to the prolongation of his father's days ; or whether[31] the cold had affected[32] his temper ; is doubtful.[33] But he gave[34] his father such a nudge in reply, that that good old gentleman[35] was taken with a cough which lasted for full five minutes,[36] without intermission, and goaded Mr. Pecksniff to that pitch of irritation, that he said at last — and very suddenly [37]—

"There is no room! [38] there is really no room in this coach for any gentleman with a cold in his head!" [39]

"Mine," [40] said the old man, after a moment's pause, [41] "is upon my chest, [42] Pecksniff."

The voice and manner, [43] together, now that he spoke out; [44] the composure of the speaker; [45] the presence of his son; and his knowledge of [46] Mr. Pecksniff; afforded a clue to [47] his identity which [48] it was impossible to mistake.

"Hem! I thought," said Mr. Pecksniff, returning to his usual mildness, "that I addressed [49] a stranger. I find that I address a relative. Mr. Anthony Chuzzlewit and his son Mr. Jonas — for they, my dear children, are our [50] travelling companions — will excuse me for an apparently harsh remark. It is not *my* desire to wound the feelings of any person with whom I am connected in family bonds. [51] I may be a Hypocrite," said Mr. Pecksniff, cuttingly, [52] "but I am not a Brute."

"Pooh, pooh!" [53] said the old man. "What signifies that word, Pecksniff? Hypocrite! why, [54] we are all hypocrites. We were all hypocrites t'other day. I am sure I felt that to be [55] agreed upon among us, or I shouldn't have called you one. [56] We should not have been there at all, if we had not been hypocrites. The only difference between [57] you and the rest was — shall I tell you the difference between you and the rest now, [58] Pecksniff?"

"If you please, my good sir; if you please." [59]

"Why, the annoying quality in *you*, is," said the old man, "that [60] you never have a confederate or partner in *your* juggling; [61] you would deceive everbody, [62] even those who practice the same art; and have a way with you, [63] as if you—he, he, he!—as if you really believed your-self.[64] I'd lay a handsome wager[65] now," said the old man, "if I laid wagers, which I don't, and never did, that you keep up[66] appearances by a tacit understanding, even before your own daughters here.[67] Now I, when I have a business scheme[68] in hand, tell[69] Jonas what it is,[70] and we discuss it openly. You're not offended, Pecksniff?"

"Offended, my good sir!" cried that gentleman, as if he had received the highest[71] compliments that language could convey.[72]

"Are you travelling[73] to London, Mr. Pecksniff?" asked the son.

"Yes, Mr. Jonas, we are travelling to London. We shall have the pleasure of your company all the way, I trust?"

"Oh! ecod,[74] you had better[75] ask father that," said Jonas. "I am not going to commit myself."[76]

Mr. Pecksniff was, as a matter of course,[77] greatly entertained by this retort. His mirth having subsided, Mr. Jonas gave him to understand that himself and parent[78] were in fact travelling to their home[79] in the metropolis ;[80] and that, since the memorable day of the great family gathering,[81] they had been tarrying in that part of the country, watching[82] the sale of certain eligible invest-ments,[83] which they had had in their copartnership eye when they came down ;[84] for it was their custom, Mr. Jonas said,[85] whenever such a thing was practicable, to kill two birds with one stone,[86] and never to throw away sprats, but as bait for whales.[87] — (DICKENS, *Martin Chuzzlewit*.)

SCENE FROM "THE SCHOOL FOR[1] SCANDAL."

Lady Sneerwell; Mrs. Candour; Joseph Surface; Maria; Crabtree; Sir Benjamin Backbite.

CRAB. Lady Sneerwell, I kiss your hand.[2] Mrs. Candour, I don't believe you are acquainted with[3] my nephew, Sir Benjamin Backbite? Egad,[4] ma'am,[5] he has a pretty wit, and is a pretty poet too.[6] Isn't he,[7] Lady Sneerwell?

SIR BEN. Oh, fie, uncle!

CRAB. Nay, egad it's true;[8] I back him at a rebus or a charade[9] against the best rhymer in the kingdom.[10] Has your ladyship heard[11] the epigram[12] he wrote last week[13] on Lady Frizzle's feather catching fire?[14] Do, Benjamin, repeat it, or[15] the charade you made last night extempore[16] at Mrs. Drowzie's conversazione.[17] Come now;[18] your[19] first is the name of a fish, your second a[20] great naval commander, and —

SIR BEN. Uncle, now — pr'ythee —[21]

CRAB. I'faith,[22] ma'am, 'twould surprise you to hear how ready he is at all these sort of things.[23]

LADY SNEER. I wonder, Sir Benjamin, you never publish any thing.

SIR BEN. To say truth,[24] ma'am, 'tis very vulgar to print;[25] and, as my little productions are mostly satires and lampoons on particular people,[26] I find they circulate more by giving copies in confidence to the friends of the parties.[27] However, I have some love elegies, which, when[28] favored with this lady's smiles, I mean to give the public. *[Pointing to* MARIA.

CRAB. [*To* MARIA.] 'Fore heaven,[29] ma'am, they'll immortalize you!—you will be handed down to posterity,[30] like Petrarch's Laura,[31] or Waller's Sacharissa.

SIR BEN. [*To* MARIA.] Yes, madam, I think you will like them, when you shall see them on a beautiful quarto page,[32] where a neat rivulet of text shall meander through a meadow of margin. 'Fore Gad, they will be the most elegant things of their kind! [33]

CRAB. But, ladies, that's true—[*To* MRS. CANDOUR]—have you heard[34] the news?

MRS. CAN. What, Sir, do you mean the report of—

CRAB. No, ma'am, that's not it.[35]—Miss Nicely is going to be married to her own footman.

MRS. CAN. Impossible![36]

CRAB. Ask[37] Sir Benjamin.

SIR BEN. 'Tis very true, ma'am : every thing is fixed, and the wedding liveries bespoke.[38]

CRAB. Yes—and they do say there were pressing reasons for it.[39]

LADY SNEER. Why, I have heard something of this before.[40]

MRS. CAN. It can't be,—and I wonder any one should believe such a story of so prudent a lady as Miss Nicely.

SIR BEN. O Lud![41] ma'am, that's the very reason[42] 'twas believed at once. She has always been so cautious and so reserved, that every body was sure there was some reason for it at bottom.

MRS. CAN. Why, to be sure, a tale of scandal[43] is as fatal to the credit of a prudent lady of her stamp as a fever is generally to those of the strongest constitutions. But there is a sort of a puny sickly reputation, that is always ailing, yet will outlive the robuster character[44] of a hundred prudes.

SIR BEN. True,[45] madam, there are valetudinarians in[46] reputation as well as[47] constitution, who, being conscious of their weak part,[48] avoid the[49] least breath of air, and supply their want of stamina by care and circumspection.[50]

MRS. CAN. Well, but this may be all a mistake.[51] You know, Sir Benjamin, very trifling circumstances often give rise to the most injurious tales.

CRAB. That they do, I'll be sworn, ma'am.[52] O Lud! Mr. Surface, pray is it true[53] that your uncle, Sir Oliver, is coming home?[54]

JOS. SURF. Not that I know of, indeed, Sir.[55]

CRAB. He has been in the East Indies a long time. You can scarcely remember him, I believe? Sad comfort, whenever he returns,[56] to hear how your brother has gone on![57]

JOS. SURF. Charles has been imprudent, Sir, to be sure ; but I hope no busy people have already prejudiced[58] Sir Oliver against him. He may reform.

SIR BEN. To be sure he may:[59] for my part, I never believed him to be so utterly void of principle as people say ; and, though he has lost all his friends, I am told nobody is better spoken of by the Jews.[60]

CRAB. That's true, egad, nephew. If the old Jewry was a ward,[61] I believe Charles would be an alderman:[62] no man more popular there, 'fore Gad! I hear[63] he pays as many annuities as the Irish[64] tontine ; and that, whenever he is sick, they have[65] prayers for the recovery of his health in all the synagogues.

SIR BEN. Yet no man lives in greater splendor.[66] They tell me, when he entertains his friends he will sit down to dinner with[67] a dozen of his own securities ;[68] have a score of tradesmen waiting[69] in the antechamber, and an officer[70] behind every guest's chair.

Jos. Surf. This may be entertainment to[71] you, gentlemen, but you pay very little regard to the feelings[72] of a brother.

Mar. [*Aside.*] Their malice is intolerable!—[*Aloud.*] Lady Sneerwell, I must wish you a good morning; I'm not very well.[73]   [*Exit.*

Mrs. Can. O dear! she changes color very much.[74]

Lady Sneer. Do, Mrs. Candour, follow her:[75] she may want your assistance.

Mrs. Can. That I will, with all my soul,[76] ma'am. Poor dear girl, who knows what her situation may be!
                                    [*Exit.*

Lady Sneer. 'Twas nothing but that she could not bear to hear Charles reflected on,[77] notwithstanding their difference.

Sir Ben. The young lady's *penchant* is obvious.

Crab. But, Benjamin, you must not give up the pursuit for that: follow her, and put her into good humor. Repeat her some of your own verses. Come, and I'll assist you.

Sir Ben. Mr. Surface, I did not mean to hurt you; but depend on't[78] your brother is utterly undone.[79]

Crab. O Lud, ay! undone as ever man was—can't raise[80] a guinea!

Sir Ben. And everything sold, I'm told, that was movable.[81]

Crab. I have seen one that was at his house.[82] Not a thing left[83] but some empty bottles that were overlooked,[84] and the family pictures, which I believe are framed in the wainscots.

Sir Ben. And I'm very sorry also to hear some bad stories against him.[85]   [*Going.*[86]

Crab. Oh! he has done many mean things, that's certain.

Sir Ben. But, however, as he's [87] your brother —

[*Going.*

Crab. We'll tell you more another opportunity.[88]

[*Exeunt* Crabtree *and* Sir Benjamin.

Lady Sneer. Ha! ha! 'tis very hard for them to leave a subject they have not quite run down.[89]

Jos. Surf. And I believe the abuse was no more acceptable to your ladyship than [90] Maria.

Lady Sneer. I doubt her affections are farther engaged than we imagine.[91]   But the family are [92] to be here this evening, so you may as well dine where you are,[93] and we shall have an opportunity of observing farther; [94] in the meantime, I'll go and plot mischief, and you shall study sentiment.[95]   [*Exeunt.*

---

20 BYRON TO THOS. MOORE.

(a familiar letter.)

August 12, 1814.

I was *not* alone, nor will be while I can help it.[1]   Newstead is not yet decided.   Claughton is to make [2] a grand effort [3] by Saturday week to complete,[4] — if not, he must give up twenty-five thousand pounds and the estate, with expenses,[5] &c. &c.   If I resume the abbacy,[6] you shall have due notice, and a cell set apart for your reception,[7] with a pious welcome.   Rogers I have not seen,[8] but Larry and Jacky came out a few days ago.[9]   Of their effect I know nothing.[10]

There is something very amusing in *your* being an Edinburgh Reviewer.[11] You know, I suppose, that Thurlow* is none of the placidest, and may possibly enact[12] some tragedy on being told that he is only a fool.[13] If, now,[14] Jeffrey were to be[15] slain on account of an article of yours,[16] there would be a fine conclusion.[17] For my part, as Mrs. Winifred Jenkins says,[18] "he has done the handsome thing by me,"[19] particularly in his last number; so, he is the best of men[20] and the ablest of critics, and I won't have him killed[21]—though I dare say many wish he were, for being so good-humored.[22]

Before I left[23] Hastings I got in a passion with an ink-bottle, which I flung out of the window one night with a vengeance;[24]—and what then? Why,[25] next morning I was horrified by seeing that it had struck, and split upon,[26] the petticoat of Euterpe's graven[27] image in the garden, and grimed her as if it were on purpose.[28] Only think[29] of my distress, — and[30] the epigrams that might be engendered[31] on the Muse and her misadventure.[32]

I had an adventure almost as ridiculous, at some private theatricals ~~near Cambridge—though of a different description~~—since I saw you last.[33] I quarrelled with a man in the dark for asking me[34] who I was (insolently enough to be sure),[35] and followed him into the green-room (a *stable*)[36] in a rage,[37] amongst a set[38] of people I never saw before.[39] He turned out to be a low comedian,[40] engaged to act with the amateurs, and to be a civil-spoken man enough,[41] when he found out that nothing very pleasant was to be got[42] by rudeness. But you would have been amused with the[43] row, and the dialogue, and

---

* A critique on Lord Thurlow's poems had recently appeared in the Edinburgh Review.

the dress — or rather the undress [44] — of the party, [45] where I had introduced myself in a devil of a hurry, [46] and the astonishment that ensued. I had gone out of the theatre, for coolness, [47] into the garden ; — there I had tumbled over [48] some dogs, and, coming away from them [49] in very ill humor, encountered [50] the man in a worse, [51] which [52] produced all this confusion.

Well — and why don't you 'launch?' Now is your time. [53] The people [54] are tolerably tired with me, and not very much enamored with Wordsworth, who has just spawned a quarto [55] of metaphysical blank-verse, [56] which is nevertheless only a part of a poem.

Let me hear from and of you and [57] my godson. If a [58] daughter, the name will do [59] quite as well.

Ever, &c. [60]

THE LAST MEETING [1] OF WAVERLEY AND FERGUS MAC-IVOR.

An officer now appeared, and intimated that the High Sheriff [2] and his attendants awaited before the gates of the castle, to claim the bodies [3] of Fergus Mac-Ivor and Evan Maccombich: "I come," [4] said Fergus. Accordingly, supporting Edward by the arm, [5] and followed by Evan Dhu and the priest, he moved down [6] the stairs of the tower, the soldiers bringing up the rear. [7] The court was occupied by a squadron of dragoons and [8] a battalion of infantry, drawn up in a hollow square. [9] Within their ranks was the sledge, or hurdle, on which the prisoners were to be drawn [10] to the place of execution, about a mile distant [11] from Carlisle. It was painted black [12] and drawn by [13] a white horse. At one end of the vehicle sat [14] the executioner, a horrid-looking fellow, as beseemed his trade,[15] with the broad axe in his hand ;[16] at the other end, next the horse,[17] was an empty seat for two persons. Through the deep and dark gothic archway, that opened on the drawbridge, were seen[18] on horseback the High Sheriff and his attendants, whom the etiquette betwixt the civil and military powers[19] did not permit[20] to come farther. "This is well *got up* for a closing scene,"[21] said Fergus, smiling disdainfully as he gazed around upon[22] the apparatus of terror. Evan Dhu exclaimed with some eagerness, after looking at the dragoons, "These are the very chields that galloped off at Gladsmuir, before we could kill a dozen of them. They look bold enough now, however."[23] The priest entreated him to be silent.

The sledge now approached, and Fergus, turning round, embraced Waverley, kissed him on each side of the face, and stepped nimbly into his place.[24] Evan sat down by[25] his side. The priest was to follow in a carriage belonging to his patron, the catholic gentleman at whose house[26]. Flora resided. As Fergus waved his hand[27] to Edward, the ranks closed around[28] the sledge, and the whole procession began to move forward.[29] There was a momentary stop[30] at the gateway, while the governor of the castle and the High Sheriff went through[31] a short ceremony, the military officer there delivering over the persons of the criminals to[32] the civil power. "God save[33] King George !" said the High Sheriff. When the formality concluded,[34] Fergus stood erect in[35] the sledge and, with a firm and steady voice, replied, "God save King James !" These[36] were the last words which Waverley heard him speak.[37]

The procession resumed its[38] march, and the sledge

vanished from beneath the portal, under which it had stopped for an instant. The dead-march was then heard, and its melancholy sounds were mingled with those of a muffled peal, tolled from a neighboring cathedral.[39] The sound [40] of the military music died away as [41] the procession moved on; the sullen clang of the bells was soon heard to sound alone.[42]— (WALTER SCOTT, *Waverley*.)

A FEW WORDS OF ADVICE TO YOUNG PEOPLE.

The great [1] source of independence, the French express in a precept of three words,[2] " *Vivre de peu*," which [3] I have always admired. " *To live upon little*," is the great security [4] against slavery; and this precept extends to dress and other things besides food and drink. When Doctor [5] Johnson wrote his Dictionary, he put in the word pensioner thus : [6] " PENSIONER. *A slave of state*." After this he himself became [7] a *pensioner !* And thus, agreeably to his own definition, he lived and died " *a slave of state !* " What must this man of great genius and of great industry too, have felt at receiving [8] this pension ! Could he be so callous as [9] not to feel a pang upon [10] seeing his own name placed before his own degrading definition? And, what could induce him to submit to this? His wants, his artificial wants, his habit of indulging in [11] the pleasures of the table; his disregard of the precept, " *Vivre de peu*." This [12] was the cause; and, be it observed, that [13] indulgences of this sort,[14] while they tend to make [15] men poor and expose them to commit mean acts, tend also to enfeeble the body, and, more especially, to cloud and to weaken the mind.

*　　*　　*　　*　　*

In your *manners* be neither boorish nor blunt, but even these[16] are preferable to simpering and crawling.[17]   I wish[18] every English youth could see those of the United States of America, always *civil*, never *servile.*/Be *obedient*, where obedience is due; for, it is no act of meanness, and no indication of want of spirit,[19] to yield implicit and ready obedience to[20] those who have a right[21] to demand it at your hands.[22]/In this respect England has been, and, I hope, always will be, an[23] example to the whole world.[24] To this habit of willing[25] and prompt obedience in apprentices, in servants, in all inferiors in station,[26] she owes, in a great measure,[27] her multitudes of matchless merchants, tradesmen, and workmen of every description, and also the achievements[28] of her armies and navies.   It is[29] no disgrace, but the contrary,[30] to obey, cheerfully, lawful and just commands.[31]   None are so saucy and disobedient as slaves ;[32] and, when you come[33] to read history, you will find that in proportion as nations have been *free* has been their reverence for the laws.[34]   But there is a wide difference between lawful and cheerful obedience, and that servility which represents people[35] as laying petitions "at the *king's feet*," which makes us imagine that we behold[36] the supplicants actually crawling upon their bellies.[37] There is something so abject in this expression; there is such horrible self-abasement in it,[38] that I do hope,[39] that every youth, who shall read this, will hold in detestation[40] the reptiles who make use of it.   In all other countries, the lowest individual can put[41] a petition into the *hands* of the chief magistrate, be he[42] king or emperor : let us hope, that the time will yet come when[43] Englishmen will be able to do the same.[44]   In the meantime[45] I beg you to despise these worse[46] than pagan parasites.

* * * * *

Perseverance is a prime quality in every pursuit. Yours is, too, the time of life to acquire [47] this inestimable habit. Men fail much oftener from want [48] of perseverance than from want of talent and of good disposition : as [49] the race was not to the hare but to the tortoise ; so the meed of success in study is not to [50] him [51] who is in haste,[52] but to him who proceeds with a steady and even [53] step. It is not to a want [54] of taste or of desire or of disposition to learn [55] that we have to [56] ascribe the rareness of good scholars, so much as to the want of patient perseverance.[57]

WILLIAM COBBETT.

POPE TO WYCHERLEY.

When I write to you, I foresee a long letter, and ought [1] to beg your patience beforehand ; for if it prove [2] the longest, it will be of course the worst [3] I have troubled you with.[4] Yet to express my gratitude at large for your obliging letter is not more my duty than my interest ;[5] as some people will [6] abundantly thank you [7] for one piece of kindness,[8] to put you in mind of [9] bestowing another. The more favorable you are to me, the more distinctly I see my faults.[10] Spots and blemishes, you know, are never so plainly discovered as in the brightest sunshine.[11] Thus I am fortified by those [12] commendations which were designed to encourage me : for praise to a young wit is like [13] rain to a tender flower ; if it be moderately bestowed, it cheers and revives ;[14] but if too lavishly,[15] overcharges and depresses him. Most men in years, as they are general discouragers of youth,[16] are like old trees, that being past bearing themselves,[17] will suffer no young plants to flourish beneath them, but, as if it were not enough to have out-done all your coevals in wit,[18] you will excel them in good nature too. As for my green essays,[19] if you find any pleasure in them,[20] it must be such as a man [21] naturally takes in observing the first shoots and [22] buddings of a tree which he has raised himself; and it is impossible they should be esteemed any otherwise [23] than as we value fruits for being early, which [24] nevertheless are the most insipid, and the worst of the year. In a word, I hate compliment, which is, at best,[25] but the smoke of friendship. I neither write nor converse with you to gain your praise, but your affection. Be so much my friend as [26] to appear my enemy, and to tell me my faults, if not as [27] a young man, at least as an inexperienced writer.

THE DEATH OF BAYARD. (A. D. 1524.)

At the beginning of the charge, Bonnivet, while exerting himself with much [1] valor, was wounded so dangerously, as obliged him to quit the field ; [2] and the conduct of the rear was committed to the Chevalier Bayard, who, though so much a stranger to the arts of a court [3] that he never rose to the chief command, was always called, in times of real danger, to the posts of greatest difficulty and importance. He put himself at the head of the men at arms,[4] and animating them by his presence and example to sustain the whole shock of the enemy's troops,[5] he gained time for the rest of his countrymen to make good their retreat.[6] But in this service [7] he received a wound which he immediately perceived to be mortal,[8] and being unable to continue any longer on horseback,[9] he ordered one of his attendants to place him under [10] a tree, with his[11] face towards the enemy; then fixing his eyes on the guard of his sword, which he held up instead of a cross,[12] he addressed his prayers to God, and in this posture, which became his character both as a soldier and a Christian,[13] he calmly awaited the approach of death.[14] Bourbon, who led the foremost[15] of the enemy's troops,[16] found him in this situation, and expressed regret and pity at the sight.[17] "Pity not me," cried the high-spirited[18] chevalier, "I die as a man of honor ought,[19] in the discharge of[20] my duty: they indeed are objects of pity, who fight against their king, their country, and their oath"[21] The Marquis de Pescara, passing soon after, manifested his admiration of Beyard's virtues, as well as his sorrow for his fate, with the generosity of a gallant enemy; and finding that he could not be removed with safety from that spot, ordered a tent to be pitched[22] there, and appointed proper persons to attend[23] him. He died, notwithstanding their care, as his ancestors for several generations had done, in[24] the field of battle. Pescara ordered his body to be embalmed, and sent[25] to his relations; and such was the respect paid to[26] military merit in that age,[27] that the Duke of Savoy commanded it to be received with royal honors[28] in all the cities of his dominions; in Dauphiny, Bayard's[29] native country, the people of all ranks came out in a solemn procession to meet it.[30] — (ROBERTSON, *History of Charles V.*)

THE CATARACT OF NIAGARA, IN CANADA,[1]
NORTH AMERICA.

This amazing fall of water is made by the river Saint-Lawrence, in its passage from lake Erie into lake Ontario.[2] The Saint-Lawrence is one of the largest rivers[3] in the world; and yet the whole of its waters is discharged in this place, by a fall of a hundred and fifty feet perpendicular.[4] It is not easy to bring the imagination to correspond to[5] the greatness of the scene. A river extremely deep and rapid, and that serves to draw[6] the waters of almost all North America[7] into the Atlantic Ocean, is here poured precipitately down a ledge[8] of rocks, that rises, like a wall, across the whole bed of its stream.[9] The river, a little above, is near three quarters of a mile broad;[10] and the rocks, where it grows narrower, are four hundred yards over.[11] Their direction is not straight across, but hollowing inwards like a[12] horseshoe; so that the cataract, which bends to the shape of the obstacle,[13] rounding inwards, presents a kind of theatre[14] the most tremendous in nature. Just in the middle of the circular wall of waters,[15] a little island, that has braved the fury of the current, presents one of its points, and divides the stream at top[16] into two parts; but they unite again long before they reach the bottom. The noise of the fall is heard at the distance of several leagues; and the fury of the waters, at the termination[17] of their fall, is inconceivable. The dashing[18] produces a mist that rises to the very clouds, and which forms a most beautiful rainbow,[19] when the sun shines. It will readily be supposed[20] that such a cataract entirely destroys the navigation of the stream;[21] and yet some Indians, in their canoes, as it is said, have ventured down it with safety.[22]— (GOLDSMITH.)

BRUTUS ON THE DEATH OF CÆSAR.

Romans, countrymen, and lovers![1] hear me for[2] my cause; and be silent that you may hear. Believe me for mine honor, and have respect for [3] mine honor, that you may believe.[4] Censure me in your wisdom, and awake your senses, that you may the better [5] judge. If there be any in this assembly, any dear friend of Cæsar's, to him I say [6] that Brutus's love [7] to Cæsar was no less than his. If then that friend demand why Brutus rose against Cæsar, this is [8] my answer; not that [9] I loved Cæsar less, but that I loved Rome more.[10] Had you rather Cæsar were living,[11] and die all slaves, than that Cæsar were dead, to live [12] all freemen? As Cæsar loved me, I weep for him; as he was fortunate, I rejoice at it; as he was valiant, I honor him; but as he was ambitious, I slew him.[13] There are tears for his love,[14] joy for his fortune, honor for his valor, and death for his ambition. Who's here so base, that would [15] be a bondman? If any,[16] speak; for him have I offended.[17] Who's here so rude,[18] that would not be a Roman? If any, speak; for him have I offended. Who's here so vile, that will not love his country? If any, speak; for him have I offended. I pause for [19] a reply. None? Then none have I offended; [20] I have done no more to Cæsar than you should do to Brutus. The question [21] of his death is enrolled in the Capitol; his glory not extenuated wherein he was worthy; nor his offences enforced for which he suffered death.[22]

Here comes [23] his body, mourned by Mark Anthony, who, though he had no hand in his death, shall receive the benefit of his dying,[24] a place in the Commonwealth; as which of you shall not? [25] With this I depart, that as I slew [26] my best lover for the good of Rome,[27] I have the same dagger for myself when it shall please my country to need my death.[28] — (SHAKSPEARE, *Julius Cæsar*.)

INFLUENCE OF THE FRENCH LANGUAGE
AND LITERATURE IN THE AGE OF LOUIS XIV.

France united at that period almost every species of ascendency.[1] Her military glory was at the height.[2] She had vanquished mighty coalitions. She had dictated treaties. She had subjugated great cities and provinces. She had forced the Castilian pride to yield her the precedence.[3] She had summoned Italian princes to prostrate themselves at her footstool.[4] Her authority was supreme in all matters of good breeding,[5] from a duel to a minuet. In literature, she gave law[6] to the world. The fame of her great writers filled Europe. No other country could produce[7] a tragic poet equal to Racine, a comic poet equal to Molière, a trifler[8] so agreeable as La Fontaine, a rhetorician so skillful[9] as Bossuet.

The literary glory of Italy and of Spain had set ; that of Germany had not yet dawned.[10] The genius, therefore, of the eminent men who adorned[11] Paris shone forth with a splendor which was set off to full advantage by contrast.[12] France, indeed, had at that time an empire over mankind, such as[13] even the Roman Republic never attained. For, when Rome was politically dominant, she was in arts and letters the humble pupil of Greece. France had, over the surrounding countries, at once the ascendency which Rome had over Greece and the ascendency which Greece had over Rome. French was becoming the universal language, the language of fashionable society,[14] the language of diplomacy. At several courts princes and nobles spoke it more accurately and politely[15] than their mother tongue.[16]

In our island there was less of this servility[17] than on

the continent. Neither our good nor our bad qualities were those of imitators.[18] Yet even here homage was paid,[19] awkwardly indeed, and sullenly,[20] to the literary supremacy of our neighbors. The melodious Tuscan, so familiar to the gallants[21] and ladies of the court of Elizabeth, sank into contempt. New canons[22] of criticism, new models of style, came into fashion.[23] The quaint ingenuity which had deformed[24] the verses of Donne, and had been a blemish on[25] those of Cowley, disappeared from our poetry. Our prose became less majestic, less artfully involved,[26] less variously musical,[27] than that of an earlier age;[28] but more lucid, more easy, and better fitted for controversy and narrative. In these changes it is impossible not to recognize[29] the influence of French precept and of French example. — (LORD MACAULAY, *History of England.*)

JOHN BULL.

JOHN BULL, to all appearance, is a plain, downright, matter-of-fact fellow,[1] with[2] much less of poetry about him than rich prose. There is little of romance in his nature,[3] but a vast deal of strong natural feeling.[4] He excels in humor more than in[5] wit; is jolly rather than gay; melancholy rather than morose; can easily be moved to a sudden tear, or surprised into a broad laugh;[6] but he loathes sentiment, and has no turn for[7] light pleasantry. He is a boon companion,[8] if you allow him to have[9] his humor, and to talk about himself;[10] and he will stand by a friend in a quarrel, with life and purse, however soundly he may be cudgelled.

In this last respect, to tell the truth, he has a propensity to be somewhat too ready. He is a busy-minded[11] personage, who thinks not merely for[12] himself and family, but for all the country round; and is most generously disposed to be everybody's champion. He is continually volunteering his services to settle his neighbor's affairs; and takes it in great dudgeon[13] if they engage in any matter of consequence without asking his advice; though he seldom engages in any friendly office of the kind without finishing by getting into a squabble[14] with all parties, and then railing bitterly at their ingratitude. He unluckily[15] took lessons in his youth in the noble science[16] of defence,[17] and having accomplished himself[18] in the use of his limbs and his weapons, and become a perfect master at boxing and cudgel-play,[19] he has had a troublesome life of it ever since.[20] He cannot hear[21] of a quarrel between the most distant of his neighbors, but he[22] begins incontinently to fumble with the head of[23] his cudgel, and consider whether his interest or honor does not require that he should meddle in the broil. Indeed, he has extended his relations of pride and policy so completely over the whole country, that no event can take place, without infringing[24] some of his finely-spun[25] rights and dignities. Couched[26] in his little domain, with[27] these filaments stretching forth in every direction, he is like some choleric, bottle-bellied old spider,[28] who has woven his web over a whole[29] chamber, so that a fly cannot buzz, nor a breeze blow, without startling his repose, and causing him to sally forth wrathfully from his den.[30]

Though really a good-hearted, good-tempered old fellow at bottom,[31] yet he is singularly fond of being in the midst of contention. It is one of his peculiarities, however, that he only relishes the beginning of an affray; he always goes into a fight with alacrity, but comes out of it grumbling, even when[32] victorious; and though no one fights with more obstinacy to carry a contested point, yet,[33] when the battle is over,[34] and he comes[35] to the reconciliation, he is so much taken up with the[36] mere shaking of hands, that he is apt to let his antagonist pocket all that they have been quarreling about.[37] It is not, therefore, fighting that he ought so much to be on his guard against,[38] as making friends. It is difficult to cudgel him out of a farthing;[39] but put him in a[40] good humor, and you may bargain him out of all the money in his pocket.[41] He is like a stout ship, which[42] will weather the roughest storm uninjured, but roll its masts overboard in the succeeding calm.[43] — (WASHINGTON IRVING, *Sketch-book.*)

SOPHIA'S LITTLE BIRD.

Tom Jones, when very young,[1] had presented Sophia with[2] a little bird, which he had taken from[3] the nest, had nursed up, and taught to sing.

Of this bird, Sophia, then about thirteen years old, was so extremely fond,[4] that her chief business was to feed and tend it, and her chief pleasure to play with it. By these means Tommy (for so the bird was called)[5] was become so tame, that it would feed out of[6] the hand of its mistress, would perch upon her finger, and lie contented[7] in her bosom, where it seemed sensible of its own happiness;[8] though she always kept a small string about its leg,[9] nor would ever trust it with[10] the liberty of flying away.

One day, when[11] Mr. Allworthy and his whole family dined at Mr. Western's,[12] Master Blifil, being in the garden with little Sophia, and observing the extreme fondness that she showed for her little bird, desired her to trust it for a moment in his hands.[13] Sophia presently[14] complied with the young gentleman's request, and after some previous caution delivered him her bird; of which he was no sooner in possession, than he slipped[15] the string from its leg, and tossed it into the air.

The foolish animal no sooner perceived itself at liberty, than, forgetting all the favors it had received[16] from Sophia, flew directly from her, and perched on a bough at some distance.

Sophia, seeing her bird gone, screamed out so loud,[17] that Tom Jones, who was at a little distance, immediately ran[18] to her assistance.

He was no sooner informed of what had happened,[19] than he cursed Blifil for a pitiful malicious rascal;[20] and then immediately stripping off his coat, he applied himself to climbing[21] the tree to which the bird escaped.[22]

Tom had almost recovered his little namesake, when the branch on which it[23] was perched, and that hung[24] over a canal, broke, and the poor lad plunged over head and ears into the water.[25]

Sophia's concern now changed its[26] object, and, as she apprehended the boy's life was in danger, she screamed ten times louder than before; and indeed Master Blifil himself now seconded her with all the vociferation in his power.[27]

The company, who were sitting[28] in a room next the garden, were instantly alarmed, and came all forth;[29] but just as[30] they reached the canal, Tom (for the water was luckily pretty shallow in that part) arrived safely on shore.[31]

Thwackum fell[32] violently on[33] poor Tom, who stood dripping and shivering before him, when Mr. Allworthy desired him to have[34] patience; and turning to Master Blifil, said, "Pray, child, what is the reason of all this disturbance?"

Master Blifil answered, "Indeed, uncle,[35] I am very sorry for what I have done. I have been unhappily the occasion of it all.[36] I had Miss Sophia's bird in my hand, and thinking the poor creature languished for liberty, I own I could not forbear giving it what it desired, for I always thought there was something very cruel in confining anything.[37] It seemed to be against the law of Nature, by[38] which everything hath a right to liberty; nay, it is even unchristian,[39] for it is not doing what we would be done by.[40] But if I had imagined Miss Sophia would have been so much concerned at it, I am sure[41] I would never have done it; nay[42] if I had known what would have happened to the bird itself, for when Master Jones, who climbed up that tree after it,[43] fell into the water, the bird took a second flight,[44] and presently a nasty hawk carried it away."[45]

Poor Sophia, who now first[46] heard of her little Tommy's fate, (for her concern for Jones had prevented her perceiving it when it[47] happened,) shed a shower[48] of tears. These Mr. Allworthy endeavored to assuage, promising her a much finer bird; but she declared she would never have[49] another. Her father chid her for[50] crying so for a foolish bird, but could not help telling young Blifil if he was a son of his, his back should be well flayed.[51]

Sophia now returned to her chamber, the two young gentlemen were sent home,[52] and the rest of the company returned[53] to their bottle, where a conversation ensued on the[54] subject of the bird. — (FIELDING.)

SCENE FROM "THE RIVALS."

(Enter Sir Lucius O'Trigger and Bob Acres, with pistols.)

ACRES. By my valor! then, Sir Lucius, forty yards is a good distance. Odds levels and aims!—I say it is a good distance.[1]

SIR L. It is for[2] muskets, or small field-pieces;[3] upon my conscience,[4] Mr. Acres, you must leave these things to me.[5] Stay, now[6]—I'll show you. (*Measures paces along the stage.*)[7] There now, that is a very pretty distance—a pretty gentleman's distance.[8]

ACRES. Zounds! we might as well fight[9] in a sentry-box! I tell you, Sir Lucius, the farther he is off,[10] the cooler I shall take my aim.[11]

SIR L. Faith! then[12] I suppose you would aim at him best of all if he was out of sight!

ACRES. No, Sir Lucius; but I should think[13] forty, or eight-and-thirty[14] yards—

SIR L. Pho! pho! nonsense![15] three or four feet between the mouths of your pistols is as good as a mile.[16]

ACRES. Odds bullets,[17] no! by my valor, there is no merit in killing him so near![18] Do, my dear Sir Lucius, let me bring him down at a long shot:[19] a long shot, Sir Lucius, if you love me!

SIR L. Well, the gentleman's friend[20] and I must[21] settle that. But tell me now, Mr. Acres, in case of an accident, is there any little will or commission I could execute for you?

ACRES. I am much obliged to you, Sir Lucius; but I don't understand—

SIR L. Why, you may think there's no being shot at

without a little risk;[22] and, if an unlucky bullet should carry a quietus with it—I say it will be no time then to be bothering you about[23] family matters.

ACRES. A quietus!

SIR L. For instance, now; if that should be the case, would you choose to be pickled,[24] and sent home? or would it be the same to you[25] to lie here in the Abbey? I'm told there is very snug lying[26] in the Abbey.

ACRES. Pickled! Snug lying in the Abbey—Odds tremors![27] Sir Lucius, don't talk so!

SIR L. I suppose, Mr. Acres, you never were engaged[28] in an affair of this kind before?

ACRES. No, Sir Lucius, never before.

SIR L. Ah! that's a pity;[29] there's nothing like being used to a thing.[30] Pray, now,[31] how would you receive the gentleman's shot?[32]

ACRES. Odds files! I've practiced that;[33] there,[34] Sir Lucius, there[35] — (*puts himself into an attitude*) — a side-front, hey?[36] Odd! I'll make myself small enough:[37] I'll stand edgeways.[38]

SIR L. Now, you're quite out;[39] for if you stand so when I take my aim — (*Levelling at him.*)[40]

ACRES. Zounds,[41] Sir Lucius! are you sure it is not cocked?[42]

SIR L. Never fear.

ACRES. But—but—you don't know; it may go off of its own head![43]

SIR L. Pho! be easy.[44] Well, now,[45] if I hit you in the body, my bullet has a double chance; for if it misses a vital part of your right side, 'twill be very hard if it don't succeed[46] on the left.

ACRES. A vital part!

Sir L. But there ;[47] fix yourself so — (*Placing him*)— let him see the broad-side of your full front ; there[48]— now a ball or two may pass clean through your body, and never do you any harm at all.[49]

Acres. Clean through me ! a ball or two clean through me !

Sir L. Ay, may they ;[50] and it is much the genteelest attitude into the bargain.[51]

Acres. Lookye ![52] Sir Lucius — I'd just as lieve[53] be shot in an awkward posture, as a genteel one ;[54] so, by my valor ! I will stand edgeways.

Sir L. (*Looking at his watch.*)[55] Sure they don't mean to disappoint us ;[56] ha ! no, faith. I think I see them coming.

Acres. Eh ! what ! coming ! —[57]

Sir L. Ay ; who are those yonder, getting over the stile ?[58]

Acres. There are two of them[59] indeed ! well, let them come ; hey, Sir Lucius ! we—we—we—we—won't run.[60]

Sir L. Run !

Acres. No, I say, we won't run, by my valor !

Sir L. What the devil's the matter with you ?[61]

Acres. Nothing, nothing, my dear friend ; my dear Sir Lucius ; but I—I—I don't feel[62] quite so bold, somehow, as I did.[63]

Sir L. O fie ! consider[64] your honor.

Acres. Ay, true ; my honor ; do, Sir Lucius, edge in[65] a word or two, every now and then,[66] about my honor.

Sir L. Well, here they're coming. (*Looking.*)

Acres. Sir Lucius, if I wasn't with you I should almost think I was[67] afraid. If my valor should[68] leave me ! Valor will come and go.[69]

Sir L. Then pray keep it fast, while you have it.

Acres. Sir Lucius, I doubt[70] it is going; yes, my valor is certainly going! it is sneaking off![71] I feel it oozing out, as it were, at the palms of my hands.[72]

Sir L. Your honor, your honor.—Here they are.

Acres. Oh, that I was[73] safe at Clod Hall! or could be shot before I was aware![74]

---

51 SKETCH OF CÆSAR'S CAREER AND CHARACTER.

The man who broke the power of Gallia in an eight years' war has written[1] the history of the[2] war himself. He was a[3] soldier in his youth, like most Romans of rank,[4] and he had been a governor[3] in Spain shortly before he was[5] consul. But it was not till after he was more than forty years of age[6] that his military career commenced, and[7] he obtained a field wide enough for his daring and capacious genius. It was Cæsar's ambition[8] to conquer the Gauls, and it was prudent policy in the Romans, for Italy was never safe[9] so long as the restless and warlike men beyond the[10] Alps were unsubdued. The rapidity of Cæsar's movements, the immense extent of country over which his military operations extended, his battles, his sieges, his defeats, and his victories, with their political consequences, give[11] to his work an untiring interest, if we read it with proper knowledge and in a proper way. Nor[12] let any man, who thinks that he knows[13] something of modern warfare,[14] venture to disparage either the Roman or his enemies without[15] a map always before him, and his attention well awake to the significance of a few words written in the Latin language, and written by Cæsar. The Gauls fought with courage and desperation; they showed military talent,[16] and in the arm of cavalry they were strong.[17] They were inferior in infantry and in their weapons;[18] and they were weakened by political disunion. Cæsar pursued his bold career through hazards and dangers enough to have stopped[19] a prudent man; but his eyes were always open,[20] and his vigilance never slumbered; his presence of mind never left him, and he was full of resources in his vigorous understanding and his resolute will. He,[21] who said himself[22] that he was not cruel, who spared the lives of[23] Roman citizens, his enemies, who pardoned his countrymen who would have taken his life,[24] pursued barbarians with unrelenting ferocity. He spared neither age nor sex; he slaughtered men in battle, in flight, and after submission; he plundered them, he sold them for[25] slaves; he mutilated them; he burnt their houses; he wasted their fields; he left them to perish in the winter, houseless[26] and without food. His most formidable enemy, who was cruel like himself,[27] and,[28] as active and as brave, the Gallic chief who, in the seventh year of the war, made a last effort to crush the Roman proconsul, and nobly surrendered to save his countrymen, was thrown into a Roman dungeon, to wait six years for Cæsar's triumph; and then[29] he was put to death.

Such a man, with all his great qualities, ought not to be made the[30] object of vulgar admiration,[31] as he often is by modern writers. He ought to be estimated justly. He was better than many, perhaps than most of his contemporaries; and that is all we can say.[32]—(GEORGE LONG, *Preface to his edition of the Gallic War.*)

32 THE DEAD ASS.

"And this," said he, putting the remains of a crust into his wallet,[1] "and this should have been thy portion," said he, "hadst thou been alive to have shared it[2] with me." I thought, by[3] the accent, it had been[4] an apostrophe to his child; but 't was[5] to his ass, and to the very ass we had seen dead in the road, which[6] had occasioned La Fleur's misadventure. The man seemed to lament it much; and it[7] instantly brought into my mind Sancho's lamentation for[8] his; but he did it with more true touches of nature.[9]

The mourner[10] was sitting upon a stone bench at the door, with the ass's pannel and its bridle on one side,[11] which he took up from time to time, and laid them down, looked at them, and shook his head. He then took his crust of bread out of his wallet again,[12] as if to[13] eat it, held it for some time in his hand, then laid it upon the bit of his ass's bridle......looked wistfully at the little arrangement he had made......and then gave[14] a sigh.

The simplicity of his grief drew numbers[15] about him; and La Fleur amongst the rest, whilst the horses were getting ready;[16] as I continued sitting in the post-chaise, I could see and hear over their heads.

He said he had come last[17] from Spain,[18] where he had been from the furthest borders[19] of Franconia; and had got so far on his return home,[20] when his ass died.[21] Every one seemed desirous to know what business could have taken so old and poor a man so far a journey from his own home.[22]

It had pleased Heaven, he said, to bless him with[23] three sons, the finest lads in[24] all Germany; but having in [25] one week lost two of the eldest of them by the small-pox, and the youngest falling [26] ill of the same distemper, he was afraid of being bereft of them all; and made a vow, if Heaven would not take him from him also, he would go [27] in gratitude to St. Iago [28] in Spain.

When the mourner got thus far on [29] his story, he stopped to pay nature her tribute,[30] and wept bitterly.

He said, Heaven had accepted the conditions; and that he had set out from his cottage with this poor creature, who had been a patient partner of his journey, that it had eat the same bread with him all the way, and was unto him as a friend.

Everybody who stood about,[31] heard the poor fellow with concern. La Fleur offered him money. The mourner said he did not want it......it was not the value of the ass ......but the loss of him......[32] the ass, he said he was assured, loved him......and upon this told them a long story of a mischance upon their passage over the Pyrenean mountains which had [33] separated them from each other three days, during which time [34] the ass had sought him as much as he had sought the ass, and that they had scarce either eat or drank till they met.[35]

"Thou hast one comfort, friend," said I, "at least,[36] in the loss of thy poor beast; I'm sure thou hast been a merciful master to him...."—"Alas!" said the mourner, "I thought so, when he was alive; but now that he is dead, I think otherwise. I fear the weight of myself and my afflictions together [37] have been [38] too much for him, they have [39] shortened the poor creature's days, and I fear I have [40] them to answer for."[41]—"Shame on the [42] world!" said I to myself; "did we love each other [43] as

this poor soul[44] but loved his ass, 't would be something."
—(STERNÈ, *Sentimental Journey.*)

ᴸᴮ FOX.

Mr. Fox's eloquence was of a kind which to comprehend you must have heard himself.[1]   When he got fairly into[2] his subject, was heartily warmed with it, he poured forth words and periods of fire that smote you, and deprived you of all power to reflect and rescue yourself, while he went on to seize[3] the faculties of the listener, and carry them captive along with him whithersoever he pleased[4] to rush.   It is ridiculous to doubt that he was[5] a far closer reasoner, a much more argumentative speaker than[6] Demosthenes; as much more so as Demosthenes would perhaps have been than Fox,[7] had he lived in our times[8] and had to address[9] an English House[10] of Commons.   For it is the kindred mistake of[11] those who fancy that the two were like each,[12] to imagine that the Grecian's orations are long chains of ratiocination, like Sir William Grant's arguments, or Euclid's demonstrations. They are close to the point;[13] they are full of impressive allusions; they abound in expressions of the adversary's inconsistency; they are loaded with bitter invective; they never lose sight of the subject;[14] and they never quit hold of[15] the hearer by the striking appeals they make to his strongest feelings and his favorite recollections : to the heart, or to the quick and immediate sense of inconsistency, they are always addressed,[16] and find their way thither[17] by the shortest and surest road; but to the head, to the calm and sober judgment, as pieces of argumenta tion, they assuredly are not addressed.[18] But Mr. Fox, as he went along, and exposed absurdity, and made inconsistent arguments clash,[19] and laid bare[20] shuffling or hypocrisy, and showered down upon meanness, or upon cruelty, or upon oppression, a pitiless storm of the most fierce invective, was ever forging also[21] the long, and compacted, and massive chain of pure demonstration.

There was no weapon of argument[22] which this great orator more happily or more frequently wielded than wit, the wit which exposes to ridicule the absurdity or inconsistency of an adverse argument. It has been said of him, that he[23] was the wittiest speaker of his times;[24] and they[25] were the times of Sheridan and of Windham. This was Mr. Canning's opinion, and it was also Mr. Pitt's. There was nothing more awful in Mr. Pitt's sarcasm, nothing so vexatious in Mr. Canning's light and galling raillery, as the battering and piercing wit[26] with which Mr. Fox so often interrupted, but always supported, the heavy artillery of his argumentative declamation.

In most of the external qualities of oratory,[27] Mr. Fox was certainly deficient, being of an unwieldy person,[28] without any grace of action, with a voice of little compass, and which, when pressed[29] in the vehemence of his speech, become shrill almost to a cry or squeak;[30] yet all this was absolutely forgotten in the moment when the torrent began to pour. Some of the undertones[31] of his voice were peculiarly sweet; and there was even in the shrill and piercing sounds which he uttered, when at the more exalted pitch, a power that thrilled the heart of the hearer. His pronunciation of our language was singularly beautiful, and his use of it[32] pure and chaste to[33] severity. As he rejected, from[34] the correctness of his taste, all vicious ornaments, and was most sparing, indeed, in the use of figures at all,[35] so, in his choice of words,[36] he justly shunned foreign idiom,[37] or words borrowed whether from the ancient or modern languages,[38] and affected the pure Saxon tongue,[39] the resources of which are unknown to so many who use it, both in writing and in speaking.[40]—(LORD BROUGHAM.)

THE VICAR OF WAKEFIELD AND HIS FAMILY.

I was ever[1] of opinion that the honest man, who married and brought up[2] a large family, did more service[3] than he who[4] continued single, and only talked of population.[5] From this motive, I had scarce taken orders a year before I[6] began to think seriously of matrimony, and chose my wife as she did her wedding-gown—not for a fine glossy surface, but such qualities as would wear well.[7] To do her justice,[8] she was a good-natured, notable woman,[9] and as for education, there were few country ladies who could show more.[10] She could read any English book without much spelling;[11] but for pickling, preserving,[12] and cookery, none could excel her. She prided herself also upon being an excellent contriver in housekeeping;[13] though I could never find[14] that we grew richer with all her contrivances.

However, we loved each other[15] tenderly, and our fondness increased as we grew old. There was, in fact, nothing that could[16] make us angry with[17] the world or each other.[18] We had an elegant house, situate in a fine country,[19] and a good neighborhood. The year was spent[20] in moral or rural amusements,[21] in visiting our rich neighbors, and relieving such as [22] were poor. We had no revolutions to fear, nor fatigues to undergo ; all our adventures were by the [23] fireside, and all our migrations [24] from the blue bed to the brown. [25]

As we lived [26] near the road, we often had the traveller or stranger to visit us, to taste [27] our gooseberry-wine, for which we had great reputation ; and I profess, [28] with the veracity of an historian, that I never knew one of them [29] find fault with it. [30] Our cousins, too, even to the fortieth remove, [31] all remembered their affinity, without any help from [32] the herald's office, [33] and came very frequently to see us. Some of them did us no great honor by these claims of kindred ; as we had the blind, the maimed, and the halt amongst the number. [34] However, my wife always insisted that, as they were the same *flesh and blood*, they should sit with us at the same table ; [35] so that, if we had not very rich, we generally had very happy friends about us ; [36] for this remark will hold good through life, that [37] the poorer the guest, [38] the better pleased he ever is with being treated ; [39] and as some men gaze with admiration at the colors of a tulip or [40] the wing of a butterfly, so I was by nature an admirer of happy human faces. [41] However, when any one [42] of our relations was found to be [43] a person of very bad character, [44] a troublesome guest, [45] or one we desired to get rid of, [46] upon his leaving my house, I ever took care [47] to lend him a riding-coat, [48] or a pair of boots, or sometimes a horse of small value, [49] and I always had [50] the satisfaction to find that he never [51] came back to return them. By this the house was cleared of such as we did not like ; but never was the family of Wakefield known to turn the traveller or the poor dependent out of doors. [52]

Thus we lived several years in a state of much happiness; not but that [53] we sometimes had [54] those little rubs which Providence sends to enhance the value of its favors. My orchard was often robbed by schoolboys, and my wife's custards plundered by the cats or the children. The squire [55] would sometimes fall asleep in [56] the most pathetic parts of my sermon, or his lady [57] return my wife's civilities at church with a mutilated courtesy. [58] But we soon got over the uneasiness caused by such accidents, [59] and usually in [60] three or four days began to wonder how they vexed us. [61]

My children, the offspring of temperance, as they were educated without softness, so they were at once well-formed and healthy; [62] my sons [63] hardy and active, my daughters beautiful and blooming. [64] Our eldest son was named George, after [65] his uncle, who left us ten thousand pounds. [66] Our second child, a girl, I intended to call after her aunt Grissel; [67] but my wife, who had lately been reading romances, insisted upon her being called Olivia. [68] In less than another year, we had another daughter, and now [69] I was determined that Grissel should be her name; but a rich relation taking a fancy [70] to stand [71] godmother, the girl [72] was by her directions called Sophia: so that we had two romantic names [73] in the family; but I solemnly protest I had no hand in it. [74] Moses was our next, [75] and after an interval of twelve years, we had two sons more. [76]

It would be fruitless to deny my exultation when I saw my little ones about me; [77] but the vanity and satisfaction of my wife were even greater than mine. When our visitors would say, "Well, [78] upon my word, Mrs. Primrose, you have the finest children in [79] the whole country:"

—"Ay,[80] neighbour," she would answer,[81] "they are as Heaven made them — handsome enough, if they be[82] good enough; for handsome is that handsome does."[83] And then she would bid the girls hold up their heads,[84] who, to conceal nothing,[85] were certainly very handsome. Mere outside is so very trifling a circumstance with me,[86] that I should scarce have remembered to mention it,[87] had it not been a general topic of conversation in the country. Olivia, now about eighteen,[88] had that luxuriancy of beauty, with which painters generally draw[89] Hebe — open, sprightly, and commanding. Sophia's features were not so striking at first,[90] but often did more certain execution;[91] for they were soft, modest, and alluring. The one vanquished by a single blow, the other by efforts successively repeated.

My eldest son, George, was bred[92] at Oxford, as I intended him for[93] one of the learned professions. My second boy, Moses, whom I designed for business, received a sort of miscellaneous[94] education at home. But it is needless to attempt describing the particular characters[95] of young people that had seen but very little of[96] the world. In short, a family likeness prevailed through all;[97] and, properly speaking,[98] they had but one character, — that of being all equally generous, credulous, simple and inoffensive.—(GOLDSMITH.)

THE SPELL OF WEALTH.

What a dignity it gives an old lady, that balance at the[1] banker's! How tenderly we look[2] at her faults, if she is a[3] relative (and may every reader have a score of such) ;[4] what a kind, good-natured old creature we find her ![5] How the junior partner[6] of Hobbs and Dobbs leads her, smiling to the carriage with the lozenge upon it,[7] and the fat wheezy coachman ![8] How, when she comes to pay us a visit, we generally find an opportunity to[9] let our friends know her station[10] in the world ! we say (and with perfect truth), I wish I had[11] Miss Mac Whirter's signature to a cheque for[12] five thousand pounds. She wouldn't miss it,[13] says your wife. She[14] is my aunt, say you, in an easy careless way,[15] when your friend asks if Miss Mac Whirter is[16] any relative? Your wife is perpetually sending her little testimonials of affection ; your little girls work endless worsted baskets, cushions, and foot-stools for her.[17] What a good fire there is in her room when she comes to pay you a visit,[18] although your wife laces her stays without one ![19] The house during her stay assumes a festive, neat, warm, jovial, snug appearance not visible at[20] other seasons. You yourself, dear sir, forget[21] to go to sleep after dinner, and find yourself all of a sudden[22] (though you invariably lose) very fond of a rubber.[23] What good dinners you have — game every day, Malmsey-Madeira[24] and no end of[25] fish from London. · Even the servants in the kitchen share in the general prosperity ; and, somehow, during the stay of Miss Mac Whirter's fat coachman, the beer is grown much stronger, and the consumption of tea and sugar in the nursery[26] (where her maid[27] takes her meals) is not regarded in the least.[28] Is it so, or is it not so? I appeal to the middle classes. Ah, gracious[29] powers ; I wish you would send me[30] an old aunt — a maiden aunt[31] — an aunt with a lozenge on her carriage, and a front of light coffee-colored hair[32] — how my children should work workbags for her, and my Julia and I[33] would make her comfortable ![34] Sweet—sweet vision ! Foolish—foolish[35] dream !—(THACKERAY, *Vanity Fair.*[36])

MOONLIGHT SCENERY.[1]

The wind had arisen, and swept before it[2] the clouds which had formerly obscured the sky. The moon was high, and at the full, and all the lesser satellites of heaven shone forth in cloudless effulgence.[3] The scene which their light presented[4] was in the highest degree unexpected and striking.

In the latter part of his journey our traveller approached the sea-shore, without being aware how nearly.[5] He now perceived that the ruins of Ellengowan castle were situated upon a promontory, or projection of rock,[6] which formed one side of a small and placid bay on the seashore.[7] The modern mansion was placed lower, though closely adjoining, and the ground behind it descended to the sea by a small swelling green bank,[8] divided into levels by natural terraces[9] on which grew some old trees, and terminating[10] upon the white sand.. The other side of the bay, opposite to the old castle, was a sloping and varied[11] promontory, covered chiefly with copsewood, which on that favored coast grows almost within watermark.[12] A fisherman's cottage peeped from among[13] the trees. Even at this dead hour of night there were lights moving[14] upon the shore, probably occasioned by the[15] unloading a smuggling lugger from[16] the Isle of Man, which was lying[17] in the bay. On the light from the sashed door of the house being observed,[18] a halloo from the vessel, "Ware hawk! Douse the glim!" alarmed those who were on the shore, and the lights instantly disappeared.[19]

It was one hour after midnight, and the prospect around was lovely. The grey old towers of the ruin, pártly entire, partly broken,[20] — here bearing the rusty weather stains of ages, and there partially mantled with[21] ivy, stretched along the verge of the dark rock which rose on the right hand[22] of Mannering. In front[23] was the quiet bay, whose little waves, crisping and sparkling[24] to the moonbeams, rolled successively along its surface, and dashed with a soft and murmuring ripple against[25] the silvery beach. To the left, the woods advanced far into[26] the ocean, waving in the moonlight along ground of an undulating and varied form,[27] and presenting those varieties of light and shade, and that interesting combination of glade and thicket, upon which the eye delights to rest, charmed with what it sees, yet curious to pierce still deeper[28] into the intricacies of the woodland scenery.[29] Above rolled the planets, each, by its own liquid orbit of light, distinguished[30] from inferior or more distant stars. So strangely can imagination deceive even those by whose volition it has been excited,[31] that Mannering, while gazing upon these brilliant bodies, was half-inclined[32] to believe in the influence ascribed to them by superstition[33] over human events.[34] — (WALTER SCOTT, *Guy Mannering.*)

LADY MONTAGU TO MRS. THISTLETHWAYTE.

(A FAMILIAR LETTER.)

Adrianople, April 1, 1718.

I can now tell dear[1] Mrs. Thistlethwayte that I am safely arrived[2] at the end of my very long journey. I will not tire you with the account of the many fatigues I have suffered.[3] You would rather[4] be informed of the strange things that are to be seen here;[5] and a letter out of Turkey that has nothing extraordinary in it,[6] would be as great a disappointment as my visitors will receive at London if I return thither without any rarities to show them.

What shall I tell you of?[7]—You never saw[8] camels in your life; and perhaps the description of them will appear new to you:[9] I can assure you the first sight of them was so to me;[10] and though I have seen hundreds of pictures of those animals, I never saw any that was resembling enough to give a true idea of them. I am going to make a bold observation, and possibly a false one,[11] because nobody has ever made it before me; but I do take them to be of the stag kind;[12] their[13] legs, bodies, and necks are exactly shaped like them, and their colour[14] very near the same. 'Tis true they are much larger, being a great deal higher than a horse; and so swift, that, after the defeat of Peterwaradin, they far out-ran[15] the swiftest horses, and brought the first news of the loss of the battle to Belgrade.[16] They are never thoroughly tamed; the drivers take care to tie them one to another with strong ropes, fifty in a string, led by an ass, on which the driver rides.[17] I have[18] seen three hundred in one[19] caravan. They carry the third part more than any [19a] horse; but 'tis a particular art to load them, because of the bunch on their backs. They seem to me very ugly creatures; their heads being ill-formed and disproportioned to their bodies. They carry all the burdens; and the beasts destined to the plough are buffaloes, an animal you are also unacquainted with.[20] They are larger and more clumsy[21] than an ox; they have short, thick, black horns close to their heads, which grow turning backwards.[22] They say this horn looks very beautiful when 'tis polished.[23] They are all black, with very short hair on their hides,[24] and have extremely little white eyes, that make them look like devils.[25] The country people dye their tails, and the hair of their forehead, by way of ornament.[26]

Horses are not put here to any laborious work,[27] nor are they at all fit for it.[28] They are beautiful and full of spirit,[29] but generally little and not strong, as the breed of colder countries;[30] very gentle, however, with all their vivacity, and also swift and sure-footed.[31] I have a little white favorite that I would not part with on any terms:[32] he prances under me with so much fire, you would think that[33] I had a great deal of courage to dare to mount him; yet, I'll assure you,[34] I never rid a horse so much at my command[35] in my life.

Here are some little birds held in[36] a sort of religious reverence, and for that reason they multiply prodigiously: turtles[37] on the account of their innocence: and storks, because they are supposed to make every winter the pilgrimage to[38] Mecca. To say truth, they are the happiest subjects[39] under the Turkish government,[40] and are so sensible of[41] their privileges, that they walk the streets without fear, and generally build in the low parts[42] of houses.

Happy are those whose houses are so distinguished,[43] as the vulgar Turks are perfectly persuaded that they will not be that year attacked either by fire or pestilence. I have the happiness of[44] one of their sacred nests under my chamber-window.[45]

Now I am talking of my chamber, I remember the description of the houses here will be as new to you as any of the birds or beasts.[46] I suppose you have read in most of our accounts of Turkey, that the houses[47] are the most miserable pieces of building[48] in the world. I can speak very learnedly on that subject,[49] having been in so many of them;[50] and I assure you 'tis no such thing.[51] We are now lodged in a palace belonging to the grand-signior. I really think the manner of building here very agreeable, and proper for the country. 'Tis true they are not at all solicitous[52] to beautify the outsides of their houses,[53] and they are generally built of wood, which I own is the cause of many inconveniences; but this is not to be charged on the ill taste of the people, but[54] on the oppression of the government. Every house at the death of its master is at the grand-signior's disposal; and therefore no man cares to make a great expense, which he is not sure his family will be the better for.[55] All their design is to build a house commodious, and that will last their lives; and they are very indifferent if it falls down the year after.[56]

Every[57] house great and[58] small is divided into distinct parts, which only join together by a narrow passage. The first house[59] has a large court before it, and open galleries all around it; which is to me a thing very agreeable. This gallery leads to all the chambers, which are commonly large, and with two rows of windows, the first being of painted glass:[60] they seldom build above two stories, each of which has galleries. The stairs are broad, and not often above[61] thirty steps. This is the house belonging to the lord, and the adjoining one is called the *harem*, that is, the[62] ladies' apartment (for the name of *seraglio* is peculiar to the grand-signior) ; it has also a gallery running round it towards the garden, to which all the windows are turned, and the[63] same number of chambers as the other,[64] but more gay and splendid, both in painting and furniture. The second row of windows is very low, with grates like those of convents ;[65] the rooms are all spread with Persian carpets,[66] and raised at one end of them (my chambers are raised at both ends) about two feet.[67] This is[68] the sofa, which is laid with a richer sort of carpet, and all round it a sort of couch, raised half a foot, covered with rich silk according to the fancy or magnificence of the owner. Mine is of scarlet cloth, with a gold fringe : round about this are placed, standing against the wall, two[69] rows of cushions, the first very large, and the next little ones ; and here the Turks display their greatest magnificence. They are generally brocade, or embroidery of gold wire upon white satin ;—nothing can look more gay and splendid. These seats are also so convenient and easy,[70] that I believe I shall never endure chairs as long as I live.[71] The rooms[72] are low, which I think no fault, and the ceiling is always of wood, generally inlaid or painted with flowers. They open in many places with folding-doors, and serve for[73] cabinets, I think, more conveniently than ours. Between the windows are little arches to set pots of perfume, or baskets of flowers. But what pleases me best, is the fashion of having marble fountains in the lower part[74] of the room, which throw up several spouts of water, giving at the same time an agreeable coolness, and a pleasant dashing sound, falling from one basin to another.[75] Some of these are very magnificent. Each house has a bagnio, which consists generally in two or three little rooms, leaded on the top, paved with marble, with basins, cocks of water, and all conveniences for either hot or cold water baths.

You will perhaps be surprised at an account so different from what you have been entertained with by the common voyage-writers, who are very fond of speaking of what they don't know. It must be under [76] a very particular character, or on some extraordinary occasion, that a Christian is admitted into a house of a man of quality; and their *harems* are always forbidden ground.[77] Thus they can only speak of the outside, which makes no great appearance; [78] and the women's apartments are always built backwards, removed from sight, and have no other prospect than the gardens, which are enclosed with [79] very high walls. There are none of our parterres in them; [80] but they are planted with high trees, which give an agreeable shade, and, to my fancy, a pleasing view.[81] In the midst of the garden is the *chiosk*,[82] that is, a large room, commonly beautified with a fine fountain in the midst of it.[83] It is raised nine or ten steps, and enclosed with gilded lattices, round which vines, jessamines, and honeysuckles make a sort of green wall.[84] Large trees are planted round this place, which is the scene of their greatest pleasures, and where the ladies spend most of their hours, employed by their [85] music or embroidery.

In the public gardens there are public *chiosks*, where people go who are not so well accommodated at home, and drink their coffee, sherbet, &c. Neither are they ignorant of a more durable manner of building :[86] their mosques are all of freestone,[87] and the public *hanns*, or inns, extremely magnificent, many of them taking up a large square, built round with shops under stone arches,[88] where poor artificers are lodged *gratis*. They have always a mosque joining to them,[89] and the body of the *hann* is a most noble hall, capable[90] of holding three or four hundred persons, the court extremely spacious, and cloisters round it,[91] that give it the air of our colleges. I own I think it a more reasonable piece of charity than the founding of convents.[92]

I think I have[93] now told you a great deal[94] for once. If you don't like my choice of subjects, tell me what you would have me . write upon';[95] there is nobody more desirous to entertain you than, dear Mrs. Thistlethwayte, Yours,[96] &c. &c.

SCENE FROM "SHE STOOPS TO CONQUER."

[Young Marlow and his acquaintance, Hastings, are travelling together to visit Mr. Hardcastle, an old friend of Marlow's father, who expects them, but is personally unknown to both of them. Marlow is intended as a husband for Hardcastle's daughter. They lose their way after dusk, and are directed to Mr. H.'s house, where, on being told by a mischievous boy that it is the nearest inn, they at once make up their minds to pass the night, with the intention of continuing their journey on the next day. It is well known that Goldsmith once made a similar blunder, of taking an old friend of his father for an innkeeper, under circumstances somewhat like those which he has here so cleverly portrayed.]

Hard. Gentlemen, once more you are heartily welcome. Which is Mr. Marlow? [Mar. *advances.*] Sir, you're heartily welcome. It's not my way, you see, to receive my friends with my back to the fire! I like to give them a hearty reception, in the old style,[1] at my gate; I like to see their horses and trunks taken care of.

MAR. [*Aside.*] He has got our names from the servants already. [*To* HARD.] We approve your caution and hospitality, sir. [*To* HAST.] I have been thinking, George, of changing our travelling dresses in the morning ; I am grown confoundedly ashamed of mine.

HARD. I beg, Mr. Marlow, you'll use no ceremony in this house.

HAST. I fancy, Charles, you're right : the first blow is half the battle. We must, however, open the campaign.

HARD. Mr. Marlow—Mr. Hastings—gentlemen—pray be under no restraint in this house.[2] This is Liberty-hall,[3] gentlemen ; you may do just as you please here.

MAR. Yet, George, if we open the campaign too fiercely at first, we may want ammunition before it is over. We must show our generalship by securing, if necessary, a retreat.

HARD. Your talking of a retreat,[4] Mr. Marlow, puts me in mind of[5] the Duke of Marlborough, when he went to besiege Denain. He first summoned the garrison——

MAR. Ay, and we'll[6] summon your garrison, old boy.[7]

HARD. He first summoned the garrison, which might consist of about five thousand men——

HAST. Marlow, what's o'clock?

HARD. I say, gentlemen, as I was telling you,[8] he summoned the garrison, which might consist of about five thousand men——

MAR. Five minutes to seven.[9]

HARD. Which might consist of about five thousand men, well appointed with stores, ammunition, and other implements of war.[10] Now, says the Duke of Marlborough to George Brooks, that stood next to him—you must have heard of[11] George Brooks—" I'll pawn my dukedom," says he, "but[12] I take that garrison without spilling a drop of blood." So——

MAR. What? My[13] good friend, if you give us a glass of punch in the meantime, it would help us to carry on the siege with vigor.

HARD. Punch, sir!—This is the most unaccountable kind of modesty I ever met with.[14] [*Aside.*]

MAR. Yes, sir, punch. A glass of warm punch after our journey will be comfortable.[15]

[*Enter servant, with a tankard.*]
This is Liberty-hall, you know.

HARD. Here's a cup, sir.

MAR. So this fellow, in his Liberty-hall, will only let us have[16] just what he pleases.[17] [*Aside to* HAST.]

HARD. [*Taking the cup.*] I hope you'll find it to your mind. I have prepared it with my own hands, and I believe you'll own the ingredients are tolerable.[18] Will you be so good as to pledge me,[19]sir? Here,[20] Mr. Marlow, here is to our better acquaintance.[21] [*Drinks and gives the cup to* MARLOW.]

MAR. A very impudent fellow this;[22] but he's a character,[23] and I'll humor him a little. [*Aside.*] Sir, my service to you.[24]

HAST. I see this fellow wants to give us[25] his company, and forgets that he's an innkeeper, before he has learned to be a gentleman.[26] [*Aside.*]

MAR. From the excellence of your cup, my old friend, I suppose you have a good deal of business in this part of the country.[27] Warm work, now and then, at elections, I suppose.[28] [*Gives the tankard to* HARDCASTLE.]

HARD. No, sir, I have long given that work over. Since our betters have hit upon the expedient of electing each other,[29] there's no business for us that sell ale.[30] [*Gives the tankard to* HASTINGS.]

HAST. So you have no turn for politics, I find.[31]

HARD. Not in the least. There was a time, indeed, I fretted myself about the mistakes of the government, like other people; but finding myself every day grow more angry, and the government growing no better,[32] I left it to mend itself.[33] Since that, I no more trouble my head about[34] who's in or who's out,[35] than I do about John Nokes or Tom Stiles. So my service to you.

HAST. So that, with eating above stairs and drinking below,[36] with receiving your friends within, and amusing[37] them without, you lead a good, pleasant, bustling life of it.[38]

HARD. I do stir about a good deal,[39] that's certain. Half the differences of the parish are adjusted in this very parlor.

MAR. [*After drinking.*] And you have an argument in your cup, old gentleman, better[40] than any in Westminster-hall.[41]

HARD. Ay, young gentleman, that, and[42] a little philosophy.

MAR. Well, that is the first time I ever heard of an innkeeper's philosophy. [*Aside.*]

HAST. So then, like an experienced general, you attack them on every quarter. If you find their reason manageable, you attack them with your philosophy; if you find they have no reason, you attack them with this. Here's your health,[43] my philosopher. [*Drinks.*]

HARD. Good, very good; thank you; ha! ha! Your generalship puts me in mind of Prince Eugene, when he fought the Turks at the battle of Belgrade. You shall hear.[44]

MAR. Instead of the battle of Belgrade, I think it's almost time to talk about supper. What has your philosophy got in the house for supper?

HARD. For supper, sir?——Was ever such a request[45] to a man in his own house? [*Aside.*]

MAR. Yes, sir, supper, sir;[46] I begin to feel an appetite.[47] I shall make devilish work[48] to-night in[49] the larder, I promise you.

HARD. Such a brazen dog sure never my eyes beheld.[50] [*Aside.*] Why, really,[51] sir, as for supper, I can't well tell.[52] My Dorothy and the cookmaid settle these things between them. I leave these kind of things entirely to them.

MAR. You do, do you?[53]

HARD. Entirely. By-the-bye,[54] I believe they are in actual conversation upon what's for supper this moment in the kitchen.

MAR. Then I beg they'll admit me as one of their privy-council. It's a way I have got.[55] When I travel, I always choose to regulate my own supper. Let the cook be called. No offence, I hope, sir.[56]

HARD. O no, sir, none in the least:[57] yet, I don't know how, our Bridget,[58] the cookmaid, is not very communicative upon these occasions. Should we send for her, she might scold us all out of the house.[59]

HAST. Let's see the list of the larder,[60] then. I always match my appetite to my bill of fare.[61]

MAR. [*To* HARDCASTLE, *who looks at them with surprise.*] Sir, he's very right, and it's my way[62] too.

HARD. Sir, you have a right to command here. Here,[63] Roger, bring us the bill of fare[64] for to-night's supper: I believe it's drawn out. Your manner, Mr. Hastings, puts me in mind of my uncle, Colonel Wallop. It was a saying of his, that no man was sure of his supper till he had eaten it. [*Servant brings in the bill of fare, and exit.*]

HAST. All upon the high ropes![65] His uncle a[66] colonel! We shall soon hear of his mother being a justice[67] of peace. [*Aside.*] But let's hear the bill of fare.

MAR. [*Perusing.*] What's here? For the first course; for the second course; for the dessert.—The devil,[68] sir! Do you think we have brought down the whole Joiners' Company, or the corporation[69] of Bedford, to eat up such a supper? Two or three little things, clean and comfortable, will do.

HAST, But let's hear it.

MAR. [*Reading.*] For the first course: at the top, a pig and prune sauce.[70]

HAST. D——[71] your pig, I say.

MAR. And d—— your prune sauce, say I.

HARD. And yet, gentlemen, to men that are hungry, pig, with prune sauce, is very good eating.[72]—Their impudence confounds me. [*Aside.*] Gentlemen, you are my guests, make what alterations you please.[73] Is there anything else you wish to retrench or alter, gentlemen?

MAR. Item: a pork pie, a boiled rabbit and[74] saussages, a florentine, a shaking pudding, and a dish of tiff—taff—taffety cream.[75]

HAST. Confound your made[76] dishes! I shall be as much at a loss[77] in this house, as at a green and yellow dinner at the French ambassador's table.[78] I'm for plain eating.

HARD. I'm sorry, gentlemen, that I have nothing you like; but if there be anything you have a particular fancy to——

MAR. Why, really,[79] sir, your bill of fare is so exqui-

site, that any one part of it is full as good as another.
Send us what you please. So much for supper:[80] and
now[81] to see that our beds are aired, and properly taken
care of.

HARD. I entreat you'll leave all that to me.[82] You
shall not stir a step.

MAR. Leave that to you! I protest, sir, you must
excuse me, I always look to these things myself.[83]

HARD. I must insist, sir, you'll make yourself[84] easy
on that head.

MAR. You see I'm resolved on it.[85]—A very troublesome fellow, as ever I met with. [*Aside.*]

HARD. Well, sir, I'm resolved, at least, to attend you.
—This may be modern modesty, but I never saw anything look so like old-fashioned impudence.[86] [*Aside.*]

[*Exeunt* MAR. *and* HARD.

HAST. So, I find this fellow's civilities begin to grow
troublesome. But who can be angry with those assidui-
ties which are meant to please him?

A HIGHLAND REVENGE.[1]

MESSENGERS were despatched in great haste, to con-
centrate the MacGregor's forces,[2] with a view to the proposed attack on the Lowlanders; and the dejection and
despair, at first visible on each countenance, gave[3] place
to the hope of rescuing their[4] leader, and to the thirst of
vengeance. It was under the burning influence of the
latter passion that the wife of MacGregor commanded
that the hostage exchanged for his safety should be brought
into her presence. I believe her sons had kept this unfortunate wretch out of her sight,[5] for fear of the consequen-

ces; but if it was so,[6] their humane precaution only postponed his fate. They dragged forward at her summons a wretch already half dead with terror, in whose agonized[7] features I recognized, to my horror and[8] astonishment, my old acquaintance Morris.

He fell prostrate before the female Chief[9] with an effort to clasp her knees, from which she drew back, as if his touch had been pollution, so that all he could do in token of the extremity of his humiliation, was to kiss the hem of her plaid.[10] I never heard entreaties for life poured forth with such agony of spirit.[11] The ecstasy of fear was such[12] that instead of paralysing the tongue, as[13] on ordinary occasions, it even rendered him eloquent; and, with cheeks pale as ashes,[14] hands compressed[15] in agony, eyes that seemed to be taking their last look of all mortal objects, he protested with the deepest[16] oaths, his total ignorance of any design upon the person of Rob Roy, whom he swore he loved and honored as his own soul.[17] In the inconsistency of his terror,[18] he said he was but the agent of others, and he muttered the name of Rashleigh. He prayed but for life — for life he would give all he had in the[19] world: it was but life he asked — life, if it were to be prolonged under tortures and privations: he asked only breath, though it should be drawn in[20] the damps of the lowest caverns of their hills.

It is impossible to describe the scorn, the loathing, and contempt,[21] with which the wife of MacGregor regarded this wretched petitioner for the boon of existence.

"I could have bid ye live,"[22] she said, "had life been to you the same weary and wasting burden that it is to me — that it is to every noble and generous mind. But you — wretch! you could creep through the world unaffected by its various disgraces, its ineffable miseries, its constantly accumulating masses of crime and sorrow: you could live and enjoy yourself,[23] while the noble-minded are betrayed—while nameless and birthless villains tread on the necks of the brave and the long-descended;[24] you could enjoy yourself, like a butcher's dog in the shambles, battening on garbage, while the slaughter of the oldest and best went on around you![25] This enjoyment you shall not live to partake of!—you shall die, base dog![26] and that before yon[27] cloud has passed over the sun."

She gave a brief command in Gaelic to her attendants, two of whom seized upon the prostrate suppliant, and hurried him to the brink of a cliff which overhung the flood.[28] He set up the most piercing and dreadful cries that fear ever uttered—I may well term them[29] dreadful, for they haunted my sleep for years afterwards.[30] As the murderers, or executioners, call them as you will,[31] dragged him along, he recognized me in that moment of horror, and exclaimed, in the last articulate words I ever heard him utter, "O Mr. Osbaldistone, save me!—save me!"

I was so much moved by this horrid spectacle, that, although in momentary expectation of sharing[32] his fate, I did attempt to speak in his behalf, but, as might have been expected, my interferance was sternly disregarded. The victim was held fast by some, while others, binding a large heavy stone,[33] in a plaid, tied it round his neck, and others again eagerly stript him of some part of his dress.[34] Half-naked, and thus manacled, they hurled him into the lake, there about twelve feet deep, with a loud hallo of vindictive triumph,—above which, however, his last death-shriek, the yell of mortal agony, was distinctly heard.   The heavy burden splashed in the dark-blue waters, and the Highlanders, with their pole-axes and swords, watched an instant, to guard, lest[85] extricating himself from the load to which he was attached, the victim might have struggled to regain the shore.   But the knot had been securely bound—the wretched man sunk without effort;[86] the waters, which his fall had disturbed, settled calmly over him, and the unit of that life for which he had pleaded so strongly, was for ever withdrawn from the sum of human existence.[87] —(Sir Walter Scott, *Rob Roy*.)

THE WIDOW AND HER SON.

The parents of the deceased had resided in the village from childhood.   They had inhabited one of the neatest cottages, and by various rural occupations and the assistance[1] of a small garden, had supported themselves creditably, and comfortably, and led a happy and blameless life.   They had one son, who had grown up to be the staff and pride of their age.[2]   "Oh, sir!" said the good woman, "he was such a comely lad, so sweet-tempered, so kind to every one around him, so dutiful[3] to his parents! It did one's heart good to see him of a[4] Sunday,. dressed out in his best, so tall, so straight, so cheery, supporting his old mother to church—for she was always fonder of leaning on George's arm than on her goodman's,[5] and, poor soul,[6] she might well be proud of him, for a finer lad there was not in the country round."

Unfortunately, the son was tempted, during a year of

scarcity and agricultural hardship, to enter into the service of one of the small craft that plied on a neighboring
river.[7]   He had not been long in this employ when he
was entrapped by a press-gang and carried off to sea.[8]
His parents received tidings of his seizure, but beyond
that they could learn nothing.   It was the loss of their
main prop.   The father, who was already infirm, grew
heartless[9] and melancholy, and sunk into his[10] grave.
The widow, left alone in her age and feebleness, could no
longer support herself, and came upon[11] the parish.   Still
there was a kind feeling toward her throughout the village,
and[12] a certain respect as being one of the oldest inhabitants.   As no one applied for the cottage in which she
had passed so many happy days,[13] she was permitted[14] to
remain in it, where she lived solitary aud almost helpless.
The few wants of nature were chiefly supplied from the
scanty production of her little garden, which the neighbors would now and then cultivate[15] for her.   It was but
a few days before the time at which these circumstances
were told me, that she was gathering some vegetables[16]
for her repast, when she heard the cottage-door which
faced the garden suddenly opened.[17]   A stranger came
out, and seemed to be looking eagerly and wildly around.[18]
He was dressed in seaman's clothes, was emaciated and
ghastly pale, and bore the air of one broken[19] by sickness
and hardships.   He saw her, and hastened towards her,
but his steps were faint and faltering; he sank on his
knees before her, and sobbed like a child.   The poor woman gazed upon him with a vacant and wandering eye.
"Oh my dear, dear mother![20] don't you know your son?
your poor boy George?"[21] It was indeed the wreck of her
once noble lad; who, shattered by wounds, by sickness,

and foreign [22] imprisonment, had at length dragged his wasted limbs homeward, to repose among the scenes of his childhood.

I will not attempt to detail the particulars of such a meeting, where joy and sorrow were so completely blended. Still he was alive! he was come home! he might yet live to comfort and cherish her old age! Nature, however, was exhausted in him; and if anything had been wanting to finish the work of fate, the desolation of his native cottage would have been sufficient.[23] He stretched himself on the pallet, on which his widowed mother had passed many a sleepless night, and he never rose from it again.

The villagers, when they heard [24] that George Somers had returned,[25] crowded to see him, offering every comfort and assistance that their humble means afforded.[26] He was too weak, however, to talk; he could only look his thanks.[27] His mother was his constant attendant; and he seemed unwilling to be helped by any other hand.

There is something in sickness that breaks down [28] the pride of manhood, that softens the heart, and brings it back to the feelings of infancy. Who that has languished, even in advanced life, in sickness and despondency; who that has pined on a weary bed [29] in the neglect and loneliness of a foreign land; but has thought of the mother "that looked on his childhood," that smoothed his pillow,[30] and administered to his helplessness? Oh! there is an enduring tenderness in the love of a mother to a [31] son that transcends all other affections of the heart. It is neither to be [32] chilled by selfishness, nor daunted by danger, nor weakened by worthlessness, nor stifled by ingratitude. She will sacrifice every comfort to his convenience;

she will surrender every pleasure to his enjoyment; she will glory in his fame and exult in his prosperity: and if misfortune overtake him, he will be the dearer to her from misfortune;[33] and if disgrace settle upon[34] his name, she will still love and cherish him in spite of his disgrace,[35] and if all the world beside cast him off, she will be all the world to him.[36]

Poor George Somers[37] had known what it was to be in sickness, and none to soothe; lonely and in prison, and none to visit him.[38] He could not endure his mother from his sight;[39] if she moved away, his eye would follow[40] her. She would sit for hours by his bed, watching him as he slept. Sometimes he would start[41] from a feverish dream and look anxiously up until he saw her bending over him, when[42] he would take her hand, lay it on his bosom, and fall asleep with the tranquillity of a child. In this way[43] he died.

My first impulse, on hearing this humble tale of affliction,[44] was to visit the cottage of the mourner, and administer pecuniary assistance, and, if possible, comfort. I found, however, on inquiry, that the good feelings of the villagers had prompted them to do everything that the case admitted, and as the poor know best how[45] to console each other's sorrows, I did not venture to intrude.

The next Sunday I was at the village church, when, to my surprise, I saw the poor old woman tottering down the aisle to her accustomed seat on the steps of the altar.

She had made an effort to put on something like[46] mourning for her son; and nothing could be more touching than this struggle between pious affection and utter poverty: a black riband or so,[47] a faded black handkerchief, and one or two more such humble attempts to express by outward signs that grief which passes show.[48] When I looked round upon the storied monuments,[49] the stately hatchments, the cold marble pomp, with which grandeur mourned magnificently over departed pride,[50] and turned to[51] this poor widow, bowed down by age and sorrow at the altar of her God, and offering up the prayers and praises[52] of a pious, though a broken heart, I felt that this living monument of real grief was worth them all.[53]

I related her story to some of the wealthy members of the congregation, and they were moved by it. They exerted themselves to render her situation more comfortable and to lighten her afflictions. It was, however, but smoothing a few steps to[54] the grave. In the course of a Sunday or two after she was missed from her usual seat at church,[55] and before I left[56] the neighborhood I heard, with a feeling[57] of satisfaction, that she had quietly breathed her last,[58] and had gone to rejoin those she loved in that world where sorrow is never known and friends are never parted. — (WASHINGTON IRVING, *Sketch-Book.*)

POOR RICHARD.[1]

(WRITTEN BY BENJAMIN FRANKLIN.)

I have heard,[2] that nothing gives an author so great pleasure as to find his works respectfully quoted by other learned authors. Judge then how much I have been gratified by an incident which I am going to relate to you.

I stopped my horse lately where[3] a great number of people were collected at an auction of merchants' goods.[4] The hour of sale not being come, they were conversing on the badness[5] of the times; and one of the company called to a plain, clean, old man, with white locks,[6] "Pray, father Abraham, what think ye of the times?[7] Won't these heavy taxes quite ruin the country? How shall we ever be able to pay them? What would you advise us to?" Father Abraham stood up, and replied, — "If you'd have my advice, I'll give it to you in short;[8] for 'a word to the wise is enough;[9] and many words won't fill a bushel,'[10] as Poor Richard says."[11] They joined in desiring him to speak his mind;[12] and gathering round[13] him, he proceeded as follows:

"Friends (says he) and neighbors, the taxes are indeed very heavy; and if those laid on by the government were the only ones we had to pay, we might more easily discharge them; but we have many others, and much more grievous to some of us. We are taxed twice as much[14] by our idleness, three times as much by our pride, and four times as much[15] by our folly; and from these taxes the commissioners cannot ease or deliver us, by allowing an abatement.[16] However, let us hearken to good advice, and something may be done for us; 'God helps them that help themselves,'[17] as Poor Richard says in his Almanac.

"It would be thought a hard government that should tax its people one-tenth part[18] of their time, to be employed in its service; but idleness taxes many of us much more.[19] Sloth, by bringing on diseases, absolutely shortens life. Sloth, like rust, consumes faster than labor wears, while the key often used is always bright,'[20] as poor Richard says. 'But dost thou love life? then do not squander time, for that's the stuff life is made of,'[21] as poor Richard says. How much more than is necessary do we spend in sleep! forgetting, that 'the sleeping fox catches no poultry,[22] and that there will be sleeping enough in the grave,'[23] as poor Richard says. If time be of all things[24] the most precious, 'wasting time must be (as poor Richard says) the greatest prodigality;' since, as he elsewhere tells us, 'Lost time is never found again;[25] and what we call time enough, always proves little enough.'[26] Let us then be up and doing, and doing to the purpose.:[27] so by diligence shall we do more with less perplexity. 'Sloth makes all things difficult, but industry all easy,' as poor Richard says; and, 'he that riseth late must trot all day, and shall scarce overtake his business at night;[28] while laziness travels so slowly, that poverty soon overtakes him,'[29] as we read in poor Richard; who adds, 'Drive thy business, let not that drive thee;' and, 'early to bed, and early to rise, makes a man healthy, wealthy, and wise.'[30]

"So what signifies wishing and hoping for better times? We make these times better if we bestir ourselves. 'Industry needs not wish,'[31] as poor Richard says; and, 'He that lives upon hope will die fasting.'[32] 'There are no gains without pains;[33] then help hands, for I have no[34] lands; or if I have,[35] they are smartly taxed;'[36] and (as poor Richard likewise observes) 'He that hath a trade hath an estate,[37] and he that hath a calling hath an office of profit and honor;'[38] but then the trade must be worked at, and the calling well followed, or[39] neither the estate nor the office will enable us to pay our taxes. If we are industrious,[40] we shall never starve; for, as poor Richard says, 'At the workingman's house hunger looks in, but dares not enter.'[41] Nor will the bailiff or the constable[42] enter; for, 'Industry pays debts, but despair[43] increaseth them,' says poor Richard. What though you have found no treasure, nor has any rich relation left you a legacy?[44]

'Diligence is the mother of good luck,' as poor Richard says; and 'God gives all things to industry; then plough deep while sluggards sleep, and you will have corn to sell and to keep,' says poor Dick. Work while it is called[45] to-day; for you know not how much you may be hindered to-morrow; which makes poor Richard say, 'One to-day is worth two to-morrows;'[46] and, farther, 'Never leave that till to-morrow, which you can do to-day.'[47] If you were a servant, would you not be ashamed that a good master should catch you idle?[48] Are you then[49] your own master, be ashamed[50] to catch yourself idle,' as poor Dick says. When there is so much to be done for yourself, your family, and your country be up by peep of day. Handle your tools without mittens; remember, that 'the cat in gloves catches no mice,'[51] as poor Richard says. It is true there is much to be done, and perhaps you are weak-handed; but stick to it steadily, and you will see great effects; for 'continual dropping wears away stones,[52] and by diligence and patience the mouse ate into[53] the cable; and light strokes fell[54] great oaks,' as poor Richard says in his Almanac, the year I cannot just now remember.

"Methinks I hear some of you say, 'Must a man afford himself no leisure?'—I will tell thee, my friend, what poor Richard says: 'Employ thy time well, if thou meanest to gain leisure; and since thou art not sure of a minute, throw not away an hour.' Leisure is time for doing something useful: this leisure the diligent man will obtain,[55] but the lazy man never; so that, as poor Richard says, 'A life of leisure and a life of laziness are two things.'[56] Many without labor would live by their own wits only;[57] but they break[58] for want of stock; whereas industry[59] gives comfort, and plenty, and respect. 'Fly pleasures, and they'll follow you;[60] the diligent spinner has a large shift;[61] and, now I have a sheep and a cow, every body bids me good·morrow;'[62] all which is well said by poor Richard.

"But with our industry, we must likewise be steady, settled and careful, and oversee our own affairs with our own eyes, and not trust too much to others; for, as poor Richard says,

> 'I never saw an oft-removed tree,
> Nor yet an oft-removed family,
> That throve so well as one that settled be.[63]

"And again,·'Three removes are as bad as a fire;'[64] and again,[65] 'Keep thy shop, and thy shop will keep thee;' and again,[66] 'If you would have your business done, go; if not, send.'[67]　And again,[68]

> 'He that by the plough would thrive,
> Himself must either hold or drive.'[69]

And again, 'The eye of the master will do more work than both his hands;'[70] and again, 'want of care does us more damage than want of knowledge;' and again, 'not to oversee workmen is to leave them your purse open.' Trusting too much to others' care is the ruin of many: for, as the Almanac says, 'In the affairs of this world, men are saved, not by faith, but by the want of it;'[71] but a man's own care is profitable; for, saith poor Dick, 'Learning is to the studious, and riches to the careful, as well as power to the bold, and heaven to the virtuous.' And, farther, 'If you would have a faithful servant, and one that you like, serve yourself.'[72] And again, he adviseth to circumspection and care, even in the smallest matters, because sometimes, 'A little neglect may breed great mischief;' adding, 'For want of a nail the shoe was lost;[73]

for want of a shoe the horse was lost;[74] and for want of a horse the rider was lost,' being overtaken and slain by the enemy; all[75] for want of care about a horse-shoe nail.[76]

" So much for[77] industry, my friends, and attention to one's own business; but to these we must add frugality, if we would make our industry more certainly successful. A man may, if he knows not how to save as[78] he gets, 'keep his nose all his life to the grindstone, and die not worth a groat at last.'[79] 'A fat kitchen makes a lean will,'[80] as poor Richard says; and,

> 'Many estates are spent in the getting,
> Since women for tea forsook spinning and knitting,
> And men for punch forsook hewing and splitting.'[81]

" 'If you would be wealthy, (says he, in another Almanac) think of saving, as well as of getting: the Indies have not made Spain rich, because her outgoes are greater than her incomes.'[82]

" Away then with[83] your expensive follies, and you will not have much cause to complain of hard times, heavy taxes, and chargeable families;[84] for, as poor Dick says, 'What maintains one vice would bring up[85] two children.' You may think, perhaps, that a little tea, or a little punch now and then, diet a little more costly, clothes a little finer, and a little entertainment now and then,[86] can be no great matter;[87] but remember what poor Richard says, 'Many a little makes a mickle;'[88] and farther, 'Beware of little expenses; a small leak will sink[89] a great ship;' and again, 'Who dainties love shall beggars prove;'[90] and, moreover, 'Fools make feasts, and wise men eat them.'[91]

" Here you are all got together at this sale of fineries and knicknacks. You call them *goods;* but if you do not take care, they will prove *evils* to some of you. You expect they will be sold cheap, and perhaps they may for less than they cost ;[92] but if you have no occasion for them,[93] they must be dear to you. Remember what poor Richard says, 'Buy what thou hast no need of, and ere long thou shalt sell thy necessaries.'[94] And again, 'At a great pennyworth, pause a while.'[95] He means, that perhaps the cheapness is apparent only ; or the bargain, by straitening thee in thy business,[96] may do thee more harm than good. For in another place he says, 'Many have been ruined by buying good pennyworths.'[97] Again, as poor Richard says, 'It is foolish to lay out money in a purchase of repentance ;' and yet this folly is practised every day at auctions, for want of minding the Almanac.

"Many a one, for the sake of finery on the back, have gone with a hungry belly,[98] and half starved their families : 'Silks and satins, scarlets and velvets, (as poor Richard says) put out the kitchen fire.' These are not[99] the necessaries of life ; they can scarcely be called the conveniences ;[100] and yet, only because they look pretty, how many want to have them?[101] By these and other extravagances, the genteel[102] are reduced to poverty, and forced to borrow of those whom they formerly despised, but who, through industry and frugality, have maintained their standing ;[103] in which case, it appears plainly,[104] that 'A ploughman on his legs is higher[105] than a gentleman[106] on his knees,' as poor Richard says. Perhaps they have[107] had a small estate left them, which they know not the getting of ;[108] they think, 'It is day,[109] and will never be night ;' that a little to be spent out of so much is not worth minding.[110] But 'always taking out of the meal-tub, and never putting in, soon comes to the bottom ;'[111] then, as poor Dick says,

'When the well is dry, they [112] know the worth of water.'
But this they might have known before, if they had
taken [113] his advice: 'If you would know the value of
money, go and try to borrow some; for he that goes bor-
rowing, goes sorrowing; [114] and, indeed, so does he that
lends to such people, [115] when he goes to get it again.' [116]
Poor Dick farther advises, and says,

> 'Fond pride of dress is sure a very curse:
> Ere fancy you consult, consult your purse.' [117]

And again, 'Pride is as loud a beggar [118] as Want, and
a great deal more saucy.' [119] When you have bought one
fine thing, you must buy ten more, that your appearance
may be all of a piece; [120] but poor Dick says, 'It is easier
to suppress [121] the first desire, than to satisfy all that follow
it.' And it is as truly folly for the poor to ape the rich,
as for the frog to swell, in order to equal the ox. [122]

> 'Vessels large may venture more,
> But little boats should keep near shore.' [123]

'Tis, however, a folly soon punished; for, Pride that
dines on [124] vanity, sups on contempt,' as poor Richard
says. And, in another place, 'Pride breakfasted [125] with
Plenty, dined with Poverty, and supped with Infamy.'
And, after all, of what use is this pride of appearance, [126]
for which so much is risked, so much is suffered? It cannot promote health, or ease pain, it makes no increase of
merit in the person; it creates envy; [127] it hastens misfortune.

"But what madness must it be to run in debt [128] for
these superfluities! We are offered by the terms of this
sale six months' credit; and that perhaps has induced some
of us to attend it, because we cannot spare the ready

money, and hope now to be fine without it.[129] But, ah! think what you do when you run in debt. You give to another power over your liberty. If you cannot pay at the time,[130] you will be ashamed to see your creditor : you will be in fear when you speak to him ; you will make poor, pitiful, sneaking excuses [131] and by degrees come [132] to lose your veracity, and sink into base downright lying ; [133] for, as poor Richard says, 'The second vice is lying ; [134] the first is running in debt.' And again, to the same purpose, 'Lying rides upon debt's back ;' [135] whereas a freeborn Englishman ought not to be ashamed nor afraid to speak to any man living. But poverty often deprives. a man of all spirit [136] and virtue : 'It is hard for an empty bag to stand upright,' as poor Richard truly says. What would you think of that [137] prince, or that government, who would issue an edict, forbidding you to dress like a gentleman or gentlewoman, on [138] pain of imprisonment or servitude ? Would you not say, that you were [139] free, have a right to dress as you please, and that such an edict would be a breach of [140] your privileges, and such a government [141] tyrannical? And yet you are about to put yourself under that tyranny when you run in debt for such dress ! [142] Your creditor has authority, at his pleasure, to deprive you [143] of your liberty, by confining you in gaol for life, or by selling you for a servant,[144] if you should not be [145] able to pay him. When you have got [146] your bargain, you may, perhaps, think little of payment ; but 'Creditors (poor Richard tells us) have better memories [147] than debtors :' and in another place he says, ' Creditors are a superstitious sect, great observers of set days [148] and times.' The day [149] comes round before you are aware, and the demand is made before you are prepared to satisfy it. Or if you bear your debt in mind, the term which at first seemed so long, will, as [150] it lessens, appear extremely short : Time will seem to have added wings to his heels as well as his shoulders. 'Those have a short Lent (saith poor Richard) who owe money to be paid at Easter.' [151]

"At present, perhaps, you may think yourselves in thriving circumstances, and that you can [152] bear a little extravagance without injury ; but,

> 'For age and want save while you may,
> No morning sun lasts a whole day,' [153]

as poor Richard says. Gain may be temporary and uncertain ; but ever, while you live, expense is constant and certain : and 'it is easier to build two chimneys, than to keep one in fuel,' [154] as poor Richard says. So, 'Rather go to bed supperless than rise in debt.' [155]

> 'Get what you can, and what you get hold,
> 'Tis the stone that will turn all your lead into gold,' [156]

as poor Richard says. And when you have got the philospher's stone, [157] sure you will no longer complain of bad times, or the difficulty of paying taxes. [158]

"This doctrine, my friends, is [159] reason and wisdom : but, after all, do not depend too much upon your own industry, and frugality, and prudence, though [160] excellent things ; for they may be blasted [161] without the blessing of Heaven : and therefore ask that blessing humbly, and be not uncharitable to those that at present seem to want it, but comfort and help them. [162] Remember Job suffered, and was afterwards prosperous.

"And now, to conclude, 'Experience keeps a dear school, [163] but fools will learn in no other, and scarce in that ; [164] for it is true, we may give advice, but we cannot give conduct,' as poor Richard says. However, remember this, 'They that will[165] not be counseled, cannot be helped,' as poor Richard says; and, further, that 'If you will not hear[166] Reason, she will surely rap your knuckles.'"[167]

Thus the old gentleman ended his harangue. The people heard it, and approved the doctrine, and immediately practised[168] the contrary, just as if it had been a common sermon; for the auction opened, and they began to buy[169] extravagantly, notwithstanding all his cautions, and their own fear of taxes. I found[170] the good man[171] had thoroughly studied my Almanacs, and digested all I had dropped[172] on these topics, during the course of twenty-five years. The frequent mention he made of me must have tired every one else;[173] but my vanity was wonderfully delighted with it, though I was conscious that not a tenth part of the wisdom was my own, which he ascribed to me, but rather the gleanings that I had made of the sense[174] of all ages and nations. However,[175] I resolved to be the better for the echo of it;[176] and though I had at first determined to buy stuff for[177] a new coat, I went away, resolved to wear my old one[178] a little longer. Reader, if thou wilt do the same, thy profit will be as great as mine.[179]

I am, as ever, thine to serve thee,[180]

RICHARD SAUNDERS.

DR. JOHNSON TO THE EARL OF CHESTERFIELD.

MY LORD,—I have been lately informed, by the proprietor of the "World," that two papers,[1] in which my Dictionary is recommended to the public, were written by your Lordship. To be so distinguished is an honor which, being very little accustomed to favors from the great, I know not well how to receive or[2] in what terms to acknowledge.

When, upon some slight encouragement, I first[3] visited your Lordship, I was overpowered, like the rest of mankind, by the enchantment of your address,[4] and could not forbear to wish that I might boast myself *le vainqueur du vainqueur de la terre;*—that I might obtain[5] that regard for which I saw the world contending; but I found my attendance so little encouraged, that neither pride nor modesty would suffer me to continue it. When I had once addressed your Lordship in public, I had exhausted all the art of pleasing which a retired and uncourtly[6] scholar can possess. I had done all that I could; and no man is well pleased to have his all neglected, be it ever so little.[7]

Seven years, my Lord, have now passed, since I waited in your outward rooms, or was repulsed from your door; during which time[8] I have been pushing on my work through difficulties, of which it is useless to complain, and have brought it, at last, to the verge[9] of publication, without one act of assistance, one word of encouragement, or one smile of favor. Such treatment I did not expect,[10] for I never had a patron before.

The shepherd in Virgil grew at last acquainted with[11] Love, and found him a native of the rocks.

Is not a patron, my Lord, one who looks with unconcern on a man struggling for life in the water, and, when he has reached the ground, encumbers him with help? The notice which you have been pleased to take of[12] my labors, had it been early, had been kind;[13] but it has been delayed till [14] I am indifferent, and cannot enjoy it; till I am solitary, and cannot impart it; till I am known, and do not want it. I hope it is no [15] very cynical asperity not to confess [16] obligations where no benefit has been received, or to be unwilling that the public should consider me as owing that to a patron which Providence has enabled me to do for [17] myself.

Having carried on my work thus far [18] with so little obligation to any favorer of learning, I shall not be disappointed though I should [19] conclude it, if less be possible, with less; for I have long been wakened from that dream of hope in which I once boasted myself with so much exultation,[20] my Lord, your Lordship's [21] most humble, most obedient servant.

THE NATIVE VILLAGE.

A kind of dread had hitherto kept me back; but I was restless now, till I had accomplished my wish. I set out one morning to walk; I reached Widford about eleven in the forenoon; after a slight breakfast at my inn, where I was mortified to perceive the old landlord did not know me again (old Thomas Billet, he has often made angle-rods [1] for me when a child), I rambled over all my accustomed haunts.

Our old house was vacant, and to be sold; I entered, unmolested, into the room that had been my bed-chamber. I kneeled down on the spot where my little bed had stood: I felt like a child; I prayed like one.[2] It seemed as though old times were to return again.[3] I looked round involuntarily, expecting to see some face I knew; but all was naked and mute. The bed was gone. My little pane of painted window, through which I loved to look at the sun, when I awoke in a fine summer's morning, was taken out, and had been replaced by one of common glass.

I visited by turns every chamber; they were all desolate and unfurnished, one excepted,[4] in which the owner had left a harpsichord, probably to be sold: I touched the keys; I played some old Scottish tunes, which had delighted me when a child. Past associations revived with the music; blended with a sense of *unreality*,[5] which at last became too powerful, I rushed out of the room to give vent to my feelings.

I wandered, scarce knowing where, into[6] an old wood, that stands at the back of the house; we called it the *Wilderness*. A well-known *form* was missing that used to meet me in this place: it was thine, Ben Moxam, the kindest, gentlest, politest of human beings, yet was he nothing higher than a gardener in the family. Honest creature, thou didst never pass me in my childish rambles without a soft speech and a smile. I remember thy good-natured face. But there is one thing for which I can never forgive thee, Ben Moxam, that thou didst join with an old maiden aunt of mine in a[7] cruel plot to lop away the hanging branches of the old fir-trees. I remember them sweeping to the ground.[8]

I have often left my childish sports to ramble in this place; its glooms and its solitudes had a mysterious charm for my young mind, nurturing within me that love of quietness and lonely thinking, which have accompanied me to maturer years.

In this *Wilderness* I found myself after a ten years' absence. Its stately fir-trees were yet standing, with all their luxuriant company of underwood : the squirrel was there, and [9] the melancholy cooings of the wood-pigeons ; all was as I had left it ; my heart softened at the sight ; it seemed as though my character had been suffering a *change* since I forsook these shades.

My parents [10] were both dead ; I had no counsellor left, no experience of age to direct me, no sweet voice of reproof. The Lord had taken away my *friends*, and I knew not where he had lain them. I paced round the wilderness, seeking a comforter. I prayed, that I might be restored to that *state of innocence* in which I had wandered in those shades.

Methought my request was heard ; for it seemed as though [11] the stains of manhood were passing from me, and I were relapsing into the purity and simplicity of childhood. I was content to have been moulded into a perfect child. [12] I stood still as in a trance. I dreamed I was enjoying a personal intercourse with my heavenly Father, and, extravagantly, [13] put off the shoes from my feet ; for the place, where I stood, I thought was holy ground.

This state of mind could not last long, and I returned, with languid feelings, to my inn. I ordered my dinner, green peas and a sweetbread : it had been a favorite dish with me in my childhood ; I was allowed to have it on my birth-days. I was impatient to see it come upon table ; but, when it came, I could scarce eat a mouthful ; my tears choked me. I called for [14] wine ; I drank a pint and a half [15] of red wine, and not till then had I dared to [16] visit the churchyard where my parents were interred.

The *cottage* lay in [17] my way. Margaret had chosen it for that very reason, to be near the church ; for the old lady was regular in her attendance on public worship. I passed on,[18] and in a moment found myself among the tombs.

I had been present at my father's burial, and knew the spot again; my mother's funeral I was prevented by illness from attending :[19] a plain stone was placed over the grave, with their initials carved upon it,[20] for they both occupied one grave.

I prostrated myself before the spot; I kissed the earth that covered them; I contemplated with gloomy delight the time when I should mingle my dust with theirs, and kneeled, with my arms incumbent on the grave-stone, in a kind of mental prayer : for I could not speak.

Having performed these duties, I arose with quieter feelings, and felt leisure to attend to indifferent objects. Still I continued in the churchyard, reading the various inscriptions, and moralizing upon them with that kind of levity which will not unfrequently[21] spring up in the mind in the midst of deep melancholy. I read of nothing but[22] careful parents, loving husbands, and dutiful children. I said jestingly, where be all the *bad* people buried?[23] Bad parents, bad husbands, bad children, what cemeteries are appointed for these? do they not sleep in consecrated ground? or is it but a pious fiction, a generous oversight, in the survivors, which thus tricks out[24] men's epitaphs when dead,[25] who, in their life-time, discharged the offices of life, perhaps, but lamely? Their failings, with their reproaches, now sleep with them in the grave. *Man wars not with the dead.* It is a *trait* of human nature, for which I love it.[26]—(CHARLES LAMB, *Rosamond Gray*.)

ON FORMING A TASTE FOR[1] SIMPLE PLEASURES.

The simple and innocent satisfactions of nature are usually within reach; and, as they excite no violent perturbation in the pursuit, so are they enjoyed without tumult, and relinquished without long or painful regret. It will, then, render essential service, both to happiness and morality, if we can persuade men in general to taste and to contract an habitual relish for the genuine satisfaction of uncorrupted nature.

The young mind is always delighted with rural scenery. The earliest poetry was pastoral, and every juvenile poet of the present day delights to indulge in the luxuriance of a rural description. A taste for these pleasures will render the morning walk at least as delightful as the evening assembly. The various forms which nature assumes[2] in the vicissitudes of the seasons constitute a source of complacency which can never be exhausted. How grateful to the senses is the freshness of the herbage, the fragrancy of the flowers, and all those simple delights of the field, which the poets have, from the earliest ages, no less justly than exuberantly described! "It is all[3] mere fiction," exclaims the man of the world, "the painting of a visionary enthusiast." He feels not, he cannot feel, their truth.[4] He sees no charms in herbs and blossoms; the melody of the grove is no music to his ear;[5] and this happens because he has lost by his own fault those tender sensibilities which nature had bestowed. They are still daily perceived in all their perfection by the ingenuous and innocent, and they have been most truly described by feeling poets, as contributing to pure, real, and exalted delight.

Yet the possessor of extensive lands, if he is a man of fashion and spirit, forsakes the sweet scenes of rural nature, and shuts himself up in a crowded metropolis, and leaves that liberal air, which breathes over his lawns and agitates his forests, to be inhaled by his menial rustics.[6] He perverts the designs of nature and despises the hereditary blessings of Providence ; he receives the adequate punishment in a restless life, perpetually seeking, and never finding, satisfaction. But the employments of agriculture, independently of their profit, are most congenial and pleasing to human nature. An uncorrupted mind sees, in the progress of vegetation, and in the manner and excellences of those animals which are destined to our immediate service, such charms and beauties as art can seldom produce. Husbandry may be superintended by an elegant mind ; nor is it by any means necessary that they who engage in it should contract a coarseness of manners or a vulgarity of sentiment. It is most favorable to health, to plenty, to repose, and to innocence ; and great, indeed, must be the objects which justify a reasonable creature in relinquishing these. Are plays, are balls, are nocturnal assemblies of whatever denomination, which tend to rob us of sleep, to lessen our patrimony, to injure our health, to render us selfish, vicious, thoughtless, and useless, equivalent to these? Reason replies in the negative ;[7] yet the almost universal departure from innocence and simplicity will leave the affirmative established by a corrupt majority.

It is not without a sigh that a thinking man can pass by a lordly mansion, some sweet retreat, deserted by its falsely refined possessor, who is stupidly carousing in a polluted city. When he sees the chimney without smoke in the venerable house where all the country was once welcomed to partake of[8] princely hospitality, he cannot help[9] lamenting that progress of refinement which, in rendering the descendants of the great fine gentleman, has left them something[10] less than men through the defect of manly virtues.

The superintendence of a garden might of itself occupy a life elegantly and pleasurably; nothing is better able to gratify the inherent love of novelty, for nature is always renewing her variegated appearance. She is infinite in her productions, and the life of man may come to its close before he has seen half of the pictures which she is able to display. The taste for gardening in England is at present pure. Nature is restored to her throne, and reigns majestically beautiful in rude magnificence. The country abounds with cultivated tracts truly paradisiacal.[11] But as the contemplative observer roams over the lawn and enjoys the shade of the weeping willow, he is often led to inquire, "Where is now the owner of this wilderness of sweets?[12] Happy man!" he exclaims, "to possess such a spot as this, and to be able at all times to taste the pleasure which I feel springing in my bosom." But, alas! the owner is engaged in other scenes. He is rattling over the streets[13] of London, and pursuing[14] all the sophisticated joys which succeed to supply the place where nature is relinquished. If he condescends to pay an annual visit to the retreat, he brings with him all his acquired inclinations; and while he sits at the card-table, or at the banquet, and thinks of little else than promoting his interest at the next election, he leaves the shrub to blossom and the rose to diffuse its sweets [15] in unobserved solitude.—(KNOX, *Essays*.)

SCENE FROM THE PLAY OF "MONEY."

(BY SIR EDWARD BULWER LYTTON.)

[GEORGINA, and SIR JOHN VESEY (*Bart.*, *Knight of the Guelph*, *F.R.S.*, *F.S.A.*), *her father.*]

GEOR. And you really feel sure that poor Mr. Mordaunt has made me his heiress?

SIR J. Ay, the richest heiress in England. Can you doubt it? Are you not his nearest relation? Niece by your poor mother, his own sister.[1] All the time he was making his enormous fortune in India, did we ever miss sending him little reminiscences of our disinterested affection? When he was last in England, and you only so high,[2] was not my house his home?[3] Didn't I get a surfeit out of complaisance to his execrable curries and pillaws?[4] Didn't he smoke his hookah—nasty old—that is, poor dear man—in my best[5] drawing-room? And did you ever speak without calling him your "handsome uncle?"—for the excellent creature was as vain as a peacock,[6]—

GEOR. And so ugly,[7]—

SIR J. The dear deceased! Alas, he *was*, indeed.[8] And *if*, after all these marks of attachment, you are *not* his heiress, why then the finest feelings of our nature—the ties of blood—the principles of justice—are implanted in us in vain.

GEOR. Beautiful, sir.[9] Was not that in your last

speech at the Freemason's Tavern upon the great Chimney-sweep Question?

SIR J. Clever girl![10]—what a memory she has! Sit down, Georgy. Upon this most happy—I mean melancholy occasion, I feel that I may trust you with a secret. You see this fine house — our fine servants — our fine plate — our fine dinners: every one thinks Sir John Vesey a rich man.

GEOR. And are you not, papa?

SIR J. Not a bit of it[11]—all humbug, child—all humbug,[12] upon my soul! As you hazard a minnow to hook in a trout, so one guinea thrown out with address is often the best bait for a hundred. There are two rules in life —First, Men are valued not for what they *are*, but what they *seem* to be. Secondly, if you have no merit or money of your own, you must trade on the merits or money of other people. My father got the title by services in the army and died penniless. On the strength of[13] his services I got a pension of 400*l.* a-year — on the strength of 400*l.* a-year[14] I took credit for[15] 800*l.*: on the strength of 800*l.* a-year I married your mother with 10,000*l.*: on the strength of 10,000*l.*, I took credit for 40,000*l.*, and paid Dicky Gossip three guineas a-week to go about everywhere calling me "Stingy Jack!"[16]

GEOR. Ha! ha! A disagreeable nickname.

SIR J. But a valuable reputation. When a man is called stingy, it as much as calling him rich; and when a man's called rich, why he's a man universally respected. On the strength of my respectability I wheedled a constituency,[17] changed my politics, resigned my seat to a minister, who, to a man of such stake[18] in the country, could offer nothing less in return than a patent office of

2,000*l.* a-year. That's the way to succeed in life. Humbug, my dear!—all humbug,[19] upon my soul!

GEOR. I must say that you —

SIR J. Know the world, to be sure. Now, for your fortune,—as I spend more than my income, I can have nothing to leave you; yet, even without counting your uncle, you have always passed for an heiress on the credit[20] of your expectations from the savings of "Stingy Jack." The same with your education. I never grudged anything to make a show[21]—never stuffed your head with histories and homilies; but you draw, you sing, you dance, you walk well into a room;[22] and that's the way young ladies are educated now-a-days, in order to become a pride to their parents, and a blessing to their husband —that is when they have caught him. Apropos of a husband: you know we thought of[23] Sir Frederick Blount.

GEOR. Ah, papa, he is charming.

SIR J. He *was so*, my dear, before we knew your poor uncle was dead; but an heiress such as you will be should look out for[24] a duke.—Where the deuce is Evelyn this morning?

GEOR. I've not seen him, papa. What a strange character he is,[25] so sarcastic; and yet he can be agreeable.

SIR J. A humorist[26]—a cynic! one never knows how to take him. My private secretary,—a poor cousin,—has not got a shilling,[27] and yet, hang me,[28] if he does not keep us all at a sort of a distance.[29]

GEOR. But why do you take him to live with us, papa, since there's no good to be got by it?

SIR J. There you are wrong;[30] he has a great deal of talent; prepares my speeches, writes my pamphlets, looks up my calculations. My report on[31] the last Commission has got me a great deal of fame, and has put me at the head of the new one.　Besides, he *is* our cousin — he has no salary :[32] kindness to a poor relation always tells well[33] in the world ; and benevolence is a useful virtue, — particularly when you can have it for nothing !　With our other cousin, Clara, it was different : her father thought fit to leave me her guardian, though she had not a penny — a mere useless incumbrance : so, you see, I got my half-sister, Lady Franklin, to take her off my hands.[34]

Geor. How much longer is Lady Franklin's visit to be ?

Sir J. I don't know, my dear ; the longer the better,[35] — for her husband left her a good deal of money at her own disposal.　Ah, here she comes.

LORD CHATHAM'S SPEECH FOR THE IMMEDIATE REMOVAL OF THE TROOPS FROM BOSTON, IN AMERICA. — (June 20, 1775.)

Too well apprized of the contents of the papers, now at last laid before the House, I shall not take up their[1] Lordships' time in tedious and fruitless investigations, but shall seize the first moment to open the door of reconcilement ; for every moment of delay is a moment of danger. As I have not the honor of access to his Majesty, I will endeavor to transmit to him, through the constitutional channel of this House, my ideas of America, to *rescue* him from the misadvice of his present ministers.　America, my lords, cannot be reconciled, she ought not to be reconciled, to this country, till the troops of Britain are withdrawn from the continent ; they are a bar to all confidence; they are a source of perpetual irritation; they threaten a fatal catastrophe. How can America trust you with the bayonet at her breast? How can she suppose that you mean less than bondage or death? I therefore, my lords, move, that an humble address be presented to his Majesty, most humbly to advise and beseech his Majesty, that, in order to open the way towards a happy settlement of the dangerous troubles in America, it may graciously please his Majesty to transmit orders to General Gage for removing his Majesty's forces from the town of Boston. I know not, my Lords, who advised the present measures; I know not who advises to a perseverance and enforcement of them: but this I will say,[2] that the authors of such advice ought to answer it[3] at their utmost peril. I wish, my Lords, not to lose a day in this urgent pressing crisis; an hour now lost in allaying ferments in America may produce years of calamity. Never will I desert, in any stage of its progress, the conduct of this momentous business. Unless fettered to my bed by the extremity of sickness, I will give it unremitting attention. I will knock at the gates of this sleeping and confounded ministry, and will, if it be possible, rouse them to a sense of their danger. The recall of your army I urge as necessarily preparatory to the restoration of your peace. By this it will appear[4] that you are disposed to treat amicably and equitably, and to consider, revise, and repeal, if it should be found necessary, as I affirm it will, those violent acts and declarations which have disseminated confusion throughout the empire. Resistance to these acts was necessary, and therefore just; and your vain declarations of the omnipotence of parliament, and your imperious doctrines of the necessity of submission, will be found equally impotent to convince or enslave America, who feels that tyranny is equally intolerable, whether it be exercised by an individual part of the Legislature, or by the collective bodies which compose it. The means of enforcing this thraldom are found to be as ridiculous and weak in practice as they are unjust in principle. Conceiving of General Gage as a man of humanity and understanding, entertaining, as I ever must, the highest respect and affection for the British troops, I feel the most anxious sensibility for their situation, pining in inglorious inactivity. You may call them an army of safety and defence, but they are in truth an army of impotence and contempt, and to make the folly equal to the disgrace, they are an army of irritation and vexation. Allay then the ferment prevailing in America by removing the obnoxious hostile cause. If you delay concession till your vain hope shall be accomplished of triumphantly dictating reconciliation, you delay for ever : the force of this country would be disproportionately exerted against a brave, generous, and united people, with arms in their hands, and courage in their hearts — three millions of people, the genuine descendants of a valiant and pious ancestry, driven to those deserts by the narrow maxims of a superstitious tyranny. But is the spirit of persecution never to be appeased? Are the brave sons of those brave forefathers to inherit their sufferings, as they have inherited their virtues? Are they to sustain the infliction of the most oppressive and unexampled severity, beyond what history has related or poetry has feigned?

> Rhadamanthus habet durissima regna,
> Castigatque, *auditque* dolos.

But the Americans must not be heard ; they have been

condemned unheard. The indiscriminate hand of vengeance has devoted thirty thousand British subjects of all ranks, ages, and descriptions, to one common ruin. You may, no doubt, destroy their cities; you may cut them off from [5] the superfluities, perhaps the conveniences of life; but, my lords, they will still despise your power, for they have yet remaining [6] their woods and their liberty. What though [7] you march from town to town, from province to province; though you should be able to enforce a temporary and local submission: how shall you be able to secure the obedience of the country you leave behind you, in your progress of [8] eighteen hundred miles of continent, animated with the same spirit of liberty and of resistance? This universal opposition to your arbitrary system of taxation might have been foreseen: it was obvious from [9] the nature of things, and from the nature of man, and, above all, from the confirmed habit of thinking, from the spirit of whiggism, flourishing in America. The spirit which now pervades America, is the same which formerly opposed loans, benevolences, [10] and ship money [11] in this country; the same spirit which roused all England to action at the revolution, and which established at a remote era your liberties on the basis of that great fundamental maxim of the constitution, that no subject of England shall be taxed but by his own consent. What shall oppose this spirit, aided by the congenial [12] flame glowing in the breast of every generous Briton? To maintain this principle is the common cause of the whigs on the other side of the Atlantic and on this: it is liberty to liberty engaged. In this great cause they are immoveably allied: it is the alliance of God and nature, immutable, eternal, fixed as the firmament of Heaven. As an [13] Englishman, I recognize to the Americans their supreme, unalterable right of property. As an American, I would equally recognize to England her supreme right of regulating commerce and navigation. This distinction is involved in the abstract nature of things : property is private, individual, absolute ; the touch of another annihilates it. Trade is an extended and complicated consideration : it reaches as far as ships can sail or winds can blow ; it is a vast and various machine. To regulate the numberless movements of its several parts, and to combine them in one harmonious effect, for the good of the whole, requires the superintending wisdom and energy of the supreme power of the empire. On this grand practical distinction, then, let us rest : taxation is theirs ; commercial regulation is ours. As to the metaphysical refinements,[14] attempting to show that the Americans are equally free from legislative control and commercial restraint, as from taxation for the purpose of revenue, I pronounce them futile, frivolous, groundless. When your lordships have perused the papers transmitted us from America, when you consider the dignity, the firmness, and the wisdom with which the Americans have acted, you cannot but respect their cause. History, my lords, has been my favorite study ; and in the celebrated writings of antiquity have I often admired the patriotism of Greece and Rome ; but, my lords, I must declare and vow that, in the master-senates[15] of the world, I know not the[16] people, nor the senate, who in such a complication of difficult circumstances, can stand in preference to[17] the delegates of America assembled in General Congress at Philadelphia. I trust it is obvious to your lordships that all attempts to impose servitude upon such men, to establish despotism over such a mighty continental nation,

must·be vain, must be futile. Can such a national prin-
cipled union [18] be resisted by the tricks of office or minis-
terial manœuvres? Heaping papers on your table, or
counting your majorities on a division,[19] will not avert or
postpone the hour of danger. It must arrive, my lords,
unless these fatal acts are done away with : it must arrive
in all its horrors ; and then these boastful ministers, in
spite of all their confidence and all their manœuvres, shall
be compelled to hide their heads.[20] But it is not repealing this or that[21] act of parliament, it is not repealing a
piece of parchment, that can restore America to your
bosom : you must repeal her fears and resentments, and
then you may hope for her love and gratitude. But now,
insulted with an armed force, irritated with a hostile array before her eyes, her concessions, if you *could* force
them, would be suspicious and insecure. But it is more
than evident that you *cannot* force them to your unworthy
terms of submission — it is impossible — *we* ourselves shall
be forced ultimately to retract : let us retract while we
can, not when we must. I repeat it, my lords, we shall
one day be *forced* to undo these violent acts of oppression ;
they must be repealed ; you will repeal them. I pledge
myself for it,[22] that you will in the end repeal them. I
stake my reputation on it ;[23] I will consent to be taken for
an *idiot* if they are not repealed. Avoid then this humili-
ating, disgraceful necessity. With a dignity becoming
your exalted situation, make the first advances to concord,
to peace, and to happiness. Concession comes with better
grace, and more salutary effect from superior power ; it
reconciles superiority of power with the feelings of man,
and·establishes .solid confidence on the foundations of affection and gratitude. On the other hand, every danger

and every hazard impend to deter you from perseverance in the present ruinous measures : foreign war hanging over your heads by a slight and brittle thread ; France and Spain watching your conduct, and waiting for the maturity of your errors, with a vigilant eye to America and the temper[24] of your colonies, *more than to their own concerns, be they what they may.*[25] To conclude, my lords, if the ministers thus persevere in misadvising and misleading the king, I will not say that they *can* alienate the affections of his subjects from the crown ;[26] but I affirm they will make the crown not worth his wearing. I will not say that the *king is betrayed*, but I will pronounce that the *kingdom is undone.*

THE DEFEAT OF THE SPANISH ARMADA.
[1588.]

It was on Saturday, the 20th of July, that Lord Effingham came in sight of his formidable adversaries. The " invincible " Armada was drawn up[1] in form of a crescent, which from horn to horn measured some seven miles.[2] There was a south-west wind ; and before it the vast vessels sailed slowly on.[3] The English let them pass by ; and then following in the rear,[4] commenced an attack on them. A running fight[5] now took place, in which some of the best ships of the Spaniards were captured ; many more[6] received heavy damage ; while the English vessels, which took care not to close with[7] their huge antagonists, but availed themselves of their superior celerity in tacking[8] and manœuvring, suffered little comparative loss.[9] Each day added not only to the spirit, but to the number of Effingham's force.

Raleigh justly[10] praises the English admiral for[11] his skilful tactics.[12] He says, "Certainly, he that will happily perform a fight at sea, must be skilful in making choice of vessels to fight in ; he must believe that there is more belonging to a good man-of-war, upon the waters, than great daring ;[13] and must know that there is a great deal of difference between fighting loose, or at large, and grappling.[14] The guns of a slow ship pierce as well, and make as great holes, as those in a swift. To clap ships together,[15] without consideration, belongs[16] rather to a madman than to a man of war."

The Armada lay off[17] Calais, with its largest ships ranged outside. The English admiral could not attack them in their position without great disadvantage, but on the night of the 29th he sent eight fire-ships among them, with almost equal effect to that of the fire-ships which the Greeks so often employed against the Turkish fleets in their late war of independence. The Spaniards cut their cables and put to sea[18] in confusion. One of their largest galeasses[19] ran foul of[20] another vessel aud was stranded.[21] The rest of the fleet was scattered about on the Flemish coast,[22] and when the morning broke,[23] it was with difficulty and delay that they obeyed their admiral's signal to range themselves round him near Gravelines. Now was the golden opportunity for the English to assail them, and prevent them from ever letting loose Parma's flotilla against England ; and nobly was that opportunity used.[24] Drake and Fenner were the first English captains who attacked the unwieldy leviathans : then came Fenton, Southwell, Burton, Cross, Raynor, and then the lord admiral, with Lord Thomas Howard and Lord Sheffield. The Spaniards only thought of forming and keeping close together,[25] and were driven by the English past Dunkirk,[26] and far away from the Prince of Parma, who in watching their defeat from the coast, must, as Drake expressed it, have chafed like a bear robbed of her whelps. This was indeed the last and the [27] decisive battle between the two fleets. It is, perhaps, best described in the very words of the contemporary writer as we may read them in Hakluyt.[28]

"Upon the 29th of July in the morning, the Spanish fleet after the above mentioned tumult,[29] having arranged themselves again into order,[30] were, within sight of Grave-lines, most bravely and furiously encountered by the English ; where [31] they once again got the wind of[32] the Spaniards : who suffered themselves to be deprived of the commodity of the place in the Calais road,[33] and of the advantage of the wind near unto Dunkirk, rather than they would change [34] their array or separate their forces now conjoined and united together, standing only upon their defence.[35]

"And howbeit [36] there were many excellent and war-like [37] ships in the English fleet, yet were there scarce 22 or 23 among them all, which matched 90 of the Spanish ships in the bigness,[38] or could conveniently assault them. Wherefore the English ships using their prerogative of nimble steerage,[39] whereby they could turn and wield themselves with the wind which way they listed,[40] came often very near upon the Spaniards, and charged them so sore,[41] that now and then they were but a pike's length asunder : and so continually giving them one broadside after another,[42] they discharged all their shot both great and small [43] upon them, spending one whole day from morning till night in that violent kind of conflict, until powder and bullets [44] failed them. In regard of which want [45] they thought it convenient not to pursue the Spaniards any longer, because they had many great advantages of the English, namely, for the extraordinary bigness of their ships, and also for that they were so nearly conjoined, and kept together in so good array, that they could by no means be fought withal one to one. The English thought, therefore that they had right well acquitted themselves, in chasing the Spaniards first from Calais, and then from Dunkirk, and by that means to have hindered them from joining with [46] the Duke of Parma's forces, and getting the wind of them, to have driven them from their own coasts.

"The Spaniards that day sustained great loss and damage, having many of their ships shot through and through, [47] and they discharged likewise great store of ordinance [48] against the English; who, indeed, sustained some hindrance, but not comparable to the Spaniards' loss: for they did not lose either one ship or person of importance, although Sir Francis Drake's ship was pierced with shot about forty times."

It reflects little credit on the English government [49] that the English fleet was so deficiently supplied with ammunition, as to be unable [50] to complete the destruction of the invaders. But enough was done to ensure it. Many of the largest Spanish ships were sunk or captured in the action of this day. [51] And at length the Spanish admiral, desparing of success, fled northward with a southerly wind, in the hope of rounding Scotland, and so returning to Spain without a farther encounter with the English fleet. Lord Effingham left a squadron to continue the blockade of the Prince of Parma's armament; but that wise general soon withdrew [52] his troops to more promising fields of action.[53] Meanwhile the lord admiral himself and Drake chased [54] the vincible [55] Armada, as it was now termed, for some distance northward; and then, when it seemed to bend away [56] from the Scotch coast towards Norway,[57] it was thought best, in the words of Drake, "to leave them to those boisterous and uncouth northern seas."

The sufferings and losses which the unhappy Spaniards sustained in their flight round Scotland and Ireland, are well known. Of their whole. Armada only fifty-three shattered vessels brought back their beaten and wasted crews to the Spanish coast which they had quitted in such pageantry and pride.—(CREASY, *The Fifteen Decisive Battles of the World.*)

LITTLE EPPIE'S MISCHIEF.

Silas had chosen a broad strip of linen as a means of fastening little Eppie to his loom when he was busy: it made a broad belt about her waist, and was long enough to allow of her reaching the truckle-bed and sitting down on it, but not long enough for her to attempt any dangerous climbing.[1] One bright summer's morning, the weaver had been more engrossed than usual in "setting up" a new piece of work,[2] an occasion on which his scissors were in requisition. These scissors had been kept carefully out of Eppie's reach; but the click of them had a peculiar attraction for her ear, and, watching the results of that click, she had derived the philosophic lesson that[3] the same cause would produce the same effect. Silas had seated himself in his loom, and the noise of weaving had began, but he had left his scissors on a ledge[4] which Eppie's arm was long enough to reach; and now, like a small mouse watching her opportunity, she stole quietly from her corner, secured the scissors, and toddled to the bed again, turning her back as a mode of concealing the fact. She had a distinct intention as to the use of the scissors; and having cut the linen strip in a jagged, but effectual manner, in two moments she had run out at the open door where the sunshine was inviting her, while poor Silas believed her to be a better child than usual.[5]

It was not until he happened to need[6] his scissors that the terrible fact burst upon him: Eppie had run out by herself—had perhaps fallen into the stone-pit. Silas, shaken by the worst fear that could have befallen him, rushed out calling "Eppie!" and ran eagerly about the unenclosed space, exploring the dry cavities into which she might have fallen, and then gazing with questioning dread at the smooth surface of the water.[7] The cold drops stood on his brow.[8] How long had she been out? There was one hope, that[9] she had crept through the stile and got into the fields where he habitually took her to stroll. But the grass was high in the meadow, and there was no descrying her,[10] if she were there, except by a close search that would be a trespass on Mr. Osgood's crop. Still the misdemeanor must be committed, and poor Silas, after peering all round the hedgerows, traversed the grass, beginning with perturbed vision to see[11] Eppie behind every group of red sorrel, and to see her moving always farther off as he approached. The meadow was searched in vain; and he got over the stile into the neat field, looking with a dying hope towards a small pond which was now reduced to its summer shallowness, so as to leave a wide margin [12] of good adhesive mud. Here, however, sat Eppie, discoursing cheerfully to her own small boot, which she was using as a bucket to convey the water into a deep hoof-mark, while her naked foot was planted comfortably on a cushion of olive-green mud. A red-headed calf was observing her with alarmed doubt through the opposite hedge.

Here was clearly a case of aberration in a child which demanded severe treatment, but Silas, overcome with convulsive joy at finding his treasure again, could do nothing but snatch her up and cover her with half-sobbing kisses. It was not until he had carried her home, and had begun to think of the necessary washing that he recollected the need that he should punish Eppie, and "make her remember." The idea that she might run away again and come to harm,[13] gave him unusual resolution, and for the first time he determined to try the coal-hole, a small closet near the hearth. "Naughty, naughty Eppie," he suddenly began, holding her on his knee, and pointing to her muddy feet and clothes — "Naughty to cut with scissors and run away. Eppie must go into the coal-hole for being naughty. Daddy must put her in the coal-hole."

He half expected that this would be shock enough,[14] and that Eppie would begin to cry. But instead of that, she began to shake herself on his knee, as if the proposition opened a pleasing novelty.[15] Seeing that he must proceed to extremities,[16] he put her into the coal-hole, and held the door closed, with a trembling sense that he was [17] using a strong measure. For a moment there was silence, but then came a little cry, "Opy, opy," and Silas let her out again, saying, "Now Eppie will never be naughty again, else she must go in the coal-hole — a black, naughty place." The weaving must stand still a long while this morning, for now Eppie must be washed and have clean clothes on; but it was ·to be hoped that this punishment would have a lasting effect, and save time in future — though, perhaps, it would have been better if Eppie had cried more.

In half-an-hour she was clean again, and, Silas having turned his back to see what he could do with the linen band, threw it down again, with the reflection that Eppie would be good without fastening for the rest of the morning, he turned round again, and was going to place her in her little chair near the loom, when she peeped out at him with black face and hands again, and said, "Eppie in de toal-hole." This total failure of the coal-hole discipline shook Silas's belief in its efficacy.[18] "She takes it all for fun," he observed to himself.

So Eppie was reared without punishment, the burden of her misdeeds being borne vicariously by father Silas.

(G. ELIOT, Silas Marner.)

THE MONKEY AND THE TWO CATS.

Two cats, having stolen some cheese, could not agree about dividing their prize. In order, therefore, to settle the dispute, they consented to refer the matter to a monkey.[1] The proposed arbitrator very readily accepted the office,[2] and producing a balance,[3] put a part into each scale.—"Let me see," said he, "ay! this lump outweighs

Mr. L. Such as balls,[23] ninepins, marbles, tops, and wooden horses.

B. No, sir; but our Tom[24] makes footballs to kick[25] in the cold weather, and we set traps for birds; and then I have a pair of stilts to walk through the dirt with; and I had a hoop, but it is broken.

Mr. L. And do you want nothing else?

B. No, sir: for I always ride the horses to field, and tend the cows, and run to town for errands;[26] and that is as good as play, you know.[27]

Mr. L. Well, but you could buy apples or gingerbread at the town, I suppose, if you had money?

B. Oh! I can get apples at home; and as for gingerbread, I don't mind it much,[28] for my mother gives me a pie now and then, and that is as good.

Mr. L. Would you not like a knife to cut sticks?

B. I have one — here it is — brother Tom gave it me.

Mr. L. Your shoes are full of holes — don't you want a better pair?[29]

B. I have a better pair for Sundays.

Mr. L. But these let in water.[30]

B. Oh, I don't care for that.[31]

Mr. L. Your hat is all torn, too.

B. I have a better at home; but I had as lief have none at all,[32] for it hurts my head.

Mr. L. What do you do when it rains?

B. If it rains very hard, I get under the hedge till it is over.

Mr. L. What do you do when you are hungry before it is time to go home?

B. I sometimes eat a raw turnip.

Mr. L. But if there are none?

B. Then I do as well as I can; I work on, and never think of it.[33]

Mr. L. Are you not thirsty sometimes this hot weather?

B. Yes, but there is water enough.

Mr. L. Why, my little fellow, you are quite a philosopher.[34]

B. Sir?

Mr. L. I say, you are a philosopher, but I am sure you do not know what that means.

B. No, sir—no harm, I hope![35]

Mr. L. No, no! (*laughing.*)[36] Well, my boy, you seem to want nothing at all, so I shall not give you money to make you want anything. But were you ever at school?

B. No, sir; but daddy says I shall go after harvest.

Mr. L. You will want books then?

B. Yes, the boys have all a spelling-book[37] and a New Testament.

Mr. L. Well, then, I will give you them. Tell your daddy so,[38] and that it is[39] because you are a very good little boy. So now go to your sheep again.

B. I will,[40] sir. Thank you.

Mr. L. Good-bye, Peter.

B. Good-bye, sir.   (J. AIKEN, 1747—1822.)

THE BROKEN FLOWER-POT.

My father was seated on the lawn before the house, his straw hat over his eyes (it was summer), and his book on his lap. Suddenly a beautiful Delft[1] blue-and white flower-pot, which had been set on the window-sill of an upper story, fell to the ground with a crash, and the fragments spluttered up round my father's legs.[2] Sublime in his studies,[3] as Archimedes in the siege, he continued to read. *Impavidum ferient ruinæ!*

"Dear, dear!"[4] cried my mother, who was at work in the porch; "my poor flower-pot, that I prized so much! who could have done this? Primmins, Primmins!"

Mrs. Primmins popped her head out of the fatal window, nodded to the summons,[5] and came down in a trice, pale and breathless.

"Oh!" said my mother mournfully, "I would rather have lost all the plants in the greenhouse in the great blight last May — I would rather the best teasel were broken! The poor geranium I reared myself, and the dear, dear flower-pot which Mr. Caxton bought for me my last birthday! that naughty child must have done this!"

Mrs. Primmins was dreadfully afraid of my father, why, I know not, except that very talkative social[6] persons are usually afraid of very silent, shy ones.[7] She cast a hasty glance at her master, who was beginning to evince signs of attention, and cried promptly, "No, ma'am, it was not the dear boy — it was I!"

"You? How could you be so careless? and you knew how I prized them both.[8] Oh! Primmins!

Primmins began to sob.

"Don't tell fibs,[9] nursey," said a small shrill voice; and Master Sisty (coming out of the house as bold as brass [10]) continued rapidly, "don't scold Primmins, mamma: it was I who pushed out the flower-pot."

"Hush," said nurse, more frightened than ever, and looking aghast at my father, who had very deliberately taken off his hat,[11] and was regarding the scene with serious eyes wide-awake.[12]

"Hush! And if he did break it, ma'am, it was quite an accident; he was standing so,[13] and he never meant it.[14] Did you, Master Sisty? Speak! (this in a whisper)[15] or pa will be so angry."

"Well," said my mother, "I suppose it was an accident; take care in future, my child. You are sorry, I see, to have grieved me. There's a kiss; don't fret."

"No, mamma, you must not kiss me; I don't deserve it. I pushed out the flower-pot on purpose."

"Ha! and why," said my father, walking up.[16]

Mrs. Primmins trembled like a leaf.

"For fun!" said I, hanging my head—"just to see how you'd look,[17] papa; and that's the truth of it. Now beat me, do beat me."

My father threw his book fifty yards off, stooped down, and caught me to his breast. "Boy," he said, "you have done wrong; you shall repair it by remembering all your life that your father blessed God for giving him a son who spoke truth in spite of fear. Oh! Mrs. Primmins, the next fable of this kind you try to[18] teach him, and we part for ever."

Not long after that event, Mr. Squills, who often made me little presents, gave me one far exceeding in value those usually bestowed on children—it was a beautiful large domino-box in cut ivory, painted and gilt. This domino-box was my delight. I was never weary of playing at dominos with Mrs. Primmins, and I slept with the box under my pillow.

"Ah!" said my father one day when he found me ranging the ivory parallelograms in the parlor—"ah!

you like that better than all your playthings, eh?"

"Ah! yes, papa."

"You would be very sorry if your mamma was to throw that box out of the window and break it for fun."

I looked beseechingly [19] at my father, and made no answer.

"But perhaps you would be very glad," he resumed, "if suddenly one of those good fairies you read of [20] could change the domino-box into a beautiful geranium in a beautiful blue-and-white flower-pot, and that you could have the pleasure of putting it on your mamma's window-sill."

"Indeed I would!" said I, half crying. [21]

"My dear boy, I believe you; but good wishes don't mend bad actions — good actions mend bad actions."

So saying, he shut the door and went out. I cannot tell you how puzzled I was to make out what my father meant by his aphorism. [22] But I know that I played at dominoes no more that day. The next morning my father found me seated by myself [23] under a tree in the garden: he paused and looked at me with his grave bright eyes very steadily.

"My boy," said he, "I am going to walk to ——, a town about two miles off; will you come? And, by the by, [24] fetch your domino-box; I should like to show it to a person there." [25] I ran in for the box, [26] and not a little proud of walking with my father on the high road, we set out.

"Papa," said I by the way, [27] "there are no fairies now."

"What then, my child?" [28]

"Why, how then can my domino-box be changed into[29] a geranium and a blue-and-white flower-pot?"

"My dear," said my father, leaning his hand on my shoulder, "everybody who is in earnest to be good[30] car-ries two fairies about with him—one here," and he touched my forehead; "and one here," and he touched my heart.

"I don't understand, papa."

"I can wait till you do,[31] Pisistratus!"

My father stopped at a nursery gardener's, and, after looking over the flowers, paused before a large double geranium. "Ah, this is finer than that which your mamma was so fond of. What is the cost, sir!"

"Only 7s. 6d.," said the gardener.

My father buttoned up his pocket. "I can't afford it to-day," said he gently; and we walked out.

On entering the town, we stopped again at a china warehouse. "Have you a flower-pot like that I bought some months ago? Ah, here is one marked 3s. 6d. Yes, that is the price. Well, when[32] your mamma's birthday comes again, we must buy her another. That is some months to wait. And we can wait, Master Sisty. For truth that blooms all the year round is better than a poor geranium; and a word that is never broken is better than a piece of Delft."

My head, which had drooped before, rose again; but the rush of joy at my heart almost stifled me.[33]

"I have called to pay your little bill," said my father, entering the shop[34] of one those fancy stationers[35] com-mon in country towns, and who sell all kinds of pretty toys and nick-nacks.[36] "And by the way,"[37] he added, as the smiling shopman looked over his books for the entry,[38] "I think my little boy here[39] can show you a much handsomer specimen of French workmanship than that workbox which you enticed Mrs. Caxton into raffling for last winter.[40] Show your domino-box, my dear."

I produced my treasure, and the shopman was liberal in his commendations.[41] "It is always well, my boy, to know what a thing is worth, in case one wishes to part with it. If my young gentleman gets tired of his plaything, what will you give him for it?"

"Why, sir," said the shopman, "I fear we could not afford to give more than eighteen shillings for it, unless the young gentleman took some of those pretty things in exchange."

"Eighteen shillings!" said my father, "you would give that. Well, my boy, whenever you do grow tired of your box, you have my leave to sell it."

My father paid his bill, and went out. I lingered behind a few moments, and joined him at the end of the street.

"Papa, papa!" I cried, clapping my hands, we can buy the geranium — we can buy the flower-pot." And I pulled a handful of silver from my pocket.

"Did I not say right?" said my father, passing his handkerchief over his eyes. "You have found the two fairies!"

Ah! how proud, how overjoyed I was, when, after placing vase and flower on the window-sill, I plucked my mother by the gown, and made her follow me to the spot.

"It is his doing and his money!" said my father, "good actions have mended the bad."

"What," cried my mother, when she had learned all; "and your poor domino-box that you were so fond of!

We will go back to-morrow, and buy it back, if it cost us double." [42]

"Shall we buy it back, Pisistratus?" asked my father.

"Oh, no—no—no!—it would spoil all," I cried, burying my face on my father's breast.

"My wife," said my father solemnly, "this is my first lesson to our child—the sanctity and happiness of self-sacrifice—undo not what it should teach him to his dying hour." [43]

And that is the history of the broken flower-pot.

(SIR E. BULWER LYTTON.)

SYDNEY SMITH BUILDS HIS HOUSE.

I was suddenly caught up by the Archbishop of York, and transported to my living [1] in Yorkshire, where there had not been a resident clergyman for a hundred and fifty years. Fresh from London, [2] not knowing a turnip from a carrot, I was compelled to farm [3] three hundred acres, and without capital to build a parsonage house. [4]

I asked and obtained three years' leave from the archbishop, in order to effect an exchange, if possible, and fixed myself meantime at a small village two [5] miles from York, in which was a fine old house of the time of Queen Elizabeth, where resided the last of the squires with his lady, who looked as if she had walked straight out of the ark, or had been the wife of Enoch. He was a perfect specimen of old! he smoked, hunted, drank beer at his door with his grooms and dogs, and spelt over the county paper on Sundays.

At first he heard [6] I was a Jacobin and a dangerous

fellow, and turned aside as I passed; but at length, when he found the peace of the village undisturbed, harvests as usual, he first bowed, then called, and at last reached such a pitch of confidence[7] that he used to bring the papers, that I might explain the difficult words to him; actually discovered that[8] I had made a joke, laughed till I thought[9] he would have died of convulsions, and ended by inviting me to see his dogs.

All my efforts for an exchange having failed, I asked and obtained from my friend the Archbishop another year to build in. And then I put my shoulder to the wheel in good earnest;[10] sent for[11] an architect; he produced plans which would have ruined me. I made him my bow: "You build for glory, sir; I for use." I returned him his plans, with five-and-twenty pounds, and sat down in my thinking-chair;[12] and in a few hours Mrs. Sydney and I concocted a plan which has produced what I call the model of parsonage-houses.

I then took to horse, to provide bricks and timber; was advised to make my own bricks of my own clay;[13] of course, when the kiln was opened, all bad; mounted my horse again, and in twenty-four hours had bought thousands of bricks and tons of timber. Was advised by neighboring gentlemen to employ oxen; bought four: Tug and Lug, Haul and Crawl; but Tug and Lug took to fainting,[14] and required buckets of sal volatile, and Haul and Crawl to lie down in the mud. So I did as I ought to have done at first — took the advice of the farmer instead of the gentleman; sold my oxen, bought a team of horses, and at last, in spite of the frost which delayed me six weeks,[15] in spite of walls running down with wet,[16] in spite of the advice and remonstrances of friends who predicted our death, in spite of an infant six months old, who had never been out of doors, I landed my family in my new house nine months after laying the first stone, on the 20th of March ; and performed my promise to the letter [17] to the archbishop, by issuing forth at midnight with a lantern to meet the last cart, with the cook and the cat, which had stuck in the mud, and fairly established myself and them before twelve o'clock at night in the new parsonage-house ; a feat, taking ignorance, inexperience, and poverty into consideration, requiring, I can assure you, no small degree of energy.[18]

It made me a very poor man for many years, but I never repented it. I turned schoolmaster, to educate my son, as I could not afford to send him to school. Mrs. Sydney turned schoolmistress, to educate my girls, as I could not afford a governess. I turned a farmer, as I could not let my land. A man-servant was too expensive ; so I caught up a little garden-girl, made like a milestone, christened her *Bunch*,[19] put a napkin in her hand, and made her my butler. The girls taught her to read, Mrs. Sydney to wait, and I undertook her morals ; Bunch became the best butler in the country.

I had little furniture, so I bought a cart load of deals ; took a carpenter (who came to me for parish relief), called Jack Robinson, with a face like a full moon, into my service' established him in a barn, and said, "Jack, furnish my house."

At last it was suggested that a carriage was much wanted in the establishment. After diligent search, I discovered in the back settlements[20] of a York coachmaker an ancient green chariot, supposed to have been the earliest invention of the kind. I brought it home in triumph to my admiring family. Being somewhat dilapitated[21] the village tailor lined it, the village blacksmith repaired it: nay, but for Mrs. Sydney's earnest entreaties, we believe the village painter would have exercised his genius upon the exterior; it escaped this danger, however, and the result was wonderful. Each year added to its charms; it grew younger and younger; a new wheel, a new spring. I christened it the *Immortal.* It was known all over the neighborhood; the village boys cheered it, and the village dogs barked at it;[22] but "*Faber meæ fortunæ*" was my motto, and we had no false shame.

My house was considered the ugliest in the country, but all admitted it was one of the most comfortable; and we did not die, as our friends had predicted, of the damp walls of the parsonage.

(SYDNEY SMITH, 1769 — 1845.)

THE TEMPTATION.

Ravenscroft was a man, I have heard say, of all men least calculated for a treasurer. He had no head for accounts, paid away at random, kept scarce any books, and summing up at the week's end, if he found himself a pound or so deficient, blest himself that it was no worse.

Now Barbara's weekly stipend was a bare half-guinea. By mistake he popped into her hand — a whole one. Barbara tripped away.

She was entirely unconscious at first of the mistake. Ravenscroft would never have discovered it.

But when she had got down to the first of those uncouth landing-places, she became sensible of an unusual weight of metal pressing her little hand.

Now mark the dilemma.

She was by nature a good child. From her parents and those about her she had imbibed no contrary influence. But then they had taught her nothing. Poor men's smoky cabins are not always porticoes of moral philosophy. This little maid had no instinct to evil, but then she might be said to have no fixed principle. She had heard honesty commended, but never dreamed of its application to herself. She thought of it as something which concerned grown-up people, men and women. She had never known temptation, or thought of preparing resistance against it.

Her first impulse was to go back to the old treasurer, and explain to him his blunder. He was already so confused with age, besides a natural want of punctuality, that she would have had some difficulty in making him understand it. She saw that in an instant. And then it was such a bit of money! And then the image of a larger allowance of butcher's meat on their table next day came across her, till her little eyes glistened and her mouth moistened. But then Mr. Ravenscroft had always been so good-natured, had stood her friend so often....... But again, the old man was reputed to be worth a world of money. He was supposed to have fifty pounds a-year clear of his profession. And then came staring upon her the figures of her little stockingless and shoeless sisters. And when she looked at her own neat white cotton stockings, which her situation made it indispensible for her mother to provide for her, with hard straining and pinching from the family stock, and thought how glad she should be to cover their poor feet with the same.........
In these thoughts she reached the second landing-place —

the second, I mean, from the top—for there was still another left to traverse.

Now virtue support Barbara!

And that never-failing friend did step in; for at that moment a strength not her own, I have heard her say, was revealed to her—a reason above reasoning—and without her own agency, as it seemed (for she never felt her feet to move), she found herself transported back to the individual desk she had just quitted, and her hand in the old hand of Ravenscroft, who in silence took back the refunded treasure, and who had been sitting (good man) insensible to the lapse of minutes, which to her were anxious ages; and from that moment a deep peace fell upon her heart, and she knew the quality of honesty.

A year or two's unrepining application to her duty set the whole family upon their legs again, and released her from the difficulty of discussing moral dogmas upon a landing-place.

I have heard her say, that it was a surprise, not much short of mortification to her, to see the coolness with which the old man pocketed the difference, which had caused her such mortal throes.

This anecdote of herself I had in the year 1800, from the mouth of the late Mrs. Crawford, then sixty-seven years of age.　　　　(CHARLES LAMB, 1775—1834.)

B. FRANKLIN TO MISS HUBBARD.
(ON THE DEATH OF HIS BROTHER.)
Philadelphia, 23d February, 1756.

I condole with you. We have lost a most dear and valuable relation. But it is the will of God and nature, that these mortal bodies be laid aside, when the soul is to enter into real life. A man is not completely born until he be dead. Why then should we grieve, that a new child is born among the immortals, a new member added to their happy society?

We are spirits. That bodies should be lent us, while they can afford us pleasure, assist us in acquiring knowledge, or in doing good to our fellow-creatures, is a kind and benevolent act of God. When they become unfit for these purposes, and afford us pain instead of pleasure, instead of an aid become an incumbrance, and answer none of the intentions for which they were given, it is equally kind and benevolent, that a way is provided by which we may get rid of them. Death is that way. We ourselves, in some cases, prudently choose a partial death. A mangled painful limb, which cannot be restored, we willingly cut off. He who plucks out a tooth parts with it freely, since the pain goes with it; and he, who quits the whole body, parts at once with all pains, and possibilities of pains and diseases, which it was liable to, or capable of making him suffer.

Our friend and we were invited abroad on a party of pleasure, which is to last for ever. His chaise was ready first; and he is gone before us. We could not all conveniently start together; and why should you and I be grieved at this, since we are soon to follow, and know where to find him? Adieu.

LETTER I.

Marseilles, May 10, 1864.

My dear sister,

When I last wrote to you, I was on the point of setting off for Marseilles, where I arrived the day before yesterday.   I did not find the journey so agreeable as that from Paris to Lyons.   The roads are excessively dusty, and the country rocky and mountainous; the weather however is very fine, tho' somewhat hot.

I have already paid several visits, and seen a great part of the town, which I like very much, particularly that called *the New Town;* the streets are very clean and well paved; the principal one is elegant, and leads directly to the port, which is very capacious, and frequented by ships of all nations.

You will perhaps ask how I can be so well acquainted with these things, after a residence of two days; I will tell you.   Our excellent friend Mr. H. has been kind enough to conduct me about the town, and to describe every thing worthy of notice; he has also invited me to dine with his family, at his country-house, on Sunday next.

You do not say, in your last, whether you have received a little parcel I sent you from Lyons; do not fail to let me know it in your next.   If I continue to like Marseilles, I shall stay some time; therefore your next letter will, in all probability, find me at No. 45, rue Beauveau.   Pray send me all the news you can, and present my kind remembrances to our dear friend.   Farewell, dear Anna; accept the best wishes of

Your affectionate sister.

LETTER II.

TO A FRIEND ASKING ADVICE CONCERNING THE ENGLISH LANGUAGE.

Thursday, Sept. 3, 18—.

My dear Friend,

I observed last night, and not without some degree of envy, the pleasure you experienced in ~~being able to~~ partake of, and join in, the conversation of the English ladies whom I had the honor of meeting at your house,

Tell me by what means you have acquired such a facility of speaking, and of understanding every thing you hear. I have studied the language some time, and can read, translate, and, I flatter myself, write tolerably well; but always find myself embarrassed when I attempt to converse with the English, not only to express myself, but also to understand them. It is clear that our methods must be very different, or that I am excessively stupid.

~~However~~, be that as it may, I am determined to conquer all difficulties, and will thank you, who have already done it, to give me some advice how to set about it. ~~Adieu~~ till Sunday, (when) I expect the pleasure of your company to dinner.   Yours, etc.

LETTER III.

ANSWER.

Friday, Sept. 4, 18—.

Dear Thomas,

You flatter me very highly in applying to me for advice on the study of the English language, and I offer you, with pleasure, the result of the observations I have made.

The first, and most important thing, is to be particularly careful in the choice of a master; it will save you much pains, time and money. ~~When you have~~ once commenced, pursue the study without intermission; let no day pass without practice, such as reading, copying and translating. The study of rules is not absolutely necessary in the beginning, but occupy yourself as much as possible with practice.

Experience has proved to me that one good practical lesson is worth a whole week of theoretical study. The principal difficulty lies in the great difference that exists between the written and the spoken language, and to acquire the knowledge of the latter, it is absolutely necessary to listen very attentively; to receive the sounds before you attempt to emit them; be assured that when once your ear is formed, half the difficulty is over. There are several minor circumstances to be observed, which we will discuss when I have the pleasure of seeing you.

Heartily yours.

LETTER IV.

LETTER TO A FRIEND, AFTER A JOURNEY.

Geneva, July 14, 18——.

Dear Juliet,

Three times have I taken up my pen to give you a few lines, and as often been prevented. Everybody is so extremely polite here that they will not let me have a moment to myself. One proposes an excursion on the lake, another a visit to Ferney, then an excursion to Mont-Blanc. So that I have been obliged to be down-

right uncivil, and disoblige half a dozen, in order to obtain this opportunity of writing to you.

I intended to give you, in this, a description of our
journey; but must leave it for the next, when my head
will be more steady, and I shall have had an opportunity
of looking over my journal. We are delightfully situated here, and in fact nothing but your agreeable company is wanting, to render our abode a perfect paradise.
From my window I have a view of an immense extent of
the lake and surrounding mountains; and within five
minutes' walk there is a delightful *promenade* called *the
Bastions*. I assure you that Geneva pleases me more
than any place I have yet seen, and my present intention
is to stay as long as the weather continues fine. Write
to me as soon as possible, and direct your letter to the
care of Mr. Pictet.

LETTER V.

FROM A YOUNG MAN, CONCERNING HIS WANT OF PUNCTUALITY.

Tuesday Evening.

My Dear Frank,

My conduct may appear very astonishing to you, and
upon my soul it is equally unaccountable to myself.
With a most ardent desire to please everybody, I seldom
succeed in pleasing any one. Last night, for instance,
determined to be punctual to my engagement with you at
eight, I left home at half after seven, and, having plenty of time, called at J—'s, just to say *how do you do.*
When I entered the drawing-room, I found myself in a

brilliant circle; a ball in honor of the birth-day of Miss Juliet, the eldest daughter,). (~)))~~

After the usual compliments I was about to retire, but found it impossible. Mr. J— insisted, Mrs. J— begged; in vain I pleaded an engagement, the answer was: "You often disappoint us for your other friends, now you must disappoint them for us."—"But, Madam," said I, "I was not invited."—"No, we knew if we invited you we should have nothing but promises; now we have you, we will keep you."

Now pray what could I do? what would you have done in such a case? I could not leave without being perfectly rude. I really consider myself a most unfortunate fellow. Do make my peace with the S— family, and I will promise faithfully to be at the concert on Friday. You say you will call to-morrow morning, I will endeavor to be at home, but I have an appointment at eleven.

ANSWER.

My dear Weathercock,

You have taken an infinite deal of useless trouble, and wasted much of your *valuable time* in composing such an elaborate apology.—Perhaps however I make a mistake, as the necessity of writing to me may be pleaded as an excuse for having disappointed some one else.

Seeing you so *full of contrition*, I offer you a little consolation, in assuring you that we were not so much disappointed as you seem to imagine. Knowing your *punctuality*, we calculated accordingly, and the pleasure of which your absence deprived us was in some degree compensated by several very good jokes which circulated at your expense.

Lest the time occupied in reading my note should cause you to break an appointment, I hasten to subscribe myself

Yours, etc.

Quiz.

LETTER VI.

A LETTER OF ADVICE TO A YOUNG MAN GOING TO LONDON.

Paris, June 20, 18—.

Dear Henry,

Understanding that you are about visiting London, I think it my duty, as a friend of your late father, to offer you a little advice, which experience has taught me is perfectly necessary to those who visit that capital for the first time.

In the first place, never lose sight of your portmanteau till you have seen it safe at your lodging. Whenever you engage a hackney-coach, be sure to remark the number. You will find at London a great number of hackney-coaches and cabriolets, but unfortunately for foreigners the prices are not regulated by the *course*, but according to distance, and the coachmen are in general such rogues that if you do not know the *fare* you are sure to be taken in. To avoid disputes you would do well to buy a little pocket-almanack containing the hackney-coach *fares*, they are sold by all the stationers. It is not customary to give the coachmen money to drink, as in Paris. When you visit the theatres, leave your watch and money (except what you will want) at home : it is true that the police officers come, about five minutes before the opening of the doors, to warn people to take care of their property ; but it often happens that the *transfer* has been made before their arrival.

Avoid all crowds, for fear of pick-pockets, and be sure you never listen to strangers who may accost you in the streets or public places, and with an air of mystery offer you excellent bargains in jewelry or other articles, which they pretend distress compels them to sell at less than half the real value, but which, should you be so imprudent as to purchase them, you would find entirely worthless. There are other things also to be avoided, such as buying fruit or other articles of people in the street, and giving them silver to change; for they frequently change your piece with great dexterity, returning you a bad one, and declaring you gave it them. You must not suppose, however, because I have shown you the black side of the picture, that London is a much viler place than other capitals. A perusal of Vidocq's *Paris Unveiled* would convince you that Paris is far from being the most virtuous, or the most honest place in the world.

ANSWER.

Dear Sir,

Did not the hurry of preparation for my departure prevent me, I would call and thank you personally for your very friendly advice. Be assured that I will not neglect it. Tell me if I can in any way be of service to you while in London; or if on my return I can render you a service by bringing any thing you may want. My brother will write to me every week, so that you have only to acquaint him with your wishes; and I assure you I shall feel pleasure in executing them.

I set off to-morrow morning at six.

Yours ever, etc.

LETTER VII.

TO A YOUNG MAN WHO IS ACCUSTOMED TO BREAK HIS WORD.

Tuesday morning.

The old story, never punctual, never keep your word! What do you think of yourself? and what do you suppose others think of you? The first question I leave you to answer; the second might perhaps embarrass you, therefore I will tell you what they think, or at least what they say. Last night, for instance, your friend Miss S. asked me when I had seen you: I told her it was some time since, but that I expected you that evening. "And why," said she, "do you expect him this evening?"—"Because, Miss, he promised to come." She laughed heartily at the word *promise*, and asked me how I could possibly be so silly as to rely on your promises, which she compared to a weathercock.

If this have no effect upon you, you are past redemption. A man may be callous to the railleries of his male acquaintance; but to be insensible to the poignant satire of the ladies, is what I cannot conceive. I have made a promise that you will assist at an amateur concert on Friday at Mr. N's. Now, though you have so little regard for your own promises, I hope you will have some consideration for mine, and, for once in your life, be punctual. I shall be in your neighborhood to-morrow morning and will call on you.

LETTER VIII.

TO A YOUNG MAN, ON EARLY RISING.

Sunday, 6 o'clock, morning.

Dear Somnus,

Twice in the course of last week I called at your lodgings at nine o'clock in the morning, and was told you were not stirring. What, in the name of health! can induce a young man to lie in bed till that hour, at this beautiful season of the year? You will perhaps say you have nothing to do, but I will not admit that as an excuse: every man who does not abandon himself to sloth, can find something to do. Have you no books to improve your mind? Are there no walks to offer you wholesome [5] exercise? You are not aware how conducive early rising is to health, and how very debilitating, both to mind and body, is a habit of lying late in bed. It shortens life in two ways; first it undermines the health, and consequently hastens death; and certainly one cannot be said to be enjoying life, when one lies snoring in bed. Pluck up courage, my boy, rise a few minutes earlier every morning; believe me you will soon become accustomed to it, and wonder that you could have wasted so much of your life. You must not plead going to bed late; that is no excuse, it is worse than none, because nothing requires your sitting up late. I shall call and pull you out of bed to-morrow at six o'clock.

NOTES TO THE TRANSLATOR.

THE DERVIS.

[1] *qui voyageait.* The use of a participle twice in this way, without any conjunction, is inelegant.

[2] *entra par mégarde dans* . . &c., *qu'il prit pour.* This turn, 'thinking it to be,' would not be French; but we might say, correctly enough *pensant que c'était.*

[3] 'about,' here, *autour de lui.*

[4] *il enfila;* to avoid an awkward repetition of *entra.*

[5] 'upon it;' simply, *dessus.* — 'after,' *à.*

[6] *Il n'y avait pas longtemps qu'il était* . . . &c., *lorsqu'il fut;* or, *Il n'était pas depuis longtemps* . . . &c., *qu'il fut.* (*Que,* in the latter phrase, is used elliptically, and rather elegantly, for *lorsque.*) The student will observe here a difference in the use of the imperfect tense *était,* and of the preterite *fut.* The preterite, in French, implies a beginning and an end of the fact; the imperfect does not.

[7] *ce qu'il venait faire.*

[8] This ellipsis of the conjunction 'that' is not allowed in French.

[9] *se loger pour la nuit.*

[10] *lui firent savoir.*

[11] *d'un air très en colère.*

[12] The ellipsis of the relative pronoun is not permitted in French; nor is the preposition to be thus placed after the verb.

[13] *Le hasard voulut* (with the next verb in the subjunctive), or, *Le hasard fit* (with the indicative).—The use of *arriver,* here, would not so explicitly indicate chance.

[14] *de.*

[15] *comment il pouvait être assez sot pour ne pas.*

[16] *permettez-moi de faire à Votre Majesté.*

[17] *Qui* (or, *Qui est-ce qui*) *logea.*

[18] *dans les premiers temps;* or, *quand elle était neuve.*

[19] *Et qui* . . . *y a logé en dernier lieu?*

[20] *que c'était lui-même.*

[21] *qui change si* (or, *aussi*) *souvent d'habitants.* Notice this use of the preposition *de,* after the verb *changer,* with reference to objects of the same kind.

[22] *et reçoit ainsi une suite perpétuelle.*

A TURKISH TALE.

[1] *On* (or, *L'histoire*) *nous apprend.*

[2] 'abroad,' in this sense, *au dehors,* or *à l'extérieur,* or *à l'étranger ;* 'at home,' likewise, *au dedans,* or *à l'intérieur.*

[3] *de.*   [4] *de.*

[5] *était-ce un plaisant.*   [6] *on ne nous le dit point.*

[7] *des oiseaux.*

[8] *si bien que pas un d'entre eux ne pouvait ouvrir le bec sans que* (followed by the subjunctive).—We say *la bouche* d'un homme (of a man); *la gueule* d'un chien, &c. (of a dog, &c.); and *le bec* d'un oiseau (of a bird).

[9] *ce qu'il disait.*   [10] *à.*

[11] *un couple de hiboux.* The French substantive *couple* is feminine when it simply means two of the same species, or kind, and near in place, or considered together; but it is masculine when it refers either to two individuals, male and female, or to any two beings united by a common will or sentiment, or any other cause which fits them to act in concert. Thus, *une couple de pommes, d'œufs* ('a couple of apples, of eggs'); and *un couple de fripons* ('a couple of rogues').

[12] *Je voudrais bien savoir.*

[13] *ce que se disent ces deux hiboux.* In subordinate sentences, like the present, it is often more elegant to put the nominative *(ces deux hiboux)* after the verb *(se disent).*

[14] *rends-m'en compte.*—'listen'; use the second person singular.

[15] *en feignant de ;* or, *en faisant semblant* (or, *mine*) *de.*

[16] Translate, 'to the words of the two owls.'

[17] Simply, *Revenu près du.*

[18] *Sire* (speaking to a sovereign); *monsieur* corresponds to 'sir,' the common term of civility.

[19] Translate, 'a part.'   [20] *de quoi il s'agit.*

[21] *ne voulut pas se contenter de.*   [22] *Vous saurez* (future of *savoir*).

[23] *et ils sont maintenant en pour-parler sur les conditions d'un mariage entre ces derniers.*   [24] Translate, 'has said.'

[25] *assez haut pour que je l'entendisse.*

[26] *pourvu que vous constituiez en dot* (or, *assigniez pour—en—dot*) *à votre fille cinquante,* &c. Always observe, as a rule, in French, the closest connexion of ideas : thus, *constituiez cinquante,* &c., *en dot à votre fille,* would not be a good French construction.

[27] Translate, 'has replied.'

[28] *si cela vous fait* (or, *peut vous faire*) *plaisir ;* or, *si vous le voulez.* —*S'il vous plaît* would correspond to 'if you please,' if used as a common term of civil request.

[29] *au sultan.* Nouns of title (such as 'Sultan,' 'King,' 'Queen,' 'Doctor,' 'Dean,' 'Colonel,' 'Captain,' &c.), used before proper names, are preceded, in French, by the definite article.

[30] *nous ne manquerons jamais de.*   [31] *On dit.*

TIT FOR TAT.

[1] *A bon chat, bon rat.*   [2] See A TURKISH TALE, note [29].

[3] 'as a present;' *en présent* (or, *en cadeau*—familiar).

[4] *fait de semblables commissions.*

[5] *Après qu'on l'eut fait entrer.*   [6] *déposant.*

[7] *Monsieur* (or, *Mon maître*) *vous envoie.*   [8] *son fauteuil.*

[9] *est-ce ainsi que tu t'acquittes de ton message* (or, *de ta commission*— or, ... *que tu fais ta commission*)?

[10] *Laisse-moi te donner une leçon de politesse* (or, *de savoir-vivre*).

[11] 'situations;' use *rôle* (singular), and see DERVIS, n. [21].

[12] *comment il faut.*   [13] *s'avança vers*—'with;' *de.*

[14] *profond.*

[15] *vous présente* (or, *vous fait*) *ses compliments affectueux.*

[16] *que vous vous portez bien;* or, more politely still, *de vouloir bien accepter* .... 'your kind acceptance of').

[18] *Vraiment!*   [19] *remercie le bien de ma part.*

[20] *et voilà une demi-couronne pour toi.* The adjective *demi* is invariable when placed before the substantive, but agrees with it in gender when after, as *une couronne et demie* ('a crown and a half').

[21] *entraîné à.*

RABELAIS A TRAITOR.

[1] *coupable de haute trahison.*

[2] *Rabelais, si célèbre par son esprit.*

[3] Translate 'to pay his expenses.'—'thither,' *jusque-là.*

[4] *en étant donc aux expédients;* or, *étant donc reduit à sa dernière ressource;* or, *étant donc presque à bout de ressources* (or, *à bout de voie*); or, *ne sachant donc plus de quel bois faire flèche.*—In the more usual sense of, 'to be famished,' 'to be sharp set' is, *avoir les dents longues.*

[5] *ramassa.*

[6] *en plusieurs petits paquets dans du papier.*—'wrote.'

[7] *Monsieur,* used absolutely, was said of the eldest of the brothers of the king of France.

[8] *Dauphin* was the title originally borne by princes of the province of France called *Dauphiné,* and which was afterwards transferred to the eldest son of every French king, from the time of the annexation of that province to the crown until the first revolution, in 1789.

[9] *Après avoir ainsi pourvu à la consommation de.*

[10] *fidèle.*

[11] *pût les voir.* The subjunctive (the mood which expresses *doubt,* among other things) is here used, instead of the indicativee (*pût* instead of *put*), because an intention only—implying a *doubt* as to the result—and not a positive fact, is stated.

[12] *comme il le désirait.* The pronoun *le* ('it'), which is used in French in such cases as this, carries back the mind to the fact mentioned before, namely, here, that 'it' (the plot) should succeed. It also corresponds to 'so,' or to any other *resuming* expression, either expressed or understood, in English.—Yet this pronoun may be left out after the adverbs of comparison *plus, moins, comme,* and after *si,* &c.

[13] *avertit immédiatement.*

[14] 'sent down;' *envoya sur les lieux,* or, simply, *envoya.*

[15] *en lui faisant fournir sur la route, aux frais du rois, le logement et les vivres nécessaires.*

[16] *on reconnut en lui;* or, *on le reconnut pour.* See DERVIS, note [2].

[17] *après,* followed by no article.   [18] Translate, 'having been.'

[19] *l'on ne fit que rire du tour.* Notice this use of *ne* before a verb, and *que* after it.

THE HARE AND THE TORTOISE.

[1] *raillait une torture sur* (or, *de*).

[2] *qu'elle la vaincrait à la course quand il voudrait.* — *A la course,* 'running;' in the same way we say, *passer une rivière* à la nage ('swimming'); *tuer un oiseau* au vol ('flying'), &c.

[3] *Allons.*

[4] *ce que peuvent mes jambes.* See TURKISH TALE, note [13].

[5] *n'attendit pas un instant, et se mit en route tout doucement, de son pas ordinaire et régulier.*

[6] *commencerait par faire.*

[7] *continua de s'évertuer.* When translating such strongly elliptical expressions as the present, formed with a verb and a preposition, we are compelled to render in full the idea only partly expressed by the words used. Thus, 'kick him out,' *faites-le sortir à coups de pied;* 'to refine people out of their veracity,' (HERVEY,) *polir les gens au point de leur faire perdre leur véracité,* &c.

[8] See RABELAIS A TRAITOR, note [19].

[9] *Hâtez-vous lentement.* This proverbial expression, which has been used by Regnard, Boileau, and La Fontaine, is nothing more than the old Greek proverb, *speude bradeos,* which the Latins took from the Greeks, and translated by *festina lente,* and which the English often render by 'most haste, worst speed,' or, hasten slowly.

MULY MOLUC.

[1] *se mourait de.*

[2] 'he himself.'—'knew was,' *savait être.* This turn is French (in the case where, as here, the nominatives, or subjects, of the two verbs are different), only after a relative pronoun. Thus we cannot say, *je le sais être savant* ('I know him to be learned'); it should be, *je sais*

qu'il est savant. See DERVIS, n. *2*.—Sometimes the following elegant turn, which comes nearer to the English construction above, is used: *je le crois savant, on le dit habile,* &c.

[3] *à recevoir.*   [4] *tellement épuisé par.*

[5] *à passer la journée.*   [6] *résulteraient pour.*

[7] *avant d'avoir mis fin.* Contrary to the case mentioned above (n. *2*), this turn is the only one allowed, in most instances, in French, when the two verbs, thus following each other, have the same subject, or nominative.

[8] *officiers, s'il expirait . . . . , de cacher.*   [9] *à.*

[10] *et de s'approcher de.*   [11] *son corps serait.*

[12] 'usual;' *à l'ordinaire.*

[13] *l'action;* to avoid an awkward repetition of *bataille,* occurring inevitably just below.

[14] *il parcourut* (to avoid repeating *porté), dans une litière découverte, tous les rangs de l'armée, formée* (we also say *rangée) en bataille.*

[15] *et encouragea les siens.*   [16] *pour la.*

[17] Translate, 'of their religion and of their country.' Remember this rule which enjoins, in French, the repetition of the pronoun, article, &c., as well as of the preposition in certain cases, before each of the substantives, whatever their number may be.

[18] Use *voir.*   [19] *tourner.*

[20] 'very near,' . . . &c.; simply, *à l'agonie.*

[21] *ce qui.* Whenever 'which' does not relate to a word in particular, as its antecedent, in the first part of the sentence, but rather to the whole of that first part, or to the fact mentioned in it; in short, whenever it can be turned by 'a thing which,' or 'a fact which,'— the French for it is *ce qui,* instead of *qui* (nominative), and *ce que,* instead of *que* (accusative). It corresponds to the Latin, *id quod,* similarly used. Likewise, in such a case, the genitive would be *ce dont,* instead of *dont* ('of which').

[22] *ses troupes,* or *son monde.*   [23] *que.*

DESTRUCTION OF THE ALEXANDRIAN LIBRARY.

[1] Alexandria was taken by the Saracens in 640. Its great library had been created about the year 287 B. C., and contained upwards of 700,000 volumes.

[2] John Philoponus, a philosopher and grammarian.

[3] *était un ami des lettres ;* or, *aimait les lettres.*

[4] *un savant.*   [5] Simply, *Un jour.*

[6] *vous avez mis le scellé sur.*

[7] *qui s'y trouvent.* The English (as the Latin) passive is to be translated into French, wherever there is a certain vagueness about the *person* or persons that could serve as a nominative to the verb, if conjugated actively, by the active voice with *on,* or, sometimes also, by the reflective form, as here. Ex.: *dicitur,* (Latin;) 'it is said,'

(English;) *on dit* (French).   'That is done every day,' *cela se fait tous les jours.*   The reflective form is also used where the name of a *thing* is the nominative to express the motions of or changes in it, or its appearance; as, *la porte se referma d'elle-même* (closed of itself), *l'eau se congèle* (congeals), *le château se dessinait sur un ciel bleu* (the outline of the castle came out on the blue sky).

[8] *je prétends n'en rien dire.*

[9] *qui ne vous sont d'aucun usage* (or, *d'aucune utilité*).

[10] *me conviendraient peut-être davantage.*   When 'more' is taken absolutely, *davantage* is used instead of *plus.*

[11] 'you want;' *vous voudriez.*   [12] *déposés.*

[13] *pour* (or, *sur*) *laquelle.*   The relative pronoun *lequel* is always used instead of *qui*, with a preposition, when speaking of a *thing*, not of a person.

[14] *On écrivit en conséquence* (or, *donc*).   See RABELAIS A TRAITOR, note [16].

[15] *et Omar répondit en ces termes.*

[16] *si ce qu'ils contiennent.*   [17] *c'est-à-dire.*

[18] *on trouve autre part qu'en eux.*

[19] *s'il s'y trouve quelque chose de contraire.*   Notice this use of the preposition *de* after *quelque chose*, as also after *rien*, and *quoi.*

[20] *nous n'avons nullement besoin* (or, *nous n'avons que faire*) *de ces ouvrages.—Nous n'en avons nullement besoin* might be considered ambiguous, *en* meaning 'of it,' as well of 'of them.'

[21] *Faites-les donc détruire tous.*   'To order, to cause a thing to be done—to have, to get it done,' is elegantly expressed, in French, by the verb *faire*, followed by an infinitive.

[22] *ordonna qu'on les distribuât* (or, *les fit distribuer*) *dans.*

[23] 'in making' . . . &c.; *pour chauffer les bains.*   [24] *De.*

THE ART OF PLEASING.

[1] *est d'un grand secours à qui le possède; mais il n'est pas aisé de l'acquérir.*

[2] *Il est difficile de l'assujettir* (or, *de le soumettre*) *à des règles.*

[3] *que je ne pourrais vous en dire.*

[4] *Agissez envers les autres comme vous voudriez que les autres agissent envers vous.*—'method;' *moyen.*

[5] The subjunctive is generally used, in French, after a superlative.

[6] *sensible à.*   [7] Use the singular.   [8] *comptez que.*

[9] Translate, 'and the same attention.'

[10] See DERVIS, n. [12].   [11] *folâtre.*

[12] 'as,' for 'according as,' *suivant* (or, *selon*) *que*; or, more concisely, as well as more elegantly, 'as you find,' simply *selon* (according to).

[13] Translate, 'which every individual must have for.'

[14] See DESTRUCTION ALEX. LIB., n. [19].

[15] *qui puisse fort à propos s'appliquer.*

[16] *donnez à entendre.*   [17] *de celle-ci.*

[18] Translate, 'has tempted you.'—'Of;' *Sur.*

[19] *le moi.*   [20] Simply, *tout autre.*

[21] *observer un trop grand secret sur ses propres affaires.*

[22] *Quelque idée que vous ayez de vos talents.*

[23] *n'en faites point parade.*

[24] See TURKISH TALE, note [13].—'nor labor;' *ne cherchez point.*

[25] *de les faire briller.*   [26] See DESTR. ALEX. LIB., n. [7].

[27] This turn is not French; we use *sans que* with the personal pronoun *(vous,* here), and the subjunctive.—'to point out,' here, *prendre la peine de faire valoir.*

[28] *quand même vous seriez persuadé que vous avez raison.*

[29] *c'est;* or, but less elegantly here, in the way pointed out in MULY MOLUC, note [21].

[30] *si cela* (or, *s'il*—'if it') *ne réussit pas.*

[31] *en disant d'un ton de.*

[32] Translate as if the English were, 'besides, that is not necessary,' or, 'and that is not necessary.' The conjunction *ni,* in French, is only used to connect together two negative propositions, not a negative with an affirmative, as, 'nor does' in English, and *nec* in Latin.

[33] *d'autre chose.*   [34] *à observer.*

[35] *Voilà une partie.*   [36] *dans le grande monde.*

[37] *Je voudrais les avoir mieux connus.*

[38] *cette science m'a coûté cinquante-trois années. Je n'en regretterai pas le prix.*

DESCRIPTION OF ENGLAND.

[1] See TURKISH TALE, note [7].

[2] *Quoique les points de vue, dit . . . , ne s'y montrent relativement que dans de petites proportions.*

[3] *par toute cette succession agréable et alternative de sites variés.*

[4] *Ici.*

[5] *jusqu'où la vue peut porter.* We also say, *tant* (or, *aussi loin) que la vue peut s'étendre;* but this same verb, *s'étendre,* coming just before, an awkward repetition must be avoided. '*Farther* than the eye can reach,' would be *à perte de vue.*

[6] *Là.*   [7] *des coteaux à pente douce.*

[8] *couverts de bois ondoyants* (or, *ondulants).*

[9] 'Some tracts,' *Plus loin.*   [10] *rapides.*

[11] 'nor,' &c.; *rien n'y manque, pas même, comme pour faire contraste avec.*

¹² *l'aspect, tour à tour, de.*

¹³ Put the two adjectives, in French, after the substantive, with the conjunction *et* between both.

¹⁴ *Voilà.*   ¹⁵ *qui excitent,* or, *propres à exciter.*

¹⁶ *que le sol recèle dans son sein.*   ¹⁷ *tout cela donne à.*

¹⁸ *dont nulle autre nation ne jouit au même degré.*

\0 MAHOMET'S MIRACLES.

¹ *à mesure qu'ils s'éloignent.*   ² See MULY MOLUC, note ¹⁷.

³ *allèrent à sa rencontre.*

⁴ *qu'il procurait des subsistances, guérissait les malades d'une manière miraculeuse, et ressuscitait les morts.*

⁵ *poussa des gémissements devant.*

⁶ *lui adressa des plaintes ;* or, *se plaignit à lui.*

⁷ *qu'elle était.* This turn, viz., 'my,' 'thy,' 'his,' 'its,' &c., followed by a present participle, is not French ; see ART OF PLEASING, note ²⁷.

⁸ 'Both,' followed by 'and,' is usually rendered, in French, the same as in Latin, by *et* repeated ; but here, we should thus have *et* occurring three times, and we must, therefore, leave 'both' out and change a little the construction accordingly.

⁹ *comme un événement réel, comme un acte corporel.*

¹⁰ *la Mecque.* The definite article is used, exceptionally, before the names of some towns ; as, *le Havre, le Mans* (in France), *le Caire* (Cairo, in Egypt), &c.

¹¹ *demeures.* — 'the patriarchs,' &c. ; see MULY MOLUC, note ¹⁷.

¹² *Il eut seul la permission* (or, *Il fut permis à M— seul) de s'avancer au delà,* &c. As *permettre,* like some other verbs, when active, does not admit, in French, of a noun of person for its object, (or accusative), it does not, for an obvious reason, admit of it either, when it is passive, for its subject (or nominative), and therefore we must use another turn. Ex. : 'you are allowed,' &c., *on vous permet,* &c. ; or, *il vous est permis,* &c. (as in Latin, *tibi permitto, tibi permittitur).*

¹³ *il se trouva à deux portées de trait* (or, *d'arc).*

¹⁴ *jusqu'au cœur.*   ¹⁵ *il redescendit.*

¹⁶ *plusieurs milliers d'années.*

COWPER TO MR. SAMUEL ROSE.

¹ *Quoiqu'il y ait longtemps que j'ai reçu votre dernière lettre.*

² *ni le bien vif plaisir que m'ont aussi procuré.*

³ *entretiens.*   ⁴ *Je ne chercherai point à m'excuser de.*

⁵ *parce que vous n'ignorez pas quelles sont.* — 'occupation ;' use the plural.

 [6] *et qu'ainsi ce serait brouiller* (or, *barbouiller—gâter—gâcher*) *du papier* (or, *ce serait mal employer mon papier*) *que de m'étendre sur une excuse qui se présentera à vous naturellement.* Notice, here, *se présentera à vous*, instead of *se vous présentera*.

 [7] *de l'emploi convenable.*

 [8] *laquelle consiste à en bien sentir le prix.* The pronouns *qui, que, dont*, are replaced by *lequel, duquel*, to avoid ambiguity : these always relate to the former noun (with which they must agree in gender and number), while *qui, que, dont*, relate to the latter. This, of course, where the construction cannot be altered.

 [9] *Si j'avais été;* or, *Si j'eussé été;* or, *Eussé-je été.* In *eussé-je*, an acute accent is put over the last *e* for euphony's sake.

 [10] *quand j'étais à votre âge;* or, better, not to repeat *être* so nearly, *quand j'avais votre âge;* or, simply, *à votre âge:* this English ellipsis, at any rate, after 'when' (*quand*), is not permitted in French.

 [11] *aussi pénétré de.*　　　　[12] See RABELAIS A TRAITOR, n. [12].

 [13] Turn, 'as I have done.'　　　　[14] *premières années.*

 [15] *fait tomber—*or, *entraîne—les neuf dixièmes.*

 [16] *et la gaieté* (or, *gaîté*).　　　　[17] *cet âge*, to avoid ambiguity.

 [18] *que lorsque les ans* (or, *les années;* or, *la vieillesse;* or, *l'âge avancé;* or, simply, *l'âge*).

 [19] *de.*

 [20] *Combien des milliers d'entre nous eussent été plus sages.*

 [21] The particle *ne* is used before the verb which follows *plus* or *moins*, unless the preceding verb, which accompanies *plus* or *moins*, is conjugated with a negative.

 [22] Turn, 'if a puny . . . or some . . . had constrained,' &c.

 [23] *infirmité intermittente.*　　　　[24] *faute d'un frein de ce genre.*

 [25] *C'est pourquoi je.*

 [26] *vous qui.* A personal pronoun, in the objective case, which is the antecedent of a relative pronoun, must be used twice in this way, first in its conjunctive form, immediately before the verb which governs it, and then in its disjunctive form, immediately before the relative : here it so happens that both forms are *vous;* in the first person singular they are *me* and *moi;* in the second, *tu* and *toi;* &c. See any grammar.

 [27] See RABELAIS A TRAITOR, note [12].

 [28] *établir son bien-être.* This use of the possessive *son* is a deviation from custom ; the reason of it is, that the possessor figures as subject (or nominative) in the same proposition wherein the thing possessed is the object (or accusative).—'should,' *doivent.*

 [29] *recueillis de bonne heure.*　　　　[30] *n'a pas été enseveli.*

 [31] *Il vit encore.* Notice the use of the pronoun, before *vit;* the pronoun is necessary, the two verbs *être enseveli*, and *vivre*, being in different tenses.

 [32] *et est un des objets les plus chers à votre cœur;* or, *et a part à vos plus vives affections.*

SIR ROGER DE COVERLEY.

[1] See TURKISH TALE, n. [26]; 'an invitation,' &c., *l'invitation de*, &c.

[2] *je l'y accompagnai la semaine dernière, et je me suis fixé.*

[3] *de rédiger plusieurs des articles qui doivent suivre* (or, simply, *de mes prochains articles.*

[4] *qui connaît très bien.*

[5] *quand il me plaît.* The verb *plaire* does not govern the objective case, in French, but requires an indirect regimen with the preposition *à* (dative case), expressed or implied : *me* is here in the dative.

[6] *selon que je le juge à propos ;* or, *comme bon me semble.*

[7] *et aussi rester silencieux et tranquille sans m'inviter à la gaîté.*

[8] *Quand les notables des environs* (or, *des alentours*) ; or, *Quand les gens les plus considérables de l'éndroit.*

[9] Translate, ' he shows me to them,' *il me montre à eux*—not *me leur montre,* this construction being used with the first pronoun in the accusative, only when that pronoun is in the third person, as, *le* (*la,* or *les*) *leur montre ;* but we should say, *me le* (*la,* or *les*) *montre,* the first pronoun being in the dative—though yet even here, *vous montre à moi,* not *me vous montre.*

[10] *j'ai aperçu plusieurs de ces messieurs qui m'observaient en cachette* (or, *furtivement*—or, *à la dérobée*).

[11] *et j'ai.* When the verbs have each a separate object, although they are in the same tense, the pronoun is usually repeated.

[12] *les prier ;* or, *qui les priait ;*—but not *les priant.*

[13] *de ne pas se laisser voir de moi.*

[14] *par la raison que je déteste les regards des curieux.*

[15] *Je suis d'autant plus à mon aise* (or, *Je me trouve d'autant mieux*) *au milieu de la maison de Sir Roger, qu'elle se compose.* The word *famille,* in the sense of 'household,' from the Latin *familia,* is no longer French. We find it so used in La Fontaine, among other old writers. We now use *maison, gens* (plural), *domestiques* (plur.), *domestique* (sing.), *monde.*

[16] *du ;* we use the preposition *de* (genitive case), after a superlative.

[17] See DERVIS, n. [21].

[18] *de tout ce qui l'entoure* (more emphatic than *tous ceux qui l'entourent*), *quand on le sert on n'a aucune envie de le quitter.*

[19] *aussi tous ses gens sont-ils* (or, *sont*) *âgés ayant vieilli au service de.* The interrogative form (*sont-ils,* here) is elegantly used after *aussi* (in the sense of 'therefore'), *peut-être, encore* (yet), *toujours* (still), *en vain, du moins, au moins, à peine, ainsi,* &c.

[20] *a les cheveux gris.*

[21] See ART OF PLEASING, n. [5].

[22] Whenever a past participle is joined with the auxiliary *avoir,* it agrees, in gender and number, with the *régime direct* (accusative) of the verb, but only if that direct regimen *precedes* the verb.

[23] *a tout l'air.*   [24] *jusque.*

[25] *qu'on garde;* or, *que l'on conserve.* The *l* here is merely euphonic.

[26] *en considération de.*

[27] *bien qu'il* (or, *quoiqu'il*) *ne serve plus à rien depuis.*

[28] *Je ne puis qu'observer avec beaucoup;* or, *Il me fut impossible d'observer sans beaucoup.*

[29] *se peignit sur.*

[30] *à.*

[31] *Quelques-uns d'entre eux ne pouvaient retenir leurs larmes.*

[32] *s'empressait autour de lui afin de se rendre utile* (or, *de s'utiliser*).

[33] *mortifié.*

[34] *lorsque, par moments, il ne se trouvait rien à faire.*

[35] *leur adressait, tout en s'enquérant de ses propres affaires.*

[36] These two nouns, being nearly synonymous, had better follow each other without a conjunction, but with the pronoun repeated.

[37] *captive* (or, *lui gagne — lui concilie*) *tous les cœurs.* Whenever two substantives, being nearly synonymous, thus follow one another immediately, the verb, and also the adjective or participle, must be in the singular.

[38] *quand il plaisante* (or, *badine*) *l'un ou l'autre de ses gens, il les met tous de.*

[39] *mais principalement celui sur le compte duquel* (or, *de qui —* but not *dont*) *il se divertit.* See DERVIS, n. [12].

[40] *ou s'il laisse voir.*

[41] *il est facile à qui se trouve présent de deviner à leur air qu'ils lui portent tous un vif intérêt.*

[42] *m'a confié tout particulièrement à la garde* (or, *aux soins*).

[43] *et qui est aux petits soins avec moi, comme le sont d'ailleurs les autres domestiques.*

COWPER TO MR. J. NEWTON.

[1] *Elle était tout à l'heure* (or, *il n'y a qu'un instant*) *pure de toute tache et de toute souillure.*

[2] *barbouiller,* or *noircir.*

[3] *il n'est pas probable que je,* with the subjunctive.

[4] *avant.* See MULY MOLUC, note [7].

[5] See SIR ROGER DE COVERLEY, n. [22].

[6] ' that,' &c., *bien indigne, à mon avis, d'être acceptée de vous.*

[7] *jusqu'à un certain point;* or, *en quelque manière* (or, *sorte —* or, *degré*).

[8] Turn, ' by the reflection.'   [9] *à.*

[10] *d'autre part;* or, *elle ne . . . . non plus,*

[11] *Mais à l'heure qu'il est, les choses sont changées* (or, *le cas n'est plus le même*). Put a colon here.

[12] *il vous faut payer en espèces de la viande creuse.*

[13] 'pick your pocket;' use *vous voler.*—'absolutely;' *dans toute la force du terme.*

[14] *votre argent ne laisse pas d'être* (or, . . . *ne laisse pas que d'être) déboursé, et vous n'en êtes pas* (or, *sans que vous en soyez) plus avancé.* This expression, *ne pas laisser de* (or, *que de*), followed by an infinitive, denotes a fact accomplished notwithstanding what has been stated previously.

[15] *Les douces chaleurs et le calme de l'automne en font.*

[16] 'much more,' *bien plus,* or *bien autrement;* see COWPER TO SAMUEL ROSE, n. [21]: the rule referred to applies to *autre* and *autrement,* as well as to *plus and moins.*

[17] 'brisk,' *assez forts.*   [18] *en laissant entrer.*

[19] Turn, 'from it *(en).'*

[20] *je reste les fenétres et la porte toutes grandes ouvertes.* Although *tout,* before an adjective or a participle, when it is an adverb (used for *tout à fait,* 'quite'), is in its nature an invariable word, yet it agrees, for the sake of euphony—in the feminine singular and plural, but never in the masculine plural,—if the adjective or the participle, being feminine, begins with a consonant or an aspirate *h.*

[21] *et je suis.* Notice the repetition of the pronoun, here also, besides the cases we have seen above. See SIR ROGER DE COVERLEY, note [11].

[22] *de.*   [23] *le rendre.*

[24] 'to keep,' here, *avoir.*   [25] Use *habiter* (active).

[26] *du.*   [27] *un carré,* or *une planche.*

[28] 'for' is not to be translated. In French, the reverse of the English takes place here: it is the thing bought which is the direct regimen, and the person paid is the indirect regimen. Thus, *me* (dative) *payent* (or, *paient) le miel* (accusative) *qu'elles en tirent.*

[29] *de;* or, *avec.*   [30] *un peu;* or, *assez.*

[31] *m'est aussi agréable à entendre;* or, simply, *m'est aussi agréable,* as the word *entendre* inevitably occurs just below.

[32] *fait entendre.*

[33] *Je ne trouverais peut-être pas très gai* . . . &c.

[34] *je ne sache point de quadrupède.*—*Je ne sache* is frequently used with *pas, point, rien, aucun, personne,* for *je ne sais,* or, *je ne connais, pas,* &c. This Gallicism is only used in the first person, singular and plural: thus we say, likewise, *nous ne sachons,* &c., for &c., &c. Yet it is only employed in the sense of 'I am not aware;' for we could not say, *e. g., je ne sache* (it should be *sais) pas ma leçon.*

[35] *dont je ne tienne la voix mélodieuse* (or, *pour mélodieuse).* Notice here, first, the use of the subjunctive *(tienne)* after a verb conjugated with a negative and followed by a relative pronoun *(je ne sache point . . . . dont);* secondly, the suppression of *pas* or

point (though *ne* shows the sentence to be negative) in this latter part of the proposition, for the sake of elegance, as *point* is already expressed in the former; and, thirdly, the position of the thing possessed *(voix)* after the verb, because it is here the *object* of the verb, whereas if it were the *subject* of the verb, it would precede it in that case in French, as it does in either case in English.

[36] 'and fowls;' *y compris ceux de basse-cour.*

[37] 'to think,' here, *s'aviser.*   [38] *afin de.*

[39] *par goût pour.*   [40] *dans la campagne.*

[41] *est parfaitement en situation.*   [42] 'as to,' *quant aux.*

[43] *si l'escarbot et, de fait, tout le reste des scarabées, veulent bien éviter de se trouver sur mon chemin* (or, *sur mon passage), aucun des autres ne me répugne.*

[44] *dans quelque clé qu'ils;* with the subjunctive.

[45] 'from,' *depuis;* 'treble,' *dessus* (masculine); 'to,' *jusqu'à.*

[46] *je crois découvrir* (MULY MOLUC, note [7]) *un exemple très remarquable de la bonté de la Providence envers l'homme, dans ce fait, que.* Whenever 'to' expresses certain relations of behavior, &c., and has the sense of 'towards,' translate it by *envers.*

[47] *un accord aussi parfait a été ménagé* We must here keep to the passive, as in English, instead of using *on* with the active voice, and this for a very obvious reason. See DESTRUCTION ALEX. LIBRARY, n. [7].

[48] 'with which,' *dont;* 'to visit,' here, *frapper.* See TURKISH TALE, note [26].

[49] *Personne au monde n'ignore.*   [50] *sur le moral.*

[51] *ce monde de pécheurs.*

[52] *de sang à cailler* (or, better, *à faire tourner—à tourner—à glacer).*

[53] *et à faire du.*

[54] *je ne sais si,* with the conditional; or, *je ne sache pas que,* with the imperfect subjunctive. — Notice here, that it is more elegant, when conjugating *savoir* negatively, to omit *pas* or *point,* and only use *ne;* except in the case of emphasis, when we should say, for instance, *je ne sais pas,* instead of *je ne sais.*

[55] *sans cesse;* or, *constamment.*

[56] *uniquement se donner à elles-mêmes du plaisir.*

[57] *à son auteur.* This use of the possessive *son* is another deviation from custom; the reason of it here is, that the object possessed *(auteur)* is what the French call the *complément* of a preposition (the prep *à).*—'though without knowing it;' see TURKISH TALE, n. [26].

[58] *conforme à l'Ecriture sainte* (or, simply, *à l'Ecriture).*

[59] *que la musique fait partie des joies du Paradis.*

[60] Leave out 'of it.'—'is found.' See DEST. ALX. LIB., n. [7].

[61] 'so,' &c., *lugubres au point de rendre.*

[62] *et d'aiguiser jusqu'au.*

[63] *à propos* (or, *à temps) de serrer.*

[64] *dans des abîmes qui ne lui sont que* (RABELAIS A TRAITOR, n. [19]) *trop familiers.*

THE COMPARISON OF WATCHES.

[1] See DERVIS, n. [6].　　　　　　　　[2] *assez longtemps.*

[3] *il était à craindre qu'il n'oubliât.* See MAHOMET'S MIRACLES, note [7]; and notice this use of *ne* and the subjunctive with *craindre:* this verb, however, rejects *ne* when conjugated negatively.

[4] See DERVIS, n. [21].

[5] *qu'il n'était pas rentré à la minute* (or, *à point nommé*).

[6] *un regard courroucé qui.*　　　　　[7] *fait reculer Mars lui-même.*

[8] *avait pu voir.* Notice this difference between the tenses of the two verbs, respectively, in French and in English.

[9] *visage.*

[10] *Il y a une heure que la dîner t'attend* (or, *Le dîner t'attend depuis une heure*), *mon ami* (or, *mon cher*). Mark this difference of construction; the English turn, 'dinner has been waiting,' is also used in French, but it would imply that the dinner is no longer waiting at the time when the words are spoken.

[11] *pourquoi as-tu attendu, ma petite* (or, *ma chère*)?

[12] *Je suis vraiment désolé d'être* (MULY MOLUC, n. [7]) *si en retard.* Instead of *tard*, use *en retard* when 'late' means behind a fixed time.

[13] *regardant à; regardant*, without the preposition *à*, would not imply looking at the dial to see the time.

[14] *six heures et demie* (TIT FOR TAT, n. [20]) *à ma montre.*—'it is only;' see RABELAIS A TRAITOR, n. [19].

[15] 'by me,' *à la mienne.*

[16] *Ils se firent voir leurs montres l'un à l'autre, lui d'un air d'excuse, elle, d'un air de reproche* (or, elliptically, *elle de reproche*).

[17] *que tu avances* (or, *que ta montre avance*).

[18] *que c'est toi qui retardes* (or, *que c'est la tienne qui retarde*).

[19] *Jamais ma montre ne retarde* (or, better, *ne se dérange*) *d'une.*— *Ne se dérange* means 'varies,' and it is to be preferred here to *retarde*, 'loses,' as the wife, who is told her watch is too fast, or gains, immediately after answers, to deny the fact, "Nor mine a second." It should have been, "Nor does mine *gain* a second." Evidently this was a negligence on the part of the authoress.

[20] *vingt-quatre.* The larger of two numbers always comes first in French, unless one multiplies the other, as, *trois cents* (100x3), *quatre-vingts*, 'eighty' (20x4), &c.

[21] *J'ai lieu de croire que je vais bien.*—*Avoir raison* means 'to be right,' and *avoir tort*, 'to be wrong,' but not when we speak of time.

[22] *Lieu de croire!*

[23] *Quel motif imaginable peux-tu; or, Quel motif peux-tu donc.*— Never couple together, in French, in the same phrase, such ideas as

those contained in the words 'can' and 'possible,' or 'possibly;' it would be considered, and not without reason, more a pleonasm than elegant emphasis. See DERVIS, n. [15].

[24] *Le seul motif* (or, *La seule raison*) *que j'aie d'en douter, c'est.* Notice this use of the subjunctive, after *le seul*, followed by a relative pronoun. As to the pronoun *ce*, it is not strictly necessary here before the verb *être*, but its use is more conformable to the genius of the French language.

[25] *j'ai réglé ma montre* (or, *j'ai mis ma montre à l'heure*—or, *j'ai pris l'heure*) *sur le soleil* (or, *sur le cadran solaire*).

[26] *Il n'y a pas là de quoi rire.*

[27] *la variation, la déclinaison, doit être mise en ligne de compte* (or, *il faut tenir compte—il faut faire la part—de la variation, de la déclinaison*) *quand on calcule l'heure du soleil en même temps que celle de l'horloge* (or, *. . . calcule le temps vrai . . . que le temps moyen* —scientific terms).

[28] *Voyons*, or *Allons*.   [29] *tu sens bien.*

[30] See DERVIS, n. [8], and above, n. [21].

[31] *Eh bien, ma petite* (or, *mon cœur*), *si tu n'en doutes pas toi-même, cela suffit* (or simply, *suffit*—or, *n'en parlons plus*). *A quoi bon se disputer pour une pareille vétille? Va-t-on servir le dîner.*

[32] *Oui, si les domestiques te savent rentré; mais je ne sais vraiment pas ce qui en est. Dites-moi, de grâce* (or, *je vous prie*); or, simply, *Dites-moi.*

[33] *une de ses amies.*   [34] *au.*

[35] *qui* (DERVIS, n. [12]) *ait en horreur autant que moi les disputes sur des riens.* Notice the use of the subjunctive *(ait)* after the impersonal verb 'there is,' conjugated with a negative.

[36] *j'aime bien à convaincre les autres.*

[37] Turn, 'was stopped.'

[38] *C'était bien contrariant* (or, *impatientant*, or *ennuyeux*); or, *Comme c'était contrariant*, &c.; or, lastly, *Quel ennui!—Quel contretemps!—Quel malheur!*

[39] *de ne pouvoir trouver tout de suite le moyen.*

[40] *en se mettant à faire le procès à.*   [41] *sur ce cas particulier.*

[42] *s'avouait coupable.*   [43] See MULY MOLUC, n. [21].

[44] For the right place of 'something,' see TURKISH TALE, n. [26].

[45] *passe ainsi, avec un air de triomphe, du particulier au général.*

[46] 'peculiarly,' *spécialement;* — 'offensive,' *blessant*, to be followed by *pour*.

[47] 'every,' *tout*, here, which is more general, more absolute than *chaque*.— 'susceptible,' *sensible*, in this sense: the French word *susceptible*, used absolutely and applied to a person, simply means 'irascible,' 'easily offended,' 'touchy.'

[48] See TURKISH TALE, note [13]; 'especially,' *surtout;* 'be,' indicative in French.

[49] *nos chères lectrices.*

[50] *d'éviter de soumettre à cette épreuve* (or, *de mettre ainsi à l'épreuve*) *la* . . . &c. See TURKISH TALE, n. [26].

[51] 'to temper with,' in this sense, *assaisonner de.*

[52] *sinon, très certainement les chôses finiront mal* (or, *tourneront à mal*).

HEARERS AND DOERS.

[1] *Préceptes et Pratique.*   [2] *vient de sonner.*—'nine.'

[3] *ayant déjeuné, se lève* (or, *sort*) *de table.* Nouns collective general, such as *nation, peuple, armée, parlement, famille,* &c., require the verb, adjective, pronoun, &c., in connexion with them, to be in the singular, in French.

[4] *Un coup de sonnette se fait entendre* (or, *On sonne*) *à la porte.*

[5] *commis.* The word *clerc* means only a lawyer's clerk (and also an ecclesiastic); thus, *clerc d'avoué, clerc de notaire* (attorney's and notary's clerk).

[6] *est ici; il espère que vous ne trouverez pas mauvais qu'il vous prie de vouloir bien régler son compte, ce dont* (see MULY MOLUC, note [20]) *il vous sera très obligé.*

[7] *est venu.*—'last week.'

[8] *Il dit qu'il ne vous dérangerait pas ainsi, s'il ne se trouvait dans un cas d'urgence.* After *si* (especially when in the sense of *à moins que,* 'unless'), it is often more elegant to leave out *pas* or *point,* and only use *ne.*

[9] *Urgence ou non.*   [10] *à moi;* or, *à perdre.*

[11] 'with,' &c., *en haussant.*—'his.'

[12] Turn, 'whilst he was giving;' see COWPER TO MR. S. ROSE, n. [10].

[13] *qu'il mettait en ce moment.*   [14] Use *partir.*

[15] *de repasser.*   [16] *de l'époque.*

[17] *la rapidité de la vapeur.*

[18] Translate as if the English were, 'he did not allow (use *donner*) himself often enough' *(assez souvent).*

[19] *ni.* The conjunction *ou* would imply that only one of the two facts mentioned is to be denied, whereas *ni* implies the negation of both.

[20] *à.*   [21] *ses semblables.*

[22] See COWPER TO S. ROSE, n. [9].   [23] *avait au contraire plusieurs.*

[24] 'and would,' &c., *sans crainte de manquer.*

[25] *mais quand même il en aurait été autrement, il n'y avait pas à se méprendre* (or, *à se tromper*) *sur ce que la justice prescrit en pareil cas.*

[26] *Une dette dont il avait différé l'acquittement devait passer avant les affaires commerciales auxquelles il se hâtait d'aller vaquer.*

[27] *s'éloigna.*   [28] Turn, 'of the.'

[29] Turn, 'the continuance of his employer's business' *(commerce);* and see TURKISH TALE, n. [13], for the place of 'depended.'

[30] Turn, 'and that.'   [31] *nombreuse.*

[32] *peu considérables ; or, peu de chose.*

[33] Turn, 'and, relying.'

[34] *de satisfaire (or, de faire honneur) ce jour-là même à une forte obligation sous forme de billet.*

[35] *il lui devenait dès lors impossible de tenir sa promesse (or, d'acquitter son engagement).*

[36] *Le commis voyageur,* here.

[37] *un homme d'un caractère vif et jugeant sévèrement les autres.*

[38] *n'avait aucune grâce à attendre de lui, et il n'en obtint point en effet.* See A r t   o f   P l e a s i n g, n. [32].

[39] *Voilà donc toute une famille, et avec elle les gens qui étaient à son service.* See above, note [3].

[40] *n'étaient pas sans observer jusqu'à un certain point les formes extérieures de la religion ; or, ne négligeaient pas entièrement les pratiques religieuses.*

[41] *de faire leurs prières en famille.*   [42] *puiser . . . dans cette Parole.*

[43] *Ne devez rien à personne ; or, Ne soyez redevables à personne.*

[44] Construct thus, in French :—'An hour after the departure of this gentleman, his wife was,'—'to stop,' here, *arréter au passage.*

[45] *qui lui dit: "Madame.* Never fail to use *madame, mademoiselle,* or *monsieur,* when addressing people with whom you are not on very intimate terms. The habit of constantly suppressing these words (or their equivalents), in conversation, has often made, to my knowledge, some English people exceedingly disagreeable, especially in the company of ladies, not only in France, but in the more polite continental countries.

[46] *Quel est son nom, son état?*

[47] *qu'il* (see D e r v i s, n. [8]) *m'est tout à fait impossible de m'occuper d'elle à présent.*

[48] *dans leur chambre.*

[49] *moi aussi j'ai.* Notice this double use of the pronoun of the same person, in its disjunctive and in its conjunctive form, which is frequent, in French, in the case of emphasis or contradistinction.

[50] *Et, navrée de douleur, elle s'éloigna.*

[51] *qui avait passé chez elle (or, qui était venue) la veille.* See S i r R o g e r d e C o v e r l e y, n. [22].

[52] *médecin.*

[53] *que selon toute apparence elle aurait pu sauver la vie à l'enfant en employant.* Notice this turn, *sauver. la vie à,* &c.

[54] *ne le pouvait pas.* See R a b e l a i s a T r a i t o r, n. [12]. This turn, *pouvoir quelque chose,* is borrowed from the Latin ; in English, the word 'do,' expressed or elliptically understood, is necessary to the sense : 'could not' is here put for 'could not *do* so.'

[55] *et cette demande était la dernière qu'elle eût faite* (See S i r R o g e r d e C o v e r l e y, n. [22]) ; *car elle était allée dans trois maisons, et dans chacune elle avait essuyé* (see S i r R o g e r, &c., n. [22]) *la même espèce de*

refus.—Notice this French (and also Latin) use of the subjunctive (*eût*) after *dernier* (as well as after *premier, seul*—Comparison of Watches, n. ²⁴—and superlatives—Art of Pleasing, n. ⁵) followed by a relative pronoun. Most of the rules of the French grammar on the use of the subjunctive are the same as in Latin, and whoever understands them in either language can have but little difficulty in applying them in the other.

[56] . . . *être dans l'ordre.*

[57] *qu'on laisse ainsi mourir* . . . &c., 'best feelings,' *l'affection la plus tendre.*

[58] *et doit-on s'attendre à tout ceci de la part d'une personne professant* . . .*jusqu'à* ('so far as to') . . . *en famille.*

[59] *prochain,* or *semblable* (in the sense of fellow-creature).

[60] Turn, 'and I will give it (to) thee to-morrow.'

[61] 'by thee,' *par devers toi.*

[62] *une seule.*—'should,' &c.; use here the verb *devoir,* and see Comparison of Watches, n. ⁸.

[63] *se gêner.*—'would;' use here the imperfect indicative of *vouloir.*

[64] *afin d'arranger.*   [65] *Tandis qu'elle faisait trop de cas de.*

[66] *valait tout autant, sinon davantage;* or, *avait tout autant, sinon plus de prix.* See Dest. Alex. Lib., n. ¹⁰.

[67] *un patron d'ouvrage à l'aiguille.*

[68] *une lettre;* or, *un billet.*

[69] *elle faisait attendre sa couturière.* Whenever 'will' and 'would,' in English, are used merely as signs of the present and the past, not of the future and the conditional (and they are so used to express the regular recurrence of an action or state), the student must always translate into French by the present and the past. The expression, it is true, is weakened thereby, but this is inevitable, as the English form does not exist in the French language.

[70] *fournisseur.* A tradesman, in his shop, is *marchand; fournisseur* has relation to his dealings with and delivery of goods to customers.

[71] *pour.*

[72] *le temps est de l'argent;* or, *qui dit temps dit argent.*

[73] *bien plus, le pain même qui les fait vivre.*

SCENE FROM "THE GOOD-NATURED MAN."

[1] *de la part de.*

[2] *notes* (fem.); or, *mémoires* (masc.);—in this sense.

[3] *nos billets de compliment* (or, simply and better, *nos petits compliments) ordinaires.* When 'usual' means 'common,' 'frequent,' 'customary,' the French for it is *ordinaire,* or *habituel; usuel* means 'usual' only in the sense of 'in common use.'

[4] *voilà.*   [5] *celle-là.*   [6] *et cette autre.*

[7] *a eu beaucoup de peine—de mal* (or, *bien de la peine—du mal*).

[8] *à ravoir;* this verb, *ravoir,* 'to have again,' 'to recover,' 'to get back,' is only used in the present infinitive.

[9] Translate here by the preterite indefinite ('you have borrowed'), and supply the ellipsis, besides, by using the pronoun understood in English.

[10] *Je ne sais; ce qui est* (or, *ce qu'il y a de*) *certain, c'est que.*

[11] *à obtenir de lui qu'il* (with the preterite subjunctive).

[12] *ces;* or, *les.*

[13] *alliez envoyer;* or, *étiez sur le point d'envoyer.*

[14] *à la famille de ce pauvre monsieur,* (or, *gentilhomme*—obsolete, but still applicable to noblemen, and, by extension, to gentlemen of the olden time) *qui est dans la prison pour dettes*—or, *en prison pour dettes.* The former expression, *dans la prison,* &c., points to a particular place of this kind ('the Fleet,' in the text: in our days, 'the Queen's prison,' and that of 'Whitecross-street,' in London; and, in Paris, that of the *Rue de Clichy,* commonly called '*Clichy*').

[15] *le ferait taire* (or, *lui fermerait la bouche*).

[16] *Oui-da.*

[17] *les fera vivre.*—This play on words, *viz.* on the one hand, 'to stop the mouth of one,' *i. e.* 'to reduce him to silence,' and, on the other hand, 'to fill the mouth of one,' *i. e.* 'to feed, to support, or nourish him,' was to be rendered into French—in order to avoid weakening the meaning—by an equivalent, at least, if the literal translation was found to fail in that purpose. I have rendered it by putting in opposition the expressions *faire taire* and *faire vivre,* which is, I believe, the only way in which it can be managed: *fermer la bouche a quelqu'un* would have done very well, in the first instance, but, in the second, unfortunately, *remplir la bouche à quelqu'un* cannot be used figuratively in the English sense mentioned above.

[18] *il se trouve être;* or, *il lui arrive* (impersonal) *d'être.*

[19] 'to relieve,' *pour subvenir à.*—'insupportable distress.'

[20] *Morbleu!* (vulgar.)

[21] *il s'agit actuellement* (or, *à cette heure*—*aujourd'hui*) *de.*—'to relieve yourself;' see Cowper to J. Newton, n. [56].

[22] Do not forget that *avoir lieu (de)* means 'to have reason, or grounds' (to, &c.), whereas *avoir raison* means 'to be in the right.' See Comp. of Watches, n. [21].

[23] *d'être hors de moi;* or, 'hav'n't I reason to be out,' &c., *n'y a-t-il pas de quoi* (lit. 'wherewith,' 'occasion for,' 'grounds to,') *me faire sortir*—*me mettre hors*—*des gonds* (or, *me mettre hors de moi*).

[24] *à la débandade;* or, *à l'abandon;* or, *au diable* (familiar). We also say, *être sens dessus dessous.*

[25] *motif.* We say *avoir lieu* (to have reason), and also *il y a lieu* (there is reason), but we can only use *lieu,* in this sense, in an indeterminate manner, without any article: thence it follows, in accordance with the same rule, by virtue of which we cannot say *un lieu,* in this acceptation, that we cannot either say *quelque lieu que,* 'whatever reason,' any more than *quel lieu* (what reason). See Comparison of Watches, note [23].— Remember, besides, that *quelque . . . que*

('whatever,' or 'however,') requires the subjunctive after it (see C o w-
per to J. N e w t o n, n. [44]).

[26] *tu conviendras ; or, tu m'accorderas.*

[27] *que je n'ai pas tout à fait tort* (or, *qu'il n'est pas tout à fait ab-
surde à moi) de rester dans mon bon sens—de n'en pas sortir non plus.*

[28] *Personne au monde que vous ;* and leave out 'that.'

[29] *en pareil cas.*—'could do so ;' see R a b e l a i s a T r a i t o r, n. [12].
but use the conditional mood here.

[30] *Tout en voie de gaspillage!*   [31] *perdues pour vous.*

[32] *et rien autour de vous.*

[33] Remember that *de* is generally used instead of the partitive article *du, de la, des,* when the noun, taken in a partitive sense, is preceded immediately by an adjective.

[34] *qui, grâce à votre bonté, ne sont plus propres* (or, *ne sont à cette
heure rien moins que propres) à servir dans.*—'family,' see S i r R o g e r
de C o v e r l e y, n. [15].

[35] *Raison de plus pour qu'ils soient.*

[36] *Bah! or, Ta! or, Tarare! or, Vous voilà bien!* ('It is just like
you.')

[37] *que voulez-vous qu'on fasse de ; vouloir* governs the subjunctive.

[38] The time at which the fact took place not being precisely stated,
we must use here, in French, the preterite indefinite ; see above, n. [9].

[39] *Sur le fait ; or, En flagrant délit.*

[40] *En ce cas ; or, S'il en est ainsi.*

[41] 'pay him,' &c. &c., *lui donner* (or, *lui faire) son compte.*

[42] *Ah bien, oui ; son compte sera bientôt réglé* (or, *son compte est bon)*
... *à Tyburn, le gredin* (or, *drôle) ;—nous le ferons pendre, ne fût-ce
que pour faire peur aux autres* (or, *au reste de nos gens ;* see S i r
R o g e r de C o v e r l e y, n. [15]).—'To turn off;' another play on words,
like the one noticed above, n. [17], and which is here also rendered as
exactly as can be : we say, proverbially, *son compte est bon,* or, *son
compte sera bientôt réglé,* in the sense of *on lui fera un mauvais parti
—on saura bien le punir* (or, *le châtier),* 'His affair will soon be settled,' &c.

[43] *Voilà qui est charmant!*

[44] *Bon ; maintenant, c'est le laquais qui, tout à l'heure* (or, *il n'y a
qu'un instant), est venu.* Notice, by the way, that *tout à l'heure* means
also, 'by and by' (time to come), as well as 'just now' (time past).

[45] *Rien de plus juste ; et pourtant voici le sommelier, qui peut-être
vient à son tour.*

[46] *Ah, ils n'en font pas d'autres* (or, *Ah, les voilà bien), tous tant
qu'ils sont.*

[47] *ils ne font que* (or, *sont toujours à—ne cessent de ;* same remark
about *cesser,* and also *oser,* and *pouvoir,* as about *savoir,* (C o w p e r to
J. N e w t o n, n. [54]) *le quereller.*

[48] We use *l'un l'autre* ('one another,' or 'each other') when speak-

ing of two only; and *les uns les autres*, when speaking of more than two. But, here, *se quereller entre eux*, is the best rendering.

ANECDOTE.

[1] *était toujours le premier* (or, *à la tête*).

[2] *et dont je ne pouvais* (Dervis, n. [6]) *malgré tous . . ., venir à bout de prendre la place* (See Art of Pleasing, n. [32], and Cowper to J. Newton, latter part of n. [35]); or, *et auquel, malgré tous . . ., je ne pouvais venir à bout de damer le pion*. This figurative expression is derived from the game of draughts *(dames)*: *damer un pion* means, properly, 'to crown a man.' We might also translate here by *et que . . . de débusquer;* but it would be somewhat familiar.

[3] *Les jours se succédaient.*

[4] *quoi que je fisse.* Put a full stop here, and do not translate 'till.'

[5] We say *faire une question à quelqu'un*, 'to ask one a question;' accordingly, to translate here correctly, see Mahomet's Miracles, n. [12], and Dest. Alex. Lib. n. [7], 'when,' here, *toutes les fois que*.

[6] *il portait aussitôt les doigts d'un air distrait* (or, ... *doigts machinalement) à;* or, *il jouait aussitôt avec*.

[7] *gilet*, not *veste*. Formerly, 'waistcoat' was called *veste*, in French; this word, *veste*, now corresponds to 'jacket' only. It is to be regretted that the greater part of even modern dictionaries are of no use on these points, as every new edition of them is at best but the old ones reprinted, with all their blunders, antiquated words, &c. &c.

[8] *A la première question qui fut faite à notre écolier.* Here, the passive does not so much matter; it may even be better, to avoid the repetition of *on* at so short an interval (see above, n. [5]).

[9] *mais ils ne le trouvèrent plus;* or, simply, *mais en vain*.

[10] *il regarda son gilet pout tâcher de l'apercevoir.*

[11] *Efforts inutiles! il ne put pas plus le voir que le sentir.* Put a full stop before the word *Efforts*.

[12] *Jamais il . . . ; et jamais.*

[13] *de ce tort;* or, *de cette injustice—de cette injure*, in the widest acceptation of this word.

[14] *j'ai éprouvé à sa vue un vif regret—repentir—serrement de cœur—lorsque je passais près de lui;* or, *je me le suis reproché en voyant passer près de moi mon ancien camarade.*

[15] *mais cela s'est borné à;* 'good resolutions:' see Scene from Good-Natured Man, n. [33].

[16] Use, in French, the preterite indefinite ('have renewed'), and leave out 'my.'

[17] See Dervis, n. [6]. There is here repetition of the action.

[18] *une charge* (or, *un emploi) subalterne*.

[19] *cours de justice de.*

[20] *Pauvre garçon!* or *Pauvre diable!—familiar.*

[21] *il s'adonna de bonne heure à la boisson.*

A TRAVELLING INCIDENT.

[1] *Incident de voyage.*

[2] *Il est ordinaire à nous autres humains, lorsque nous nous sommes endormis en diligence.* The adjective *autre* is often thus used, in the plural, with *nous* or *vous*, for the sake of emphasis or contradistinction.

[3] *et de nous trouver embarrassés* (or, *empêchés*) *de nos jambes et agacés* (or, *irrités*) *par nos cors ; or, de trouver nos jambes un embarras, et dans nos cors un sujet d'agacement—d'irritation.*

[4] *positivement ;* and leave out 'the.'   [5] *envie.*

[6] *de s'en venger sur ses filles. Il avait déjà commencé à satisfaire cette envie sous.*

[7] 'random kicks,' *coups de pied données au hasard.*

[8] *mouvements.*

[9] *et peu après la portière s'ouvrit.* The use of the passive, instead of the reflective form, in French, in such a case as this, would convey a very different meaning; it would express a state, not an act.

[10] *Faites bien attention ;* or, *Ah ça, attention !*

[11] *voix grêle et aiguë.*

[12] *moi et mon fils—mon fils et moi—nous allons dans l'intérieur.* When we have, in a sentence, two or more personal pronouns, or a noun or nouns and a pronoun, used as subjects (nominatives) of a verb, what grammarians call a *resuming* pronoun (either *nous* or *vous*) is used before the verb, unless the subjects are all in the third person, in which latter case no resuming pronoun is used.

[13] *parce qu'il n'y a pas de place sur le dessus ;* or, *parce que le dessus est plein—complet.*

[14] *mais vous vous engagez à ne nous demander* (or, *prendre—faire payer) que le prix de l'impériale.*

[15] *n'est-ce pas ?*—'more ;' see D est. A lex. L ib. n. [10].

[16] *Très-bien* (in this one sense).

[17] *voyageurs ; passager* is said generally of a traveller on the sea, but is beginning to be also applied to a railway traveller.

[18] *entrer* (or, *monter) en toute sûreté.*

[19] *Conformément à cette.*   [20] *deux individus prirent place.*

[21] *véhicule* (only used, in this sense, in familiar and jocose style, for *voiture).*

[22] *qui était solennellement autorisé, par patente, en vertu d'un Acte du Parlement, à porter, dans l'intérieur, toute personne, jusqu'au nombre de six, q'on y pourrait faire entrer.*—Observe the following difference, not always heeded by English people : *patente,* 'a licence ;' *brevet,* 'a patent.'

[23] *Nous avons eu de la chance.*

[24] *quand la voiture se fut remise en route* (or, *fut repartie).*

[25] *Et c'a été très adroit de ta part de;* or, *Et c'a été de ta part un grand coup de l'art de* (or, more forcily, *que de*).

[26] *Hi, hi, hi!* [27] Comp. of Watches, n. [6].

[28] Remember that *mourir*, as well as some other neuter verbs, in French, is conjugated, in its compound tenses, with the auxiliary verb *être*, not with *avoir*.

[29] *S'il vint* (or, *Soit qu'il vînt.—*subj.) *dans l'idée.*

[30] *qu'il s'était jusqu'à un certain point fait tort à lui-même* (or, *trahi lui-même*). Comp. of Watches, n. [16].

[31] *ou si* (or, *soit que,—*or, *ou que—*with the subj.) It is optional either to repeat *soit,* or to use *ou,* before the second member of the sentence.

[32] *influé* (or, *agi*) *sur.*

[33] *c'est ce qu'il y a de douteux;* or, *c'est que nous ne savons pas;* or, *ne saurions le dire;* or, again, *c'est là ce qui fait question.*

[34] See D e r v i s, n. [6], and various other references on this important point, which can hardly be too much insisted upon.

[25] *que le bonhomme.* In this sense, *bonhomme* is spelt in one word.

[36] *qui dura bien cinq minutes;* or, *qui dura cinq grandes minutes— cinq minutes bien comptées.*

[37] *et qui agaça les nerfs de M. P— au point de lui faire dire à la fin, et très brusquement.*

[38] *place.* [39] *pour les voyageurs enrhumés du cerveau.*

[40] *Mon rhume.* [41] *un moment d'intervalle* (or, *de silence*).

[42] *est un rhume de poitrine.* [43] *manière de parler;* or, *ton.*

[44] *tout ensemble, alors qu'il articulait* (or, *s'exprimait*) *distinctement —clairement—net—nettement.*

[45] *le sang-froid de l'interlocuteur.*

[46] *et le fait qu'il connaissait.*

[47] *toutes ces circonstances étaient autant d'indices de.*

[48] *sur lesquels* (D e s t. A l e x. L i b. note [13]).

[49] *je croyais m'adresser* (or, *adresser la parole—*see M u l y M o l u c, note [7]) *à.*

[50] *car ce sont eux-mêmes, mes chers* (or, *chères*) *enfants, que nous avons pour* (no article is to follow).—The substantive *enfant* is of both genders; yet, in the plural, the feminine is seldom used. Notice that Mr. P. had only his daughters, and no son, with him in the coach; else, of course, the feminine could by no means be used.

[51] *Je ne voudrais pas, moi, blesser une personne, quelle qu'elle soit, à qui m'unissent des liens de famille* (or, *les liens du sang*).

[52] *d'un ton caustique.*

[53] *Bah, bah!* or, *Allons donc, allons donc!* [54] *mais.*

[55] *Et en vérité* (or, *Et je puis le dire en conscience—*or, *en bonne con-science*), *je sentais bien;* 'that to be,' see M u l y M o l u c, n. [2].

[56] *appelé ainsi;* or, *traité d'hypocrite.*

[57] *qu'il y eût entré;* see Comp. of Watches, n. [24].—'was;' turn, 'it is that.'

[58] 'now,' *voyons.*—'shall I,' &c., *faut-il vous dire* (or, *voulez-vous que je vous dise,* or, simply, *vous dirai-je) quelle était la différence entre,* &c.

[59] *Dites, mon cher monsieur, dites.* 'If you please,' is, literally, as is well known, *s'il vous plaît,* in French; but, in a case of this particular kind, it is not the phrase used.

[60] *Eh bien, ce qu'il y a d'ennuyeux chez vous en particulier, . . . c'est que ;* or, *Eh bien, vous avez, vous en particulier, . . . cela d'ennuyeux que.*

[61] *ni compère ni compagnon dans vos jongleries, à vous.*

[62] *vous feriez volontiers prendre* (or, *vous donneriez volontiers) le change—vous ne vous feriez pas faute de faire prendre* (or, *de donner) le change—à n'importe qui* (or *à qui que ce soit).*—The use of the verb *tromper* ('to deceive'), even here, would be somewhat too uncivil.

[63] *et vous* (see Cowper to S. Rose, n. [31]) *avez je ne sais*—or, *un je ne sais—quel air.*

[64] *comme si vous preniez dans le sérieux ce que vous dites ou ce que vous faites* (or, better, *comme si vous vous preniez au sérieux).* "Prendre une chose *dans le sérieux,*" is, to take a thing in earnest, to believe it to be true, although it was said in joke; whilst "prendre une chose *au sérieux,*" is to take offence at a thing, though it was said in a joke, and without any intention of offending. Authors often disregard this distinction of grammarians.

[65] *Je parierais gros.* We also say, in a similar way, *parier double contre simple ;* also, by exaggeration, *Je parierais ma tête* (or, *ma tête à couper),* and, implying no doubt whatever, *Je mettrais ma main au feu.*

[66] Use *garder ;* or, *sauver ;* or, *conserver.*

[67] *ici présentes ;* or, *que voici.*

[68] 'Now I;' *Moi, voyez-vous ;* or, *Moi qui vous parle.*—'a business scheme ;' *le plan de quelque affaire.*—'in hand.'

[69] See Hearers and Doers, n. [49].

[70] *de quoi il s'agit ;* or, *ce qui en est,*—not *ce que c'est,* here : *ce que c'est* would correspond to 'what it—or that—is,' in another sense, the sense of 'what *that thing* (in a vague way) is'—namely a *scheme ;* whereas *ce qui en est* means, 'what *that scheme* (mentioned above) is about.' We might also translate by *j'en fais part à Jonas.*

[71] *les plus grands ;* or, *les plus beaux ;* or, again, *les plus flatteurs,* after the noun. In general, no adjectives, in French, can precede a noun, when in the superlative degree, except those which are allowed to precede it when in the positive degree.

[72] Simply, *qu'on eût* (see Art of Pleasing, n. [5]) *pu lui faire ;* or, *. . . les . . . compliments possibles :—susceptibles d'être exprimés par* (or, *au moyen de) la parole,* would be awkward.

[73] *Est-ce que vous allez* (or, *vous vous rendez).*

[74] *ma foi ;* or, *parbleu* (familiar).   [75] *vous feriez mieux de.*

[76] *Ce n'est pas moi qui irai me compromettre ;* or, elliptically and

familiarly, *Pas si bête que d'aller me* ..... &c.—(The vulgar phrase would be, *Le plus souvent que j'irai* ... &c.)

[77] *comme de raison—cela va sans dire—bien entendu—naturellement.*

[78] *lui et son père.* The French word *parents* means all relatives, and is also said of the father and mother; but it is never used in the singular, in this latter sense, as in English, to signify only one of the two.

[79] *se rendaient à leur demeure.* See A Travelling Incident, n. [12].

[80] *capitale.* *Métropole* was said formerly, in French, of the capital town of a province; it only means now a town which has an archiepiscopal see, as Paris, Rouen, Bordeaux, &c., and also 'mother country,' 'parent state,' with relation to colonies.

[81] *réunion.*

[82] *ils étaient restés* (see note [28]) — or, *ils avaient séjourné — dans cet endroit* (or, *dans ce comté*) *afin de surveiller.*

[83] *propriétés qui offraient un placement avantageux.*

[84] *et que ces deux associés, Chuzzlewit et fils,* (or, *et que ces deux associés en nom collectif*) *avaient déjà en vue lors de leur départ de Londres.* There is no French expression, as concise as the English, corresponding to 'up,' and 'down,' in this sense: we say, *e. g.*, *trains se dirigeant vers Paris* ('up trains'), and *trains s'éloignant de Paris* ('down trains'); also, *trains d'aller* ('down'), and *trains de retour* ('up' or 'back').

[85] *au dire de M. J——.*

[86] *de faire d'une pierre deux coups* (proverbial).

[87] *et de ne jamais donner* (or, *se dessaisir de*) *un petit poisson que pour en avoir un gros* (proverbial); or ... *un œuf* ... *pour avoir un bœuf—* ... *un pois* ... *pour avoir une fève* (proverbial).

SCENE FROM "THE SCHOOL FOR SCANDAL."

[1] *de,*—with the article, of course.

[2] use, the plural ('hands') here, in French.

[3] 'to be acquainted with,' *connaître;* see Dervis, n. [8]; and use the subjunctive, here, as *penser* ('to think,' 'to believe') is conjugated negatively. See Cowper to J. Newton, n. [35], for another example of this. We might also very well translate the English phrase by, *permettez-moi de vous présenter.*

[4] *Parbleu* (familiar).

[5] *madame.* The abbreviation of this word, in French, belongs to very vulgar language.

[6] *c'est un garçon d'esprit, et, qui plus est, un poète.*—*c'est*, instead of *il est:* the demonstrative pronoun *ce* is generally used, instead of *il, elle, ils, elles,* as the subject of a proposition whose attribute is not an adjective; the attribute is here the substantive *garçon.*

[7] *n'est-ce pas;* literally, 'is it not' (understood, 'true,' *vrai*). This is the usual French phrase corresponding to 'am I not,' 'art thou not,' 'is he (she, or it) not,' 'are we (you, or they) not,' or 'do I not,' &c.

&c., whatever may have been mentioned in the foregoing part of the proposition.

⁸ *Pardieu* (familiar), *rien de plus vrai.* Put a full stop here.

⁹ *En fait de* (lit. 'in point of') *rébus et de charades, je parierais pour lui.*

¹⁰ See Sir Roger de Coverley, n. ¹⁶.

¹¹ *Milady connaît-elle.*   ¹² See Dervis, n. ¹².

¹³ 'he wrote;' use the indefinite preterite 'he has written,' the time at which the fact took place not being precisely stated, and not being far distant; and see, besides, Sir Roger de Coverley, n. ²².—'last week' *la semaine dernière; la dernière semaine* is French, too, but it means '*the* last week' (of the month, or year, or &c.).

¹⁴ *à propos des plumes de lady Frisure, qui avaient pris feu?*

¹⁵ *Benjamin, récitez-nous cela, ou bien.*

¹⁶ 'to make extempore,' *improviser.*

¹⁷ *cercle.*   ¹⁸ *Voyons.*

¹⁹ *mon.*   ²⁰ 'a,' *est celui d'un.*

²¹ 'pr'ythee,' *de grâce.*—'uncle;' always use the possessive pronoun 'my,' in French, before 'uncle,' 'father,' 'mother,' 'brother,' &c., in the vocative case.

²² *En vérité.*

²³ *vous seriez étonnée de voir combien il est expert dans ces choses-là.*

²⁴ *A dire vrai;* or, *A vous dire le vrai;* or, *A vous parler vrai.*

²⁵ *rien de plus vulgaire* (or, better, *commun) que de faire imprimer;* or, simply, *c'est si commun.*

²⁶ *sur des particuliers;* or, *sur telle ou telle personne.*

²⁷ *je leur assure une circulation beaucoup plus étendue, en en donnant confidentiellement des copies aux amis des parties intéressées.* 'Copy,' of a printed book or pamphlet, or of an engraving, &c., from a common type, is, in French, *exemplaire;* in the above sense, *copie* is the word used.

²⁸ See Cowper to S. Rose, n. ¹⁰.

²⁹ *Par le ciel* (familiar).

³⁰ 'to be handed down to posterity,' *passer* (or, *aller) à la postérité.*

³¹ *la Laure de Pétrarque.*

³² *imprimées en grand in-quarto* (abbreviated, *in-4);* or, *dans le format* ('size of a book') *d'un magnifique in-quarto;* or, again, *figurer dans un magnifique in-quarto.*

³³ *quand vous suivrez des yeux le gentil ruisseau du texte, qui serpentera agréablement entre les prairies d'une marge blanche;* or, *où un joli ruisseau de texte courra à travers l'étendue d'une double et vaste marge;* or, better, *où le texte serpentera entre deux vastes marges, comme un petit ruisseau dans une large prairie.*—*Vive Dieu!* (familiar) *on n'aura jamais rien vu dans ce genre de* (see Dest. Alex. Lib., n. ¹⁹) *plus élégant* (or, *oh! ce sera ce qu'il y aura de plus élégant*—or, *galant—en son genre;* or, in a more emphatic and a not uncommon way, *oh! ce sera la plus belle chose du monde!)*

[34] *savez-vous.*

[35] *ce n'est pas cela;* or, *vous n'y êtes point.*

[36] *Cela ne se peut pas;* or, *Allons donc!* (familiar) or, again, *Pas possible!* or, literally, *Impossible!*

[37] *Demandez plutôt à.*

[38] 'wedding liveries,' *livrée de noce;* this expression signifies also, in villages, 'wedding favors, or ribbons.'—'bespoke,' *commandée,* in this sense.

[39] 'it,' *ce mariage.*

[40] *J'en avais déjà entendu quelque chose* (or, *En effet, j'en ai entendu parler).*

[41] *Oh! mon Dieu* (familiar, but much used). We might also say, *Eh mais.*

[42] *c'est justement pour cela;* or, *voilà justement pourquoi.*

[43] *Ce qu'il y a de certain, c'est qu'un propos médisant.*

[44] *Mais il est* (or, *il y a*) *des* (or, *de ces*) *réputations chétives et malingres* (or, simply, *maladives*) *qui sont toujours souffrantes, et qui cependant survivent* (see H e a r e r s and D o e r s, n. [89]) *à la robuste renommée* (or, *et qui cependant vont bien plus loin que celles*).

[45] *C'est vrai.*   [46] *de.*

[47] Repeat *de,* here.   [48] *côté.*

[49] *jusqu'au* (lit. 'even to the').

[50] *et suppléent à force de soins et de précautions à la santé qui leur manque.*

[51] *Oui, mais ce bruit peut n'avoir pas le moindre fondement.*

[52] *C'est vrai, madame, sur ma parole;* or, *C'est d'honneur vrai, madame.* This familiar expression, *d'honneur,* is elliptical for *foi d'homme d'honneur;* sometimes we suppress elliptically only the word *foi,* and say *d'homme d'honneur.*

[53] *est-il vrai, dites-moi.*

[54] *soit en route pour revenir en Angleterre?* We use *soit* (subjunctive), and not *est* (indicative), because the first part of the proposition (*est-il vrai*) is interrogative, and a doubt is therefore implied as to the fact. See R a b e l a i s a T r a i t o r, n. [11], for a somewhat similar use of the subjunctive.

[55] *Non pas que je sache, monsieur.*

[56] *A son retour, ce sera fort triste pour lui.*

[57] *votre frère* (formally, we say, *monsieur votre frère,* as well as *madame votre mère,* &c. &c.) *s'est conduit.*

[58] *j'espère toutefois qu'aucun rapporteur officieux n'a encore prévenu* (or, *qu'il ne s'est point trouvé de méchant*—or, *de malveillant*—*empressé à prévenir).*

[59] *Il le peut, sans aucun doute.*

[60] *on m'assure que personne n'est en meilleure réputation* (or, *en meilleure odeur*) *auprès des* (or, *chez les*) *juifs;* or, *du moins ne parle-t-on de lui* (or, *n'en parle-t-on*)—see S i r R o g e r de C o v e r l e y, n. [19]—*qu'avec honneur chez les juifs.* This construction, 'to be spoken of,' is

not allowed in French. As to the pronoun *en*, it is more commonly used when speaking of animals and things than of persons: in the latter case we rather make use of *de lui, d'elle, d'eux, d'elles.* Voltaire has still more deviated from the rule, laid down by grammarians, on this subject, and used *en* for *de moi;* but this breach of grammar is so contrary to custom, that it should not be imitated.

[61] *un quartier* (un des quartiers de la cité de Londres); or, better, *une section* (or *circonscription) municipale.*

[62] There are no aldermen in France: the nearest to them are the *conseillers municipaux,* and 'ward' corresponds to *arrondissement* in Paris; formerly we had the *quartiniers* (for towns), and the *échevins* (for *communes).* Translate here simply by *serait alderman;* and remember that the indefinite article ('a' or 'an'), which is used in English (as here), is not used in French, before nouns which express the titles, professions, trade, country, or any other attribute of the substantive antecedent. We might however say here, more accurately, perhaps, *en serait l'alderman.*

[63] *j'ai entendu dire* (See Dervis, note [8]).

[64] *d'Irlande.*　　　　　　　　[65] *on fait.*

[66] *Et cependant, personne ne mène un train de vie plus splendide.*

[67] *Jamais il ne donne à dîner, dit-on, sans avoir à sa table.*

[68] *de ses répondants.*

[69] *une vingtaine de créanciers* (in this sense, 'creditors'); leave out 'have,' already used just above, in French, and also 'waiting,' which is not necessary to the sense.

[70] *officier de justice,* i. e., *huissier,* (and *recors),* in this sense—'bailiff' (and follower).

[71] *pour.*

[72] *mais vous ménagez bien peu* (or, *mais vous avez bien peu d'égard pour) la sensibilité.*

[73] *(A part.) Je ne peux* (or *puis) plus y tenir* (or, *Je n'y puis plus tenir);* or, literally, *Leur méchanceté est intolérable!—(Haut.) Je vous demanderai la permission de vous quitter, milady* (it is considered more familiar than civil, in France, to address people by their name; and as to *bonjour,* 'good morning'—or, *je vous souhaite le bonjour,* it is also familiar); *je ne me sens pas bien.*

[74] *O mon Dieu! avez-vous vu comme elle a changé de couleur!*

[75] 'do,' here, *je vous en prie,* and at the end of the sentence; or, better, *Veuillez la suivre, mistress* (English)—or *madame* (French) *Candeur.*

[76] Simply, *De tout mon cœur.*　　　　　[77] See note [60].

[78] See Art of Pleasing, note [8].

[79] *est un homme perdu;* or, better, *est complètement ruiné.*

[80] *Hélas oui!* (or, *Parbleu!) perdu sans ressources* (or, *aussi ruiné qu'on peut l'être).—Il ne pourrait emprunter* (or, *trouver à emprunter).*

[81] *Et on prétend que tous ses effets mobiliers sont vendus.*

[82] *chez lui (chez* means 'at—in, or to—the dwelling of').

[83] *Il n'y reste absolument rien.*

[84] *auxquelles on n'a pas fait attention.* See Dest. Alex. Library, note [13].

[85] *En outre, j'ai été fâché d'entendre tenir sur son compte des propos peu flatteurs ;* or, *En outre, il court sur son compte certains* (or, *de certains*) *bruits qui me font beaucoup de peine.*

[86] *Il va pour sortir.*

[87] See note [6].

[88] *Nous vous conterons tout cela une autre fois.*

[89] *il est cruel pour eux* (or, *il leur en coûte*) *d'abandonner un sujet avant de l'avoir épuisé* (or, *coulé à fond*).

[90] *Et je crois que* (see Dervis, n. [8]) *leurs propos médisants on déplu à milady tout autant qu'à.*

[91] *Je crains bien qu'elle ne* (See Comp. of Watches, n. [3]) *l'aime plus* (or, *qu'elle n'ait engagé ses affections plus avant*) *que nous ne l'imaginons.*

[92] See Hearers and Doers, n. [3]; and observe that 'I am,' 'thou art,' &c., followed by another verb in the infinitive, in the sense which it has here, is rendered into French by the verb *devoir.*

[93] *vous ferez donc tout aussi bien de dîner où vous êtes ;* or, *dînez avec moi, puisque vous êtes tout porté.*

[94] *de plus près ;* or, *avec plus d'attention.*

[95] *je vais comploter de nouvelles malices, et vous repasserez votre rôle sentimental.*

2. BYRON TO THOS. MOORE.

[1] *Je n'étais point seul, et je ne le serai pas* (see Art of Pleasing, n. [32], and Cowper to S. Rose, n. [31]) *tant que je pourrai faire autrement* (or, *et je ne le serai qu'autant que je ne pourrai faire autrement*). 'Newstead,' *L'affaire de N—.*

[2] See above (this page), note [92].

[3] The student may translate here literally, or use the idiomatic and familiar expression *donner un (grand,* or *bon,* here—'grand,' in the text) *coup de collier,* which, however, always means, or implies, a *new* effort.

[4] *afin d'avoir terminé samedi,* i. e., *terminé le contrat*—or, more exactly still, *la passation du contrat—d'acquisition,* 'completed the purchase').

[5] *sinon, il renonce à la propriété, et consent en outre à payer la somme de . . .* &c., *plus les frais.*

[6] *l'Abbatial.*

[7] *je vous en donnerai avis comme il convient ; et je vous promets en même temps une cellule réservée pour vous.*

[8] As we have have repeatedly seen before, this construction is not allowed in French.

[9] 'came out,' *ont paru.*

[10] See note [8]. — 'their effect;' *l'effet qu'ils* (or, *que ces écrits*) *auront produit* (or, *ont pu produire*). The future, or its compound (*auront produit*, here) is often used in French, instead of the present indicative, or its compound (*ont produit*), to imply a conjecture, instead of setting forth an affirmation, with regard to the existence of a fact; in the same way that the conditional (*auraient produit*—to take the same verb as an example) is used, also, for the indicative, to imply only a conditional belief. This is one of the many niceties of the French language which are extremely difficult to foreigners, and it is therefore well worth dwelling upon once for all. If we said here, *qu'ils ont produit*, we might affirm, perhaps, more than has actually taken place—more, at least, than is positively known or professed to be known. Let us now choose an example of the conditional so used: "D'après *les avis que* nous recevons de Trieste, des troubles *auraient eu* (not *ont eu*) lieu," &c.; that is, . . . 'have taken place' ('are said to have,' &c.), but this fact to be credited only so far as the intelligence (*les avis*) which has been received is itself worth belief. The latter kind of phrase is very frequently to be found in French newspapers, but is seldom understood as it ought to be, except by natives.

[11] *dans l'idée que vous êtes, vous, un des rédacteurs de la Revue d'Édimbourg.* See Mahomet's Miracles, n. [7], and Comparison of Watches, n. [3].

[12] *et il pourrait bien exécuter* (or, *jouer*). When we pass from affirmation to negation, and *vice versâ*, a pronoun is necessary before the second verb, although the noun or pronoun which is the subject of both verbs has been expressed before the first.

[13] *en s'entendant dire qu'il n'est qu'un imbécile* (or, *sot*); or, *en s'entendant* (or, *se voyant*) *traiter de pur imbécile*, See A Travelling Incident, note [56].

[14] *Or, si.*   [15] *allait être.*

[16] Translate as if the English were, 'one of your articles.' The construction in the text is not French: thus we say, *un de mes amis*, 'a friend of mine;' sometimes, also, familiarly, *un mien ami*, or, *cousin*, &c.

[17] *dénoûment* (or, *dénouement*),—masculine; or, *catastrophe*,—feminine; in this sense.

[18] See Turkish Tale, n. [13].

[19] *il en a bien usé* (or, *il a bien agi*) *avec moi.*

[20] See Scene from School for Scandal, note [6].

[21] *et je ne veux pas qu'on le tue;*—'have one killed,' or, &c. is not a French construction.

[22] *contrairement, sans doute, à* (or, *au contraire, sans doute, de*) *bon nombre de gens, qui le voudraient bien* (or, *qui ne demanderaient pas mieux*), *vu l'excellence de son caractère* (ironically).

[23] See Muly Moluc, note [7].

[24] *je me mis un soir en colère contre une bouteille d'encre, que je jetai* (or, *lançai*) *violemment par la fenêtre.*

[25] *Et puis? . . . Voilà donc que* (or, simply, *Eh bien*).

[26] *frappé* (or, *donné*) *en se brisant contre.*

[27] *sculptée.*

[28] *et barbouillé cette dernière comme à dessein.*

[29] *Jugez un peu;—un peu* corresponds also to 'just,' thus used in familiar conversation.

[30] See **Muly Moluc**, n. [17].

[31] Use *on* here; 'to engender,' here, *produire.*

[32] Here, the two nouns being considered together—indeed being so closely connected together as they are—the repetition of the preposition, in French, as well as in English, would be a breach of the logical rules of language.

[33] *Depuis la dernière fois que je vous vis* (or, *Depuis que je ne vous ai vu*), *j'ai eu, à une comédie bourgeoise* (or, *comédie de société—*or *d'amateurs*), . . . &c., *quoique d'un autre genre.*

[34] *sur ce qu'il me demandait.*

[35] *assurément;* or, *ma foi.*

[36] *écurie* (for horses, asses, and mules); *étable* is for cattle.

[37] See **Turkish Tale**, n. [26].

[38] *une réunion;* or, *un tas—*familiar.

[39] Use the pluperfect tense here.

[40] *Il se trouva être* (or, *Il se trouva—*impersonal—*que c'était*) *un cabotin.*

[41] *et se montra assez civil* (or, *poli—honnête*) *dans son parler;—*or, *Je reconnus bientôt que j'avais affaire à un cabotin,* . . . &c., *et à un homme au parler assez civil* (or *poli—honnête*).

[42] *du moment* (or, *dès*) *qu'il vit* (or, *s'aperçut*) *qu'il n'y avait pas grand'chose à gagner.*

[43] *Mais vous eussiez* (or, *auriez*) *bien ri, et du.—eussiez;* another form of the conditional of *avoir,* peculiar to that verb, as *je fusse,* &c., is to that of *être. J'eusse,* &c., is frequently used instead of *j'aurais,* &c. This form, which belongs exclusively to the two auxiliary verbs, is also elegantly made use of instead of the imperfect tense of the indicative, either with *si* ('if'), or in elliptical phrases wherein that conjunction is suppressed.

[44] *et de l'habillement—ou plutôt du déshabillé—.*

[45] *compagnie.*   [46] *ahuri en diable comme je l'étais.*

[47] *pour prendre le frais;* or, *pour prendre l'air;* or, *pour respirer le frais.* Construct, in French, thus, 'I had gone from the theatre into the garden for coolness.'

[48] *j'étais tombé en me heurtant contre.*

[49] *et, en m'en éloignant.*   [50] See **Cowper to S. Rose**, n. [31].

[51] *de plus mauvaise humeur encore.*

[52] See **Muly Moluc**, n. [21]. We might very well, however, and more elegantly, translate here, 'which produced,' simply by *d'où.*

[53] *Ah çà, mais pourquoi ne vous lancez-vous donc pas? C'est maintenant pour vous le bon moment.*

[54] *Le public.*

[55] *lequel* (which is somewhat more pointed than *qui*) *vient d'engendrer un* (or, *d'accoucher d'un*) *in-quarto.* The verb *frayer*, which is the proper word for 'to spawn,' would not do here.

[56] Plural, in French.

[57] *Écrivez-moi pour me donner de vos nouvelles et de celles de.*

[58] See Cowper to S. Rose, n. [10].

[59] *ira.*   [60] *Croyez-moi bien toujours,* &c.

LAST MEETING OF WAVERLEY AND FERGUS McIVOR.

[1] *entrevue.*

[2] *grand shérif,*—to make this French as much as possible.

[3] *personnes.*   [4] *J'y vais.*

[5] *donnant le bras à Édouard.*   [6] *il descendit.*

[7] *puis des soldats qui fermaient la marche.* Construct so, in French: '... by the arm, he moved down ..., &c., followed by ..., and the soldiers,' &c.

[8] Here it is necessary to repeat the preposition, if we wish to establish in our expressions that connexion which exists in our ideas; here, 'battalion' and 'drawn up' are more closely connected together than 'squadron' and 'battalion' are with each other. If, on the contrary, 'squadron' and 'battalion' were considered together, and 'drawn up' related to both (instead of to the last only, as here), the preposition should not be repeated. This is a common rule in the logic of language, which is not generally observed in English; and this, together with many other such neglects, accounts for the great obscurity which pervades the works of even the best English writers.

[9] *formé en carré.*

[10] 'were to be;' see School for Scandal, n. [92].—'to draw,' here, *conduire.*

[11] *à environ un mille.*   [12] *en noir.*

[13] *attelé de.*   [14] 'vehicle,' *voiture*; 'sat,' *était assis.*

[15] *homme hideux comme son emploi.*

[16] *et tenant sa hache à la main.* The closest connexion of ideas is not observed in the English construction of the above sentence; mend that construction in the French.

[17] *sur le devant.*

[18] *A travers le sombre arceau gothique qui s'ouvrait sous le pont-levis, on apercevait.*

[19] *qui sépare le pouvoir civil et l'autorité militaire.*

[20] 'whom ... permit;' *permettre* governs the dative, in French as well as in Latin.

[21] *Voilà qui est bien disposé* (or, *bien monté*) *pour une scène de dénoûment.*

[22] 'to gaze round upon;' simply, *regarder.*—'the;' *cet,* here.

[23] *Voilà s'écria vivement E— D—, ces braves dragons, qui galopaient si vite à G—, avant que nous en eussions tué seulement une douzaine ; ils ont l'air assez vaillant aujourd'hui.*

[24] *F—, après avoir embrassé W— sur chaque joue, y monta d'un pas leste.*

[25] *à.*

[26] 'gentleman;' see Scene from Good-Natured Man, n. [14].—'at whose house;' see Scene from School for Scandal, n. [82].

[27] *Au moment où* (or, *que*) *F— faisait un signe de la main.*

[28] *les soldats entourèrent.*—'faisait;' 'entourèrent.'

[29] *et le cortége se mit en marche.*

[30] *On fit halte quelques instants.*

[31] 'to go through,' in this sense, *accomplir.*

[32] *pour que l'officier militaire fît en cet endroit la remise des condamnés entre les mains de.*

[33] *Vive ;*—'king,' &c., see Turkish Tale, n. [22].

[34] *fut terminée ;* the verb *terminer* (or, *finir*) is always used in this sense : thus, 'to conclude a letter,' *terminer une lettre.*

[35] *se leva sur.*   [36] *Ce.*

[37] *lui entendit prononcer ;* or, *entendit prononcer à son ami.* Notice here, that the neuter verb *parler* (to speak) is never used actively in French, as it is in English.

[38] *se remit en.*

[39] *la marche funèbre se fit entendre, et à ses sons lugubres se mêlèrent les tintements sourds des cloches de la cathédrale, couvertes de crêpe.*

[40] *bruit.*   [41] *s'éloigna à mesure que.*

[42] *et bientôt on n'entendit plus que le son mélancolique des cloches.*

A FEW WORDS OF ADVICE TO YOUNG PEOPLE.

[1] *principale.*

[2] *se résume dans ces trois mots du précepte français.*

[3] *précepte que.* The repetition of the word *précepte* is here necessary.

[4] *garantie* (or, *sauvegarde—protection*) *par excellence.*

[5] See Turkish Tale, n. [22].   [6] *il y expliqua ainsi, . . .* &c.

[7] 'After this,' *Mais par la suite.* This construction, 'he himself,' is not allowed in French ; translate as if the English were, 'he became himself,'—'a pensioner.'

[8] *éprouver* (or, *ressentir*—which verb is more expressive than *sentir*) *à recevoir.*

[9] 'so . . . as,' when they thus come before a verb, are rendered into French by *assez . . . pour ;* yet *si . . . que* is better after a verb conju-

gated with a negative, as *Je ne suis pas si fou que de le croire,* 'I am not so mad as to believe it.'

[10] *un saisissement en.*

[11] *de s'abandonner* (or, *s'adonner—se livrer—se laisser aller*) *à.*

[12] *Telle en ;*—'*en,*' 'of it.

[13] *et faisons-le observer ;* leave out 'that' in the translation.

[14] *l'habitude de suivre les* (or, *de céder—de ne pas résister—de se laisser entraîner,* or *aller,*—&c., as above—*aux*) *penchants de cette nature.*

[15] 'they,' *elle* ('*l'habitude*'), the verb in the singular.—'to make ;' in this sense, see Cowper to J. Newton, n. [23].

[16] *ces défauts.*

[17] *à ceux de toujours avoir sur les lèvres un niais sourire de commande* (or, *de sourire avec affeterie à tout bout de champ—à chaque bout de champ ;* familiar—or, *à tout propos*) *et d'être toujours à ramper.*

[18] *Je voudrais* (conditional) *que ;*—followed by the imperfect subjunctive (of *pouvoir,* here).

[19] *cœur—caractère—fierté ;* in this sense.

[20] *de* (or *que de*—'*que,*' together with '*de,*' in such a case as this, is more forcible and graceful than '*de*' only, which is grammatical enough) *montrer une soumission implicite et prompte envers.*

[21] *le droit ;* or, merely, *droit :* 'right' being used here in a definite sense, we cannot use, in French, the indefinite, but must use the definite article, if we use any at all.

[22] Simply, *de l'exiger de vous.*

[23] 'been' . . . , 'will be' . . . , 'an ;' *servi* . . . , *servira* . . . , *de.*

[24] *monde entier ;— tout le monde* is more commonly used in the sense of 'every body.'

[25] *spontanée.* Construct, in French, as if the English were, 'It is to this habit . . . &c., that she owes,' &c.

[26] *tous les inférieurs envers leurs supérieurs.*

[27] *en grande partie.*

[28] In this sense, *exploits—hauts faits—faits* (or, *beaux faits*) *d'armes.*

[29] *Il n'y a.*   [30] 'but,' &c. ; *bien* (or, *tout*) *au contraire.*

[31] The verb *obéir* governs the dative (prep. *à* here).

[32] *Les esclaves sont, de tous les hommes, le plus* . . . &c., *et les plus* . . . &c.

[33] Use *à* before the next verb, here.

[34] *que le respect des lois chez les peuples a été grand à proportion qu'ils ont été libres ;* or, *que plus les nations ont été libres, plus leur respect pour les lois a été grand.*

[35] *les gens ;—peuple* only means 'people' in the sense of a 'nation' (*populus,* in Latin).

[36] A full stop, after 'king's feet.' *On s'imagine voir.*

[37] *positivement se traîner sur le ventre ;* or, simply, *positivement à plat ventre* (or, *ventre à terre*).

[38] 'self-abasement,' *abaissement* (or, *humiliation*) *volontaire*. Change the construction here.

[39] *j'espère bien;* see Comp. of Watches, note [36]. We have more ways than one, however, according to the case, of rendering the emphasis of 'do,' thus used in English; with an imperative we should use *donc*, or *je vous prie* (or, *en prie*): ex., *goûtez donc de ce pâté* (do taste this pie); &c. See Scene from School for Scandal, n. [75].

[40] *n'auront que de l'exécration pour ;—détestation* is hardly used in French, except as a religious term.

[41] *remettre.*

[42] *qu'il soit.*

[43] *espérons donc qu'un temps viendra néanmoins.*

[44] *en faire autant.*

[45] *En attendant ;* or, *Jusque-là.*

[46] *de faire moins de cas encore de ces êtres-là (être* is often so used, in French, as a term of contempt, and, sometimes also, as an expression of anger). We might also translate by, *de mettre ces êtres-là au-dessous de ;* leaving out 'than.'

[47] *Aussi bien est-ce à votre âge que s'acquiert. Aussi bien,* thus used, without *que,* serves to account in several ways for a preceding proposition. It corresponds, according to the case, to 'as,' 'for indeed,' 'the more so as,' 'after all,' 'besides,' 'too,' as used here in the text, &c. It here accounts, though somewhat indirectly, for 'perseverance' being that particularly recommended to young people. It may also be observed that this expression often takes elegantly after it the interrogative form.

[48] Simply, *faute* (or, *par manque*).

[49] 'as,' *de même que ;* . . . 'so,' *de même,* or, *ainsi.*—'the race was not to,' *le prix de la course fut remporté, non par.*

[50] *revient, non à.*

[51] 'him,' here, *celui.* When the personal pronouns 'he,' 'she,' &c., are the antecedents of a relative pronoun, they are expressed, not by *il, elle,* &c., but by *celui, celle,* &c.

[52] *se presse.*

[53] *ferme* (or, *sûr) et égal* (or, *uniforme—régulier*).

[54] *manque ;* or, *défaut.*

[55] *du désir d'apprendre ou de dispositions.* The definite article is here used before *désir,* because this noun is taken in a particular definite sense.

[56] *qu'il nous faut.*

[57] 'patient perseverance.' Construct this sentence so, in French. See Turkish Tale, n. [26]. 'It is not so much to a want of taste . . . &c., as to the want of . . . &c., that we have . . . scholars.' On this subject, the French have two proverbs which run thus, "La trop grande hâte est cause du retardement," and, "Qui trop se hâte reste en chemin (or, en beau chemin se fourvoie)."

POPE TO WYCHERLEY.

[1] See Cowper to S. Rose, n. [31].

[2] *car si cette lettre-ci* (or, *la présente lettre*—or, substantively, *la présente*) *se trouve être.*

[3] 'the worst,'—'letter' understood.

[4] See Dervis, n. [12]. 'to trouble,' here, *importuner.*

[5] *Toutefois, il n'est pas moins de mon intérêt que de mon devoir de vous exprimer au long* (or, *tout au long*) *ma reconnaissance de votre lettre obligeante* (or, *de votre bonne lettre*).

[6] 'some people,' *certaines gens.* The substantive *gens* requires adjectives, &c., preceding it to be feminine, and those following masculine. This rule has somewhat complicated exceptions.

[7] *nous,* here, will not be ambiguous; *vous* would be so,—'to thank abundantly,' *remercier tant et plus;* or, *faire mille remerciments.*

[8] 'for,' *de,* here, as at note [5].—'a piece of kindness;' simply, *une bonté* (or, *une faveur*), just as we say *une imprudence* (an act of imprudence), &c. &c.

[9] *pour nous faire songer à.*

[10] No article is used, in French, with *plus,* or, *moins,* repeated. Besides, in such a case, the following is the order usually observed in the words: 1st *plus,* or *moins;* 2nd, the nominative of the verb; 3rd, the verb; 4th, the regimen of the verb (whether an adjective or a substantive); the rest as in English.

[11] *en plein soleil.*   [12] *les mêmes.*

[13] *est à un jeune écrivain de talent* (or, *un jeune auteur qui promet*— or, *un bel-esprit en herbe*—or, simply, *un jeune homme d'intelligence*) *ce qu'est.* The word *bel-esprit,* however, is now generally taken in a bad sense.

[14] A personal pronoun, governed by several verbs, must not only be placed before the first, in French, but be repeated before each of them.

[15] See Cowper to S. Rose, n. [10].

[16] *La plupart des hommes d'âge* (or, *des gens âgés*), *décourageant* (or, *rebutant*) *la jeunesse, comme ils le font généralement.*

[17] *ayant eux-mêmes cessé de porter des fruits;* or, *ne portant plus de fruits eux-mêmes;* or, simply, *étant eux-mêmes hors d'âge de porter.*

[18] See Turkish Tale, n. [26].

[19] *premiers essais;* or, *essais de novice.*

[20] 'in them;' *y,* here, before the verb.

[21] *ce doit être un plaisir du genre de celui qu'on.*

[22] Repeat the article and numeral.   [23] Simply, *autrement.*

[24] *à cause de leur précocité, des fruits qui.*   [25] *tout au plus.*

[26] 'so much' ... 'as,' *assez ... pour,*—the same turn as the one mentioned in Advice to Young People, note [9].

[27] *voyant en moi sinon.*

THE DEATH OF BAYARD.

[1] *qui se comporta avec la plus grande.*

[2] *champ de bataille.*   Leave out 'and.'

[3] 'so much . . . &c.;' simply, *si peu courtisan.*

[4] *gens* (or, *hommes*) *d'armes.*

[5] Simply, *des ennemis.*

[6] *pour couvrir la retraite du reste de l'armée.*

[7] *cette action.*

[8] 'perceived,' *sentit.*   (See Muly Moluc, note [2].)

[9] *et n'ayant plus la force de se soutenir sur son cheval.*

[10] *de l'appuyer contre.*—'attendants;' simply, *gens,* here.

[11] Leave out 'with.'

[12] *qu'il tint élevée* (or, *qu'il tint en l'air*) *en guise de crucifix.*

[13] Se Mahomet's Miracles, n. [8].

[14] Simply, *la mort.*

[15] *la tête.*

[16] *troupes ennemies* (adjective).

[17] *le trouvant . . ., lui témoigna;* leave out 'at the sight:' 'situation,' just above, is enough for the sense, after our change of construction.

[18] *ce brave.*

[19] Either leave out 'ought,' in the translation, or supply the ellipsis, viz: 'ought to do;' see Rabelais a Traitor, n. [12].   Use the present indicative of *devoir.*

[20] *en faisant.*

[21] When in an English sentence the pronouns 'he,' 'she,' 'it,' or 'they,' are separated from the relative pronouns, 'who,' or 'which,' they must be joined in French, and the second part of the sentence is expressed the first. Construct, therefore, here, 'they who fight against . . ., are indeed objects of pity,'—*ceux qui* (See Advice to Young People, note [51]) . . . &c., *sont* . . . &c.   Yet, these pronouns can be separated, as in English, by adding the particle *là* to *celui, celle,* &c.   We might therefore also say, with the English construction, *ceux-là sont* . . . &c., *qui* . . . &c.   But, after all, the translation here will gain in elegance by our saying, simply, *il faut plaindre ceux qui.* Observe, however, that sometimes we use *il, elle,* &c., together with *celui, celle,* &c., for the sake of emphasis, and with the following construction: "Il est homme de lettres aussi, celui que le feu de son imagination porte sans cesse vers des sujets nouveaux."—(SAINTE-BEUVE.)   'country,' that is, here, 'native county,' *patrie.*

[22] 'to pitch,' *dresser.*

[23] *et y laissa des personnes chargées de prendre soin de.*

[24] *comme étaient morts ses ancêtres depuis plusieurs générations, sur.* The repetition of the verb *mourir,* here, is more forcible than would be the translation of the English 'had done;' yet, in other cases, the repetition of the verb is inelegant.

[25] *et l'envoya.*   [26] *qu'on avait pour.*

[27] See Turkish Tale, n. [26].

[28] *qu'on rendît au corps de Bayard les honneurs qu'on rend aux rois.*

[29] *de ce héros.*

[30] 'solemn,' *grande.*—'it,' *son corps.* We also use, in this sense, *les restes,* or *la dépouille mortelle,* or, simply, *la dépouille* or *les dépouilles* (d'une personne).

CATARACT OF NIAGARA.

[1] *du Niagara, au Canada.*—*au* (not *en*) *Canada.* The article is always used before the names of certain minor or distant countries, such as *le Canada, le Brésil, le Pérou, le Bengale, le Japon, les Indes, la Jamaïque, la Guadeloupe,* &c.; with these, besides, *à* (with the article) is used instead of *en,* 'in,' (without the article).

[2] *le lac,* in both instances.—'made;' we use the verb *former* in this sense.

[3] *un des plus grands fleuves.*

[4] *en tombant perpendiculairement de cent cinquante pieds* (pieds anglais) *de haut;* or, *par une chute perpendiculaire de cent cinquante pieds.*

[5] *de mettre son imagination en rapport avec.*

[6] *porter;* or, *faire écouler.*

[7] This is a monstrous geographical blunder.

[8] *se précipite ici le long d'une chaîne—ligne—rangée.*

[9] *dans toute la largeur de son lit.*—'bed of its stream.' We say *le lit d'un fleuve,* or *d'une rivière* (of a river), in this sense; but *le lit d'un courant* is a naval term, which means the *direction* of a stream, as *le lit du vent* means the direction of the wind.

[10] *a près de trois quarts de mille de large* (or, *de largeur*). Notice this use of *avoir,* whereas the English use 'to be;' and, also, that of the preposition *de,* here, before the adjective, or the noun of dimension.

[11] *environ deux cents toises en* (or, *de*) *largeur—de large.* The *toise* (six feet, or about) is out of use: the current French measure is now the *mètre* and its decimal multiples and sub-multiples. The *mètre* is very nearly three French feet and one inch: the English 'yard' is *mètre* 0,914. There was no old French measure corresponding to the 'yard.'

[12] *Ile ne traversent pas le fil de l'eau en droite ligne* (or, *en ligne directe—directement*), *mais s'échancrent* (or, *forment une courbe,* or *un demi-cercle—creusent*) *en dedans* (or, *vers l'amont*) *en.*

[13] *qui cède à l'obstacle et en prend la forme;* or, *forcée qu'elle est de prendre la forme de l'obstacle;* or, literally, *qui se plie à la forme . . . ,* &c.

[14] *un des spectacles.*   [15] *mur d'eau circulaire.*

¹⁶ *et le divise* (or, *et le partage—et le coupe*) *par le haut.*

¹⁷ *terme* (masculine). ¹⁸ *brisement.*

¹⁹ *un arc-en-ciel des plus beaux (—on ne peut plus beau—*too familiar here).

²⁰ *On pense bien.* ²¹ *fleuve.*

²² *se sont' à ce qu'on dit, hasardés à la descendre dans leurs canots, et y ont réussi sans accident.*

BRUTUS ON THE DEATH OF CÆSAR.

¹ *amis,* in this case. ² *dans.*

³ *ayez foi en.* ⁴ *croire à mes paroles.*

⁵ *et prêtez-moi votre attention, afin d'être mieux en état de.*

⁶ *je lui dirai.* ⁷ *affection.*—'to,' here, *pour.*

⁸ *voici.* This word, in a narration, or an exposition of facts, always relates to what follows, and *voilà* to what precedes.

⁹ *ce n'est pas que;* with the subjunctive.

¹⁰ Leave out 'that,' here, and use the indicative.

¹¹ *Aimeriez-vous mieux voir César vivant.*

¹² *et de vivre.*—'to live' is here put for 'and live.'

¹³ Use here the indefinite preterite (I have slain him).

¹⁴ *amitié.*

¹⁵ *Quel est ici l'homme assez lâche pour consentir à.*

¹⁶ *S'il en est un.*—'speak,' *qu'il parle* (lit. 'let him speak,'—imperat. mood).

¹⁷ *c'est lui que j'ai offensé;* leaving out 'for.'

¹⁸ *stupide.* ¹⁹ *J'attends.*

²⁰ Invert, putting 'none' last.

²¹ *La cause;* or, *Le sujet;* or, better, *Les motifs.*

²² 'to extenuate,' in this sense, *diminuer,* or, *amoindrir;* 'to enforce,' likewise, *exagérer.*—in the capitol; his glory,' &c., *au Capitole dans un exposé impartial où l'on n'a rien diminué de la gloire qu'il avait justement acquise, rien ajouté aux fautes qui lui ont mérité la mort.*

²³ *Voici.*

²⁴ *qu'accompagne Marc-Antoine en deuil, lui qui, sans avoir eu part à sa mort, en recueillera les bienfaisants résultats.*

²⁵ *et qui de vous n'en recueillera pas autant?*

²⁶ *Voici ma conclusion: j'ai tué.*

²⁷ 'good,' *salut;* a full stop after 'Rome.'

²⁸ 'I have;' *Je garde.*—'myself;' simply, *moi.*—'to need;' *demander.*

INFLUENCE OF THE FRENCH LANGUAGE
AND LITERATURE IN THE AGE OF LOUIS XIV.

[1] *possédait à cette époque la supériorité dans presque tous les genres.*

[2] 'height,' here, *apogée.*   [3] *le pas.*

[4] *obligé les . . . à s'humilier à ses pieds.*

[5] *en matière de bon ton* (or, *de bon goût*).—'a duel' . . . 'a minuet;' use the definite article ('the'), in French, here.

[6] *faisait la loi;* or, *donnait des lois.*

[7] *montrer,*—to avoid ambiguity.   [8] *un poète badin;* 'so,' *aussi.*

[9] *un orateur aussi puissant;* or, simply, *un orateur tel.* The word *rhétoricien* means merely one who knows rhetoric.

[10] 'had set' . . . , 'had not yet dawned,' *n'était plus . . . n'était pas encore.* The English metaphor would not be acceptable in French; but we might very well say, *s'était éteinte . . . , n'avait pas encore lui* (from the verb *luire*).

[11] *faisaient l'ornement de* (in this figurative, pointed sense; in a proper, ordinary sense, *ornaient* would be the word used).

[12] *qu'augmentait encore le contraste;* or, *qui s'augmentait encore par le contraste:* the French are not so fond as the English of the passive voice; they generally prefer the active or the reflective.

[13] See Comp. of Watches, note [6].

[14] *la haute société.*   [15] *et plus élégamment.*

[16] *leur propre langue;* or, *la langue de leur pays;* or, *leur langue maternelle* (a more poetical than prosaic expression).

[17] *cette servilité fut moindre.*

[18] Put a colon or semi-colon, after 'continent.' — *ni nos bonnes ni nos mauvaises qualités ne furent jamais celles des imitateurs;* or, better, *nous n'avons jamais eu les qualités ou les défauts des imitateurs.*

[19] 'here,' *chez nous.*—'to pay,' here, *rendre.*—'was paid,' see Dest. Alex. Lib., n. [6]. We may use here, either the imperfect or the preterite : if we wish to consider the fact mentioned only as one point in history, we shall use the preterite; but if we wish, on the contrary, to dwell on the continuance or repetition of it, on the habit in which people were, at that period, of 'paying homage,' &c., we must then use the imperfect.

[20] *quoique bien gauchement et comme à regret* (or, *et comme à contre-cœur*).

[21] *preux,* or, *chevaliers.*   [22] *règles.*

[23] *devinrent* (or, *vinrent*) *à la mode.* In the same way we say, *être hors de mode,* 'to be out of fashion,' and *passer de mode,* 'to go out of fashion.'

[24] *déparé.*   [25] Simply, *et entaché.*

[26] *moins artistement arrondie dans ses périodes* (or, simply, *arrondie*).

[27] *moins variée dans son harmonie* (or, *quant au nombre*).

[28] *qu'elle ne* (see Cowper to S. Rose, note [21]) *l'était jadis.* The word *jadis* is growing obsolete, except in poetry and in elevated style: in familiar style we use *autrefois*, as, 'I was very strong formerly,' *j'étais très fort autrefois.*

[29] Construct so :—'It is impossible not to recognise in these changes.'

[28] JOHN BULL.

[1] *Selon toutes les apparences, John Bull est un hommes sans façon, franc, positif.*

[2] 'with . . . about him,' *ayant en lui.*

[3] 'romance,' *romanesque* ; 'nature, *caractère*, here.

[4] *beaucoup de naturel et de force.*   [5] *Il a plus de gaieté que.*

[6] *il n'est ni difficile de l'émouvoir (de le toucher—de l'attendrir) jusqu'aux larmes, ni rare de l'entendre partir tout-à-coup d'un éclat de rire ;* or, more freely and concisely, *on le voit rire et pleurer avec une égale facilité.*

[7] *n'entend rien à la ;* or, *n'a pas la moindre idée d'une.*

[8] *un fort bon vivant.*   [9] *de se livrer à.*

[10] *de lui.*   [11] *affairé.*   [12] *à.*

[13] *et s'offense.*   [14] *par se mettre mal.*

[15] Use here the indefinite preterite, 'he has taken ;' speaking of a deceased person, however, we should use, in French, as in English, the definite preterite.

[16] See Turkish Tale, note [26].

[17] *défense de soi-même ;* or, *défense personnelle.*

[18] 'to accomplish oneself,' *se perfectionner ;* translate by, 'and as he has accomplished,' &c.

[19] *et qu'il s'est rendu tout a fait familier l'art de boxer et de jouer du bâton (*or, *l'art de faire jouer le poing et le bâton).*

[20] *il a dû mener depuis ce temps (*or, *depuis lors) une vie sans cesse agitée.*

[21] *entendre parler.*   [22] *sans,* with the infinitive.

[23] *à consulter.*   [24] 'to infringe,' *blesser,* here.

[25] *d'une manière plus ou moins forte ses ete.*

[26] *Retranché.*   [27] *entouré de.*

[28] *une grosse et vieille araignée colère.*

[29] *dans toute la largeur d'une* (see Cataract of Niagara, n. [9]).

[30] *et la faire sortir furieuse du repaire où elle se tien cachée.*—'la faire sortir.' The verbs *faire* and *laisser,* when followed immediately by an infinitive, take the accusative (as here, *la*) if that following the infinitive has itself no *régime direct* (i. e., no accusative, or object) ; but they take the dative, instead, if the following infinitive has a *régime direct,* and also if it is accompanied by the pronoun *en* (though this pronoun is considered by grammarians as an indirect regimen),

Ex.:—'I make them write,' *je* les (accusat.) *fais écrire;* and 'I make them write an exercise,' *je* leur (dative) *fais écrire un thème:* 'I make my brother read,' *je fais lire* mon frère (accus.); and, 'I make my brother read a book,' *je fais lire un livre* à mon frère (dat.); 'I have made him write some,' *je* lui (dat.) *en ai fait écrire:* 'I did let him depart,' *je* le (accus.) *laissai partir;* and, 'I let him eat whatever he chose,' *je* lui (dat.) *ai laissé manger tout ce qu'il a voulu:* 'I did let your sister depart,' *j'ai laissé partir* votre sœur (accus.); and, 'I let your sister eat whatever she chose,' *j'ai laissé manger* à votre sœur (dat.) *tout ce qu'elle a voulu;* 'he is like the dog in the manger,' [proverbial expression] *il est comme le chien du jardinier, qui ne mange point de choux, et n'en laisse point manger* aux autres (dat., with *en*). This peculiarity is also observable with other verbs. The above is an important point, and one especially difficult for English students, which accounts for thus insisting upon it.

[31] *Quoique fort bon enfant au fond.*

[32] See **Cowper to S. Rose**, note [10].

[33] 'yet,' after 'although,' is one of those redundancies with which the English language abounds; leave it out in the translation.

[34] *est finie.*

[35] *et que l'on en vient.*   [36] *ému au.*

[37] *qu'il laisse son adversaire mettre dans sa poche l'objet de la querelle.* See above, n. [30]. Here we use the accusative *(son adversaire)*, and not the dative, although *mettre* has a *régime direct*, but it must be observed that *mettre* does not follow immediately the verb *laisser;* this separation of the two verbs often happens with regard to *laisser*, and other verbs as well (but never with *faire*), through the exigency of construction.

[38] See **Dervis**, n. [12].   [39] See **Hare and Tortoise**, n. [7].

[40] See **Sir Roger de Coverley**, n. [38].

[41] *et vous aurez tout son argent.*

[42] *Il est comme ces vaisseaux qui.*—'will weather;' see **Hearers & Doers**, note [69].

[43] *et se brisent pendant le calme qui lui succède.*

SOPHIA'S LITTLE BIRD.

[1] See **Cowper to S. Rose**, n. [10].

[2] *avait donné à Sophie.*   [3] *dans.*

[4] *Sophie, qui avait alors environ treize ans, aimait si passionnément cet oiseau.*

[5] *(c'était le nom de l'oiseau).*

[6] See **Hearers and Doers**, note [69].

[7] *et dormait tranquillement.*

[8] Put a full stop here; and begin *Cependant.*

[9] 'about,' *à.*

[10] 'nor.'—'would;' see Hearers and Doers, note [60].—'to trust with,' *laisser*.

[11] *que*.

[12] *chez M. Western*. See School for Scandal, n. [82].

[13] 'to trust it ... in his hands;' translate, 'to entrust it to him,'..., &c.

[14] Leave out 'presently.'

[15] 'of which' ..., &c., *dès qu'il l'eut, il fit glisser*.

[16] See Sir Roger de Coverley, n. [22].—'favors;' *bienfaits*.

[17] *si fort*. We use *fort* more commonly with *crier*, and always *haut* with *parler, lire*, &c.

[18] Use here the verb *accourir* (Latin, *ad* and *currere*), not *courir*: the former generally implies running towards a particular point on which the mind is dwelling, while the latter expresses the mere act of running, and is also used when the point to be reached is not the one on which the mind is dwelling.

[19] Remember that some neuter verbs, like *arriver* ('to happen,' and also 'to arrive'), *venir, devenir, tomber*, &c., are conjugated, in their compound tenses, with the auxiliary *être*, not with *avoir*.

[20] *traita B— de misérable méchant drôle*.

[21] *mettant habit bas, il grimpa à*.   [22] *s'était posé*.

[23] *celui-ci*,—to remove the ambiguity, *il* meaning 'he,' as well as 'it.'

[24] *s'étendait*.   [25] *tomba et disparut sous l'eau*.

[26] See Dervis, note [21].

[27] 'louder,' *plus haut*, here (and not *plus fort*), as *forces* will follow close.—'with all' ..., &c., *de toutes ses forces*.

[28] 'to be sitting,' here, *être réuni*. See Hearers and Doers, n. [3].

[29] Use *accourir*, and put 'all' at the beginning of the sentence.

[30] 'as,' *au moment où*.

[31] *arrivait sain et sauf à bord*.—'reached,' 'arrived.'

[32] *s'emporta*.

[33] *contre le;* in such a case, we only suppress the article when the phrase is an exclamation, as, *pauvre Tom!*

[34] *de prendre*. We also say *patienter* (to have patience).

[35] School for Scandal, note [21].

[36] *c'est moi qui ai malheureusement tout occasionné*.

[37] *un être quelconque*.   [38] *en vertu de*.

[39] *bien plus, c'est anti-chrétien*.

[40] *car ce n'est pas faire ce que nous voudrions qu'on nous fît* (subj., after *vouloir*).

[41] 'I am sure,' *certes*, here; and put this part of the sentence first (that is, after 'but').

[42] *ou même seulement*,

[43] *pour le prendre*.—'fell;' translate, 'has fallen.'

[44] *s'est envolé de nouveau*.

[45] *et un vilain épervier vient de l'emporter.*

[46] 'now first;' translate, 'for the first time,' and after the verb.

[47] *de voir ce qui.* [48] *torrent.*

[49] Translate here by the imperfect indicative of *vouloir;* in the same way we say, e. g., *voulez-vous du bœuf,* 'will you have some beef?'

[50] *de.*

[51] *que s'il était son père, il le fouetterait d'importance.—s'il était,* literally, 'if *he* (Mr. A—);' if 'he' was used in the sense of 'that gentleman,' we should rather say *c'était* instead of *il était.*

[52] *renvoyés chez eux.*

[53] According to some grammarians, and according to the French Academy itself, *le reste* must always be followed by the verb, pronoun, &c., in the singular. I beg to dissent from this, on no less an authority than that of Madame de Staël, of Racine, and of other writers, who have used the plural. It is true, that when there is a kind of unanimity, of inseparable unity, among the persons or things mentioned, the singular may be more properly used, as in the example given by the Academy, "le reste *des hommes* est *de mon avis,*" that is, they are all of one opinion, of one mind. But here, in our text, had the rest of the company only one bottle to divide among them all? or had they, if not a bottle each, at least more than one for them all? The use of the singular, here, *(s'en revint à sa bouteille)* might perhaps seem to imply the former, rather than the latter, of these suppositions; which would be absurd.

SCENE FROM "THE RIVALS."

[1] Simply, *Par ma valeur, sir Lucius, je vous le répète, quarante pas est une bonne distance.*

[2] *Oui, pour.*

[3] *pièces de campagne.* Put a full stop here.

[4] *En conscience.*

[5] *me laisser régler* (or, *arranger) ces choses-là.*

[6] 'now,' here, *un peu.* [7] *(Il mesure un certain nombre de pas.)*

[8] *Tenez, voilà, par exemple, pour un galant homme,*—and put now, only once, 'a very pretty distance.'

[9] *Fichtre !* (very trivial) *autant vaudrait nous battre.*

[10] Use the future (he will be).

[11] *plus j'aurai de sang-froid à viser.* [12] *En ce cas.*

[13] *il me semble.* [14] See Comp. of Watches, n. [20].

[15] *Allons donc! cela n'a pas le sens commun* (or, *chansons que tout cela).*

[16] *Entre les gueules . . . ,* &c., *qu'il y ait trois . . . ,* &c., *ou un mille de distance, qu'est-ce que cela fait?*

[17] *Balles de D—* (vulgar). [18] *de si près.*

[19] 'do;' see Advice to Young People, n. [39]; 'bring him down,' &c., *l'abattre à une longue portée.*

[20] *second,* in this sense; yet, there is no objection to using *ami.*

[21] See Travelling Incident, n. [12].

[22] *Vous devez bien penser qu'on n'essuie pas le feu d'un adversaire sans courir quelques petits risques.*

[23] *et si par malheur une balle vient à* ('happen to,' 'should,') *vous étendre* (or, *coucher*—or, *jeter*—or, *laisser) sur le carreau, ce ne sera guére le moment de venir vous troubler la cervelle de.*

[24] *voudriez-vous être embaumé.*　　　　[25] *ou vous serait-il égal.*

[26] *il y a de petits coins bien tranquilles.*

[27] *Tremblements de D—* (vulgar).

[28] 'to be engaged,' here, *se trouver engagé.*

[29] *c'est dommage* (in this sense).　　　[30] *d'avoir l'habitude des choses.*

[31] *Dites-moi, je vous prie.*

[32] Use the future (will you receive); 'the gentleman's shot,' *le feu de votre adversaire.*

[33] *Serre-file de D—* (vulgar); 'to practise,' here, *s'exercer à.*

[34] *tenez.*

[35] *voyez;* or you may repeat *tenez.*　　　　[36] *hein?*

[37] Leave out 'Odd;' 'small enough,' here, *le plus petit possible.*

[38] 'to stand edgeways,' *se présenter de côté;* or, *se tenir de biais.*

[39] *Non, vous n'y êtes pas.*

[40] *(Il le vise avec son pistolet);* or, *(Il lui présente le bout de son pistolet).* In speaking of muskets (not of pistols, as here), we also say *coucher quelqu'un en joue,* in this sense.

[41] *Diable* (vulgar).　　　[42] *armé.*　　　[43] *partir tout seul.*

[44] *soyez sans crainte;* or, *rassurez-vous;* or, *tranquillisez-vous;* or, again, *soyez tranquille.*

[45] 'now,' here, *donc.*

[46] *il y a à parier qu'elle y réussira;* 'to succeed,' in the sense of 'to come to succession,' is *succéder,* and it is *réussir* in the sense of 'to have success.' We often say, familiarly, *ce sera bien le diable si,* as corresponding exactly to 'it will be very hard if,' but then generally when the thing mentioned is wished for.

[47] *Tenez.*

[48] *Présentez-vous complètement de face,—comme cela.*

[49] Leave out 'clean;'—'your body;'—'any harm at all,' turn 'the least harm.'

[50] *Eh, mais, sans doute;* or, *Oui, la chose est possible.*

[51] *en outre;* and at the beginning of the sentence.

[52] *Tenez.*　　　　[53] *j'aime autant.*

[54] Repeat both the preposition and the noun.

[55] See Comp. of Watches, note [13].

[56] *Est-ce que, par hasard, il nous manquerait de parole?*

[57] *Comment !—Qui venir ?*   [58] *le pas*, or, *la barrière.*

[59] Translate, 'they are two.'   [60] 'to run,' here, *se sauver.*

[61] *Que diable avez-vous donc ?* (We also say, in the same sense, *Qu'est-ce qui vous prend ?*)

[62] 'to feel,' here, *se sentir.*

[63] *que tout à l'heure* (lit., 'as just now'); 'somehow;' render this by *à vrai dire*, and put it after *mais* (but).

[64] *songez à.*   [65] *m'adresser.*

[66] *de temps à autre.*   [67] Translate, 'I am afraid.'

[68] *allait;* or, *venait à* (see note [23]).

[69] See H e a r e r s a n d D o e r s, note [69].

[70] *il me semble.*   [71] *elle m'échappe.*

[72] *pour ainsi dire, qui me glisse entre les doigts.*

[73] *que ne suis-je.*—'safe;' see S o p h i a's L i t t l e B i r d, note [31], and always translate it so when it means 'unscathed,' 'uninjured:' when it means 'secured,' the French for it is, *en sûreté*, and when it signifies 'affording safety' (as *e. g.*, a safe harbor) we use *sûr.*

[74] Leave out 'or;' *puissé-je être tué avant même que je m'en doute.* Notice that an acute accent is placed, for the sake of euphony, over the final *e* of *puisse* (pres. subj.). Observe also this construction, the pronoun being placed after the verb; the same thing takes place after *dusse* (imp. subj.) used in a similar way, as *dussé-je être tué, j'irai*, 'were I to be killed, I shall go there.' These kinds of sentences are elliptical, the governing verb or conjunction being understood: the first sentence is for *je désire que je puisse*, &c., and the second, for *bien que* (or, *quoique*) *je dusse*, &c.

CÆSAR'S CAREER AND CHARACTER.

[1] Translate literally, 'has written himself.'

[2] *cette.*   [3] 'a soldier;' 'a governor.'

[4] *nobles romains* (literally, 'Roman nobles').

[5] See M u l y M o l u c, note [7].

[6] *ce ne fut qu'après qu'il eut atteint l'âge de quarante ans* (or, *eut eu quarante ans révolus—or, accompli*).

[7] See T u r k i s h T a l e, note [13].   [8] Turn, 'Cæsar's ambition was.'

[9] See Scene from T h e R i v a l s, note [73].

[10] *qui habitaient au delà des.*

[11] See D e s c r i p t i o n o f E n g l a n d, note [17].

[12] See A r t o f P l e a s i n g, n. [32].   [13] See M u l y M o l u c, n. [7].

[14] *art militaire.*   [15] *sans avoir.*

[16] Use the plural, in French.

[17] *et leurs armées étaient fortes en cavalerie;* or, *et l'arme de la cavalerie étaient leur fort.*

[18] *sous le rapport de l'infanterie et des armes.*

[19] *qui auraient suffi pour arrêter.*

[20] The French construction is, in such cases, 'he had always the eyes open.'

[21] *Le même homme.*   [22] Translate, 'who has said.'

[23] *fit grâce de la vie à.*   [24] *qui en voulaient à ses jours.*

[25] *comme;* without any article.   [26] *sans abri;* or, *sans asile.*

[27] *lui.*   [28] *et de plus.*   [29] *après quoi.*

[30] *être représenté comme un.*

[31] No article, here; but whilst we say, *un objet d'admiration vulgaire,* we should say, *l'objet d'une admiration vulgaire.*

[32] *et c'est dire autant qu'on en peut dire.*

32 THE DEAD ASS.

[1] 'crust,' *croûte de pain.*   [2] *si tu avais vécu pour le partager.*

[3] *à.*   [4] *que c'était.*   [5] *c'en était une.*

[6] *et qui.*   [7] *cela.*   [8] *sur.*

[9] *mais cet homme se plaignait avec des accents plus conformes à la nature;* or, *mais l'autre avait des traits plus frappants de naturel.*

[10] *L'affligé.*

[11] Turn, 'having beside him the pannel and the bridle of the ass, which,' &c.

[12] *Ensuite il reprit . . . dans son . . . &c.*   [13] *comme pour.*

[14] *et poussa;* but we may also use *soupirer.*

[15] *nombre de gens.* The word *nombre,* thus used adverbially, for *beaucoup,* corresponds to the English 'numbers,' or to 'a number,' in the sense of 'a great number;' but in French, if we prefix the article *un* to the substantive *nombre,* it has not in that case the sense of 'a great number,' and it then requires the adjective *grand,* thus, *un grand nombre,* to give it that meaning.

[16] *pendant qu'on préparait les chevaux.*

[17] *arrivait en dernier lieu.*

[18] *de l'Espagne.* It is better to use the definite article, here, on account of *où* (where), which gives the noun a more definite meaning.

[19] *du fin fond.*

[20] *et qu'il avait déjà fait tout cela de chemin pour regagner son pays.*

[21] Translate, 'had died.'

[22] *ce qui avait pu décider un homme si vieux et si pauvre à partir de chez lui pour un si long voyage.*

[23] *de lui accorder.*—'It had pleased,' &c.

[24] See Sir Roger de Coverley, note [16].

[25] *en.* There is an essential difference between *dans* and *en* with

reference to time.   Thus, we say, 'I shall start for America *in* eleven days' (hence), *Je partirai pour l'Amérique* dans *onze jours ;* but, *on va maintenant en Amérique* en *onze jours,* means 'people now go to America *in* eleven days' (in eleven days' time), in the sense of, 'it takes eleven days to accomplish the journey.'

[26] Translate, 'having fallen.'—'ill,' here, *atteint.*

[27] See Muly Moluc, n. [7].—'in,' *par.*

[28] *Saint-Jacques.*—'in Spain.'   [29] *en fut là de.*

[30] See Cowper to J. Newton, n. [28].

[31] Simply, *Tous les assistants.*   [32] *sa perte.*

[33] *qui, à leur passage dans les Pyrénées, les avait.*

[34] Translate, ' . . . three days, during which the ass,' &c.

[35] *n'avaient presque ni mangé ni bu jusqu'à ce qu'ils se fussent* (or, simply, . . . *ni bu qu'ils ne se fussent)* retrouvés.

[36] *L'ami, dis-je, tu as . . . , du moins.*—In familiar talk, we thus use the definite article before such words as *ami, homme, femme, fille,* when addressing an inferior and unknown person.

[37] *mon poids joint à celui de mes afflictions.*

[38] See Comp. of Watches, n. [3].   [39] 'they,' use the singular.

[40] See Muly Moluc, n. [7].   [41] *à en répondre.*

[42] *au.*   [43] See Comp. of Watches, n. [16].

[44] *homme ;* and leave out 'but.'

FOX.

[1] Turn, 'Mr. Fox had a kind of eloquence which one cannot comprehend without having heard the orator himself.'

[2] *Quand il entrait en plein dans.*   [3] *tout en s'emparant de.*

[4] *il lui plaisait* (literally, 'it pleased to him'). The verb *plaire* is not used, in French, as above in the text; thus *je plais, tu plais,* &c., 'I please,' &c., are only taken in the sense of 'I give pleasure,' 'I am pleasing, or pleasant,' &c., never in that of 'I am pleased,' &c.

[5] Remember that *douter* governs the subjunctive (without *ne,* when conjugated affirmatively, and with *ne* when negatively, which is the reverse with *craindre.* See Comp. of Watches, n. [3]).

[6] Turn, 'that his reasonings were (subj.) far closer, his speeches much richer in argumentation, than those of.'

[7] Turn, 'he was by as much—or simply, as—(*d'autant,* or, simply, *aussi)* superior to Demosthenes in this double respect *(sous . . . rapport)* as Demosthenes would perhaps have been to Fox.'

[8] *temps* (singular), or, *jours* (plural).

[9] *s'adresser à.*   [10] *Chambre.*

[11] *une erreur commune chez* (or, *particulière à).*

[12] *ces deux orateurs se ressemblent.*

[13] *Elles ne s'écartent* (or, *ne s'éloignent*) *jamais de la question;* or, *Tout y est rigoureusement au fait;* or, again, *Tout y va droit au but.*

[14] The French construction is, 'they never lose the subject of sight,' or, 'they never lose of sight the subject;' but never '... lose sight of,' &c.

[15] *captivent jusqu'au bout.*

[16] Begin so, 'they are always addressed to the heart,' &c.

[17] *s'y font jour;* or, *s'y introduisent.*

[18] Invert the last part of this proposition, in the same way as in the preceding one (note [16]).

[19] 'to make clash,' *mettre en conflit.*

[20] 'to lay bare,' *mettre à nu.*

[21] *ne cessait en même temps de forger.*   [22] *argumentation.*

[23] See Sophia's Little Bird, n. [51].   [24] Use the singular.

[25] See School for Scandal, note [26].

[26] *les rudes bordées et les traits perçants de l'esprit.*

[27] *de l'orateur.*   [28] *lourd de sa personne.*

[29] See Cowper to S. Rose, n. [10].

[30] *se faisait aiguë jusqu'à* (or, *au point de) ne plus être presque qu'un cri.*

[31] *tons bas.*

[32] *et son expression;* or, *et l'usage qu'il en faisait.*

[33] *jusqu'à.*   [34] *par suite de.*

[35] *était même très réservé dans l'emploi de figures;* or, better, *était même fort sobre de figures.*

[36] Turn, 'in the choice of the words.'   [37] Use the plural.

[38] Translate as if the English were, 'from the ancient languages or from the modern languages (or, the modern ones)'.

[39] *le saxon pur.*

[40] *à un si grand nombre de personnes ...,* &c., *tant pour écrire que pour parler.*

THE VICAR OF WAKEFIELD AND HIS FAMILY.

[1] Translate, 'I have ever been.'

[2] Use the present.—'large,' *nombreuse.*

[3] 'to do more service,' *être plus utile.*

[4] See Advice to Young People, n. [51].

[5] *et se contente de disserter sur la population* (or, *de parler population;*—in the same way we say, without any preposition or article, *parler musique, littérature, théâtres,* &c., &c.)

[6] *un an, tout au plus, après avoir pris les ordres, je;* or, *à peine avais-je pris les ordres depuis un an que je;* or, *à peine étais-je depuis*

un an dans les ordres que je ; or, again, *il y avait à peine un an que j'avais pris—que j'étais dans—les ordres, lorsque je.*

[7] *non sur le brillant de l'étoffe, mais sur les qualités qui garantissaient le bon user.*

[8] 'to do justice to one,' *rendre justice à quelqu'un.*

[9] *elle était d'une excellente nature, et laborieuse ;* or, *elle avait un excellent naturel et de l'activité.*

[10] Translate, 'show more of it than she.'

[11] *assez couramment, toute espèce de livre anglais* (or, *quelque livre anglais que ce fût).*

[12] *les conserves au vinaigre* (or, simply, here, as the context is plain, *les conserves), les confitures.*

[13] *Elle se piquait d'être une femme de ménage des plus habiles.*

[14] Translate, 'I have never found ;'—'to find,' in this sense, *s'apercevoir.*

[15] See Comp. of Watches, note [16].

[16] See Cowper to J. Newton, note [35].

[17] *nous donner de l'humeur contre.*

[18] Repeat the preposition.

[19] When 'country' means the reverse of 'town,' being taken in the sense of the Latin *rus, ruris,* the French for it is rather *campagne* than *pays.*

[20] See Dest. Alexandrian Library, note [7].

[21] *à jouir des plaisirs de l'âme et des champs.*

[22] Translate, 'those who.'   [23] *au.*   [24] *voyages.*

[25] *de la chambre bleue à la chambre brune.*

[26] Remember that 'to live,' in the sense of 'to dwell,' is *demeurer,* or *habiter,* not *vivre.*

[27] Translate, 'the traveller and the stranger often came to taste.'

[28] 'to profess,' in this sense, *affirmer.*

[29] 'I never knew ;' translate, 'never I saw.'—'saw one of them,' *en ... un seul.*

[30] *y trouver à redire ;* or, *y trouver le mot à dire.*

[31] *degré.* Either leave out 'all,' which is not necessary here, or put it after the verb.

[32] *sans avoir besoin de recourir à.*

[33] *l'*Herald's office. We must keep the English expression here : there is nothing of the kind in France ; if, however, we must give a nearly equivalent French expression, we may say, . . . *à aucun registre* (or, *à aucune table) généalogique.*

[34] Begin and translate, 'as *(car),* in the number, figured' . . . , &c.

[35] Turn, 'After all, said my wife, it is *same flesh and same blood ;* and she insisted always to *(pour)* make them sit *(asseoir,* without the reflective pronoun *se,* after *faire)* at the same table with us *(que nous).*

[36] Turn, 'therefore *(aussi)* we were habitually surrounded by *(de)* friends, if not rich, at least happy.

[37] *car, et c'est une remarque dont, toute la vie, vous sentirez la justesse.*

[38] Supply the ellipsis of the verb ('is').

[39] Turn, 'more he enjoys seeing himself *(jouit de se voir)* well treated.'

[40] *restent en extase* (or, *s'extasient*) *devant les nuances . . . ou devant.*

[41] *j'aimais, par instinct* (or, *par nature*), *à contempler l'expression du bonheur sur la figure humaine.*

[42] *dans l'un.*   [43] *nous reconnaissions.*

[44] *de très mauvaises mœurs ;* or, *de très mauvaise vie.*

[45] *un fâcheux.*

[46] 'or one,' *un hôte.*—'to get rid,' in a general way, *se défaire* (literally, to rid oneself).

[47] Turn, 'I had ever care upon his leaving my house *(au moment où il nous quittait).'*

[48] *une redingote de voyage ;* or, simply, *une redingote*, which, however, more commonly corresponds to 'a frock coat.'

[49] *de peu de valeur.*   [50] Translate, 'have had.'

[51] *de voir que pas un.*—'came back ;' translate, 'has come back.'

[52] *mais la famille de Wakefield n'a jamais passé pour avoir fermé sa porte au voyageur ou au pauvre malheureux ;* or, *mais jamais on n'a pu dire que la famille de W— ait fermé sa porte au voyageur ou à l'indigent.*

[53] *non que.*   [54] See Cowper to J. Newton, n. [35].

[55] *châtelain ;* or, *seigneur de l'endroit.*

[56] 'to fall asleep,' *s'endormir.*—'in,' *à* here.

[57] *la châtelaine.*—'to return,' in this sense, *répondre à.*

[58] *par une révérence un peu écourtée.*

[59] *nous nous consolions bientôt de ces sortes d'accidents ;* or, *nous nous mettions promptement au-dessus du chagrin que nous causaient ces accidents.*

[60] 'in,' here, *au bout de.*

[61] *nous nous trouvions tout surpris de nous en être préoccupés* (or, *d'avoir pu nous en affecter).*

[62] *Mes enfants devaient, à notre tempérance et à une éducation sans mollesse, une bonne constitution et une bonne santé.*

[63] Translate, 'my sons were.'   [64] *fraîches.*

[65] *s'appela G—, du nom de.*   [66] Translate, 'who had left us.'

[67] Translate, 'Our second child was a girl; I intended to give her the name of her aunt, G—.'

[68] *insista pour le nom d'O—;* or, *insista pour* (or, *voulut absolument*) *qu'elle s'appelât* (or, *qu'elle eût nom) O—.*

[69] *et, cette fois ;* or, *et, pour le coup.*

[70] Translate, 'having taken,' and leave out 'a;' or, 'having had,' and substitute 'the' for 'a.'

[71] *d'en être la.*   [72] *la petite.*

[73] *noms de roman.* The French often form kinds of adjectives with a noun and the preposition *de;* as *de bras* d'Hercule, '*Herculean* arms,' *festin* de roi, '*kingly* festival,' &c.

[74] *que je n'y fus jamais pour rien.*

[75] *Moïse fut notre quatrième enfant.*   [76] *encore deux garçons.*

[77] *quand je me voyais entouré de ma petite famille.* Be careful here *des petites* (literally, 'little ones') is only said, in French, of the progeny of animals, and corresponds to 'young.' An analogous difference between the two languages is observable in the word *femelle* (literally, 'female'), which is, in French, properly applied to animals only.

[78] Leave this word out, here.

[79] 'in;' see Sir Roger de Coverley, n. [16].—'the whole country;' translate, 'all the country.'

[80] *Ah.*

[81] In such cases as this, always put the subject, or nominative, after the verb.

[82] Translate, 'if they are.'

[83] *est beau qui fait bien.*—There is no French proverb corresponding exactly to this English saying. The nearest are, *Les hommes ne se mesurent pas à l'aune,* i. e., men are not to be judged by their stature; and, *Le fait juge l'homme.*

[84] *se tenir droites.*—'the girls,' *ses filles* (her daughters).

[85] *pour tout dire.*

[86] *L'extérieur est, à mes yeux, chose si peu importante.*

[87] 'it,' *ces détails.*—'had it not;' turn, 'if they had not.'

[88] Translate, 'At eighteen years, Olivia.' The ellipsis of the word 'year,' or 'years,' is not allowed, in French, after a numeral indicative of age.

[89] Translate, 'which painters give, in general, to.'

[90] *au premier coup d'œil.*

[91] *effet,* in this sense; or you may translate, 'but their action was often more certain.'

[92] *étudiait.*   [93] 'To intend for,' *destiner à.*

[94] *mixte.*   [95] Use the singular.   [96] Leave out 'of.'

[97] *tous avaient un air de famille très prononcé.*

[98] *à proprement parler.*

THE SPELL OF WEALTH.

[1] *un compte ouvert chez son;* and leave out 'it,' as well as the comma.

[2] Notice that the adjective, or adverb, which follows *how (combien, comme,* or *que,* in this sense—but not *comment,* meaning 'how' in the

sense of 'in what way') in English, is always put after the verb in French. Yet, here, we shall translate more elegantly by, *Avec quelle tendresse nous*, &c.

[3] *notre.*

[4] Translate, 'of such relatives,' and put a full stop here.

[5] *Qui de nous ne la juge une bonne et excellente vieille !*

[6] *nouvel associé.*　　　　　　　[7] *sa voiture blasonée.*

[8] *garnie du gros cocher asthmatique.*

[9] Turn, 'How we know, when she . . . , how (not expressed here, in French) to find the opportunity of.'—'to pay,' here, *rendre*, without any article after it;—*rendre* (or, *faire) visite à quelqu'un*, is, to visit one, and *rendre à quelqu'un sa visite*, is, to return one a visit which we have received from him (or her).

[10] 'to let know,' *faire savoir ;* or, *apprendre.*

[11] *Je voudrais avoir.*　　　　　　[12] *pour un bon de.*

[13] *Elle ne serait pas à court ;* or, *Cela ne la gênerait point.*

[14] Here, as well as note [3], *elle* may be used, more pointedly than *ce.*

[15] When two adjectives thus follow each other immediately, in English, we must generally translate by putting the conjunction *et* between them, in French : ex., 'a tall pale man,' *un homme grand* et *pâle ;* except, 1st, when the second is so inseparably connected with the following noun, as to form together with it a kind of compound substantive, as *un beau petit garçon ;* 2d, when they are nearly synonymous ; and, 3d, when they form a climax, as here. But, in the two latter cases, a comma is placed between both adjectives.

[16] Translate, 'would not be.'

[17] *font pour elle un nombre infini de . . . ,* &c.

[18] *demeurer pour quelque temps chez vous,* in this sense.

[19] *s'en passe quand elle . . . . . . ,* &c.—'stays ;' use the singular, in French ; so with 'trowsers,' the French say *un pantalon* (sing.), in the sense of '*a pair* of trowsers.'

[20] *un air propre* ('neat'), *cossu* ('warm,' in this particular sense), *confortable* ('snug'), *joyeux*—or, *gai* ('jovial'), *un air de fête* ('festive') *qu'elle n'a point en.*

[21] Turn, 'Yourself, (A d v i c e t o Y o u n g P e o p l e, n. [7]) my dear sir, you forget.'

[22] *tout d'un coup ;* this expression must be used, instead of *tout à coup*, when we wish to indicate that a fact, which might have happened gradually, has taken place at once, immediately ; whereas, if we wish to express that a fact has happened, also at once, but unexpectedly, we must then use *tout à coup* in preference to *tout d'un coup.*

[23] *très amoureux du whist.*　　　[24] *du madère-malvoisie.*

[25] *et régulièrement du.*　　　[26] ~~See Hearers and Doers, n. 40.~~

[27] *sa bonne ;* or, *sa femme de chambre,* if we had not to avoid here the awkward repetition of the word *chambre,* coming just above in the translation.

[28] *n'est plus surveillée du tout.*　　　[29] *célestes.*

[30] 'I wish you would;' we might use *je voudrais* (conditional) *que* . . ., with the imperfect subjunctive (of *envoyer*, here), as directed in Advice to Young People, n. [18]; but here, we shall more elegantly translate by *que ne m'envoyez-vous*. Notice, by the way, that, with *que*, in the sense of *pourquoi* (why), *pas*, or *point*, is elegantly suppressed.

[31] *une tante fille.*   [32] *et un faux toupet couleur café clair.*

[33] *comme ma Julia* (or *Julie*, for the French have both names) *et moi.*

[34] *serions aux petits soins pour elle!*

[35] *O vain, trop vain.*   [36] *La foire aux vanités.*

MOONLIGHT SCENERY.

[1] *Un effet de clair de lune.*   [2] Leave these two words out.

[3] *La lune était dans son plein, et pas une étoile ne pouvait échapper à l'œil de l'observateur* (or, *et l'on voyait resplendir dans tout leur éclat sur la voûte azurée les feux du firmament*—poetic style).

[4] *ainsi éclairée de toutes ces lumières.*

[5] *jusqu'à quelle distance.*   [6] *ou rocher avancé.*

[7] Translate, 'one of the sides;' and leave out 'on the sea-shore,' mentioned just above.

[8] *par une petite colline verdoyante.*

[9] Simply, *en terrasses naturelles.*

[10] *et qui venaient mourir.*   [11] *accidenté.*

[12] *presque jusqu'à l'endroit atteint par les marées.*

[13] *perçait à travers;* or, *On y remarquait, à travers . . .* &c.

[14] *Même à cette heure avancée de la nuit, des lumières allaient et venaient* (or, *on voyait des lumières se promener*).

[15] *éclairant sans doute le.*—'smuggling lugger;' *lougre de contrebandiers.*

[16] *venant de.*   [17] 'which was lying;' simply, *et à l'ancre.*

[18] Turn, 'As soon as they perceived,' &c.; or, 'At the sight of,' &c.

[19] *on cria du navire: "Gare à vous, éteignez!" et à ce cri d'alarme, toutes les lumières du rivage disparurent à l'instant.*

[20] *les unes renversées, et les autres encore debout;* or, *les unes entières, et les autres à moitié écroulées.*

[21] *l'empreinte rouillée du temps, et là tapissées de.*

[22] *à la droite.*   [23] *Devant lui.*

[24] 'crisping and sparkling;' simply, *étincelant.*

[25] *se déroulaient successivement et expiraient* (or, *et venaient mourir*) *avec un doux murmure sur.*

[26] 'far into;' *jusque dans.*

[27] 'waving in,' &c.; simply, *suivant les nombreuses ondulations du terrain.*

[28] *de pénétrer plus avant.*—'intricacies;' *profondeurs.*

[29] 'woodland scenery;' simply, *feuillage.*

[30] 'each, by its own . . . ,' &c., *distinguées, chacune par son orbite lumineux.*

[31] *L'imagination sait si bien abuser ceux-là même qui l'ont volontairement excitée.*

[32] *presque tenté.*　　[33] See Infl. of French Literature, &c., n. [12].

[34] On account of these last words, 'over human events,' we must deviate here from the rule given in Turkish Tale, note [13], if we wish to avoid ambiguity, or, at the least, an awkward construction.

LADY MONTAGU TO MRS. THISTLETHWAYTE.

[1] If we do not address the person directly, the possessive pronoun must be used, in French; if we do, the pronoun may be dispensed with. Thus, either translate, ' . . . tell *my* dear,' &c., or, ' . . . tell *you*, dear (or, my dear),' &c.: the latter turn, however, is preferable.

[2] A past participle joined with *être*, 'to be,' impassive verbs, agrees with the nominatives.

[3] See Dervis, note [12].

[4] *Vous aimerez mieux (aimer mieux* is used like the Latin *malo).*

[5] *qu'on voit ici;* or, *de ce pays.*

[6] 'that has . . . in it,' *qui ne contiendrait;* or, *qui ne raconterait.*

[7] See Dervis, note [12].　　[8] Translate, 'have seen.'

[9] *Je vais vous en parler: ce sera du nouveau pour vous.* Put a full stop here, as well as after 'life.'

[10] *J'ai été, je vous assure, bien étonnée la première fois que j'en ai vu.*

[11] In such cases, the noun must be repeated, in French.

[12] *Je classe le chameau dans la famille des cerfs.*

[13] Translate, 'its.'　　　　　[14] *pelage.*

[15] *les chameaux prirent le pas sur . . ,* (or, *gagnèrent . . . de vitesse).* This expression, *prendre le pas,* however, is more frequently used in the sense of 'to take precedence.'

[16] Turn, 'and it was *(ce furent,* plural) they which brought the first to Belgrade the news of the loss of the battle.'

[17] Put a semicolon after 'ropes;' *quand ils sont ainsi maintenus, un seul homme, monté sur un âne, en conduit cinquante.*

[18] *J'en ai.* The personal pronoun *en* ('of it,' 'of them') always accompanies the indefinite pronouns *quelqu'un, quelques-uns, autre,* and the numeral adjectives or adverbs of quantity, when the noun to which they refer is not expressed in the same part of the sentence; it corresponds to 'one,' plural 'ones,' sometimes used similarly in English, 'I have a good one,' 'several good ones.'

[19] *une seule.*　　　　　　　　[19a] *un tiers en plus de la charge du.*

[20] 'an animal.'—'are also,' &c., *ne connaissez pas non plus.*

[21] *pesants.*

[22] 'close,' &c., *qui s'étendent en arrière de leurs têtes.*

[23] *. . . corne, bien polie, sert à faire de beaux ouvrages.*

[24] Translate, simply, 'Their hair *(poil,* speaking of animals) is black and short.'

[25] Turn, 'which (Muly Moluc, note [21]) renders them somewhat similar to the devil.'

[26] Turn, 'To embellish them, . . . dye their tail and the hairs of their *(la)* head.'

[27] *On ne fait pas ici travailler les chevaux.*

[28] Translate as if the English were, 'nor (and . . . not) would work suit them at all.'

[29] *vivacité.*

[30] Translate, 'and weaker than those of cold countries.'

[31] *et ont le pied très sûr.*

[32] Turn, 'I have made my favorite of a little white horse which I would give at no price.'

[33] *qu'il faut que.*　　　　　　　　[34] Use the present.

[35] *si docile;* and at the end of the sentence.

[36] *pour lesquels on a.*　　　　　　　[37] Translate, 'turtles, for instance.'

[38] *de.*—'Mecca;' see Mahomet's Miracles, note [10].

[39] *êtres.*

[40] Turn, 'in Turkey' (see Sir Roger de Coverley, note [16]).

[41] Turn, 'and they know so well.'

[42] *et font le plus souvent leurs nids au bas.*

[43] *dont ils choisissent ainsi les habitations.*

[44] *d'avoir.*　　　　　　　　[45] *ma fenêtre.*

[46] *De ma fenêtre je passe à ma chambre et crois bien que si je vous la décris, ce sera là une autre nouveauté pour vous.*

[47] *dans les relations que les maisons de Turquie.*

[48] Simply, 'miserable buildings.'

[49] *vous en parler à bon escient*—or, *sciemment—savamment—en* (or, *avec) connaissance de cause.*

[50] Turn, 'for I have seen many of them *(en,* before the verb).'

[51] *que rien n'est moins vrai;* or, *qu'il n'en est rien.*

[52] *qu'on n'est pas très soucieux.* We must use here *pas,* and not *point: point* being the strongest expression of negation, being of itself equivalent to 'not in the least,' it obviously follows that it can never be coupled with such terms as *très, peu, beaucoup,* &c., and that, in such cases, its weaker synonym, *pas,* must be substituted for it.

[53] *de la beauté des façades.*

[54] This repetition of 'but' would be inelegant in French: use another turn.

[55] *chacun met le moins d'argent possible dans les constructions, puisque sa famille n'en doit rien recueillir.*

[56] *Tout ce que l'on veut, c'est une maison commode pour la vie; peu importe qu'elle s'écroule plus tard.*

[57] See Comp. of Watches, n. [47].   [58] *ou.*

[59] Simply, *La première.*

[60] *le premier rang est orné de vitres de couleur.* Put a semicolon before *le premier,* and a full stop after *couleur.*

[61] *et n'ont pas souvent plus de.*

[62] *Tel est le corps de logis qui appartient au maître. Il communique avec le* harem *ou.*

[63] *galerie tournante, mais elle regarde* (or, *a vue—donne—sur*) *le jardin, comme toutes les fenétres. Il y a le.*

[64] *dans ce corps de logis que dans l'autre.*

[65] Turn, 'The windows of the second row are very small, and with grates *(et grilles)* like those of our convents:' a full stop here.

[66] *Les appartements sont tapissés de tapis de Perse.* The national adjective is hardly used, in such cases, except when speaking of articles of dress: thus we say, *des vins* d'Espagne, and *un chapeau* français.

[67] *et à l'un des bouts de la chambre il y a une estrade de deux pieds: chez moi, il y en a deux qui se font face.*

[68] *Là est.*

[69] A full stop after 'fringe.' *De toutes parts se trouvent adossés au mur deux.*

[70] *doux.*

[71] *je doute que je puisse revenir aux chaises désormais.*

[72] *plafonds* (ceilings),—to remove the ambiguity.

[73] *et je ne m'en plains guère; partout sont des lambris de bois ornés de marqueteries ou de fleurs peintes, qui s'ouvrent par un grand nombre de portes brisées sur.*

[74] *au fond.*

[75] A full stop after 'room.' *L'eau y vient par des conduits et répand une douce fraîcheur. De petits jets d'eau* (spouts of water), *tombant d'un bassin dans un autre, y joignent leur agréable musique.*

[76] *par l'influence de.*   [77] *sont formellement interdits.*

[78] We use *avoir* with *apparence,* and *faire* with *effet.*

[79] *loin de la vue des passants, et les jardins qui les entourent sont fermés par.*

[80] Turn, 'One does not find in them,' &c.

[81] *et, à mon gré, forment un charmant coup d'œil.*

[82] *kiosque* (masculine).

[83] *qui en occupe le centre.*—'beautified with a *fine,*' &c.

[84] 'round which,' &c., *le long desquels se développent . . . , &c., qui font un rideau de verdure.*

[85] *la plus grande partie de leur temps à faire de la.*

[86] *Les Turcs n'ignorent pas la manière de bâtir solidement.*

[87] *pierres de taille.*

[88] *forment un grand carré, avec des arcades de pierre sous lesquelles se trouvent des boutiques.*

[89] *Une mosquée y est toujours attachée.*

[90] *capable* must be used in this sense only.

[91] *avec une . . . , et une enceinte cloîtrée.*

[92] Turn, 'I own that I find that a foundation much more reasonably charitable than our convents.'

[93] See Muly Moluc, n. [7].

[94] With such a construction, in French, every one would at once ask, 'a great deal, *of what?* For the sake of more clearness, always use, in such cases, *en*, 'thereof,' 'thereon,' *i. e.*, on the matter, or subject which has just occupied us.

[95] Turn, 'If you don't like the choice of the things which I relate to you, indicate to me others for the future.'

[96] Turn, 'there is nobody that is more desirous (use *tenir à*, here and see Comp. of Watches, note [35]) not to tire *(ennuyer)* you, dear Mrs. T—, than your.'

SCENE FROM "SHE STOOPS TO CONQUER."

[1] *à l'antique.*   [2] *je vous en prie, ne vous gênez pas.*

[3] *C'est ici le palais de la Liberté.*   [4] *Ce mot de retraite.*

[5] *me rappelle.*

[6] *nous aussi, nous,* &c.; see Hearers and Doers, note [49].

[7] *mon vieux.*

[8] 'I say,' &c.; simply, *Comme je vous disais, messieurs.*

[9] *Sept heures moins cinq minutes* (or, simply, *cinq*). The word *minutes* (from five upwards) is often understood, in French; but *heures* is never so, as 'o'clock' frequently is in English.

[10] *et de tout ce qui est nécessaire à la guerre.*

[11] 'To hear of,' *entendre parler de.*

[12] *que;* and the future, 'shall take.'   [13] *Dites-moi, mon.*

[14] *Voilà une singulière réserve, comme je n'en ai jamais vu.*—[Marlow's father had represented his son, in a letter to Mr. Hardcastle, as a very modest young man.]

[15] Turn, 'will do us good *(du bien)* after our journey.

[16] *prendre.*   [17] See Sir Roger de Coverley, n. [5].

[18] *n'en sont pas mauvais.*

[19] *Voulez-vous me permettre de vous faire raison.*

[20] *Allons.* [21] *je bois à notre connaissance plus intime.*

[22] *Voilà un gaillard qui n'est pas mal familier.*

[23] *un original;* and leave out 'and.'

[24] *laissons-le faire. Monsieur, je suis votre serviteur.*

[25] *nous honorer de.* [26] *les manières d'un homme comme il faut.*

[27] *je m'imagine que vous devez avoir beaucoup à faire* (or, *beaucoup de besogne*) *dans cet endroit.*

[28] *Sans doute* (or, *Je suppose*) *que vous travaillez chaudement aux élections de temps en temps* (or, *de temps à autre*)?

[29] See Scene from G o o d - N a t u r e d M a n, note [48].

[30] Turn, 'there is nothing more to do for us landlords (*propriétaires,* here), who sell our ale.'

[31] *Ainsi donc, à ce que je vois, vous n'avez aucun goût pour la politique.*

[32] *sans que le gouvernement en allât mieux.*

[33] *s'amender tout seul.*

[34] *je ne me mets pas plus en peine de savoir.*

[35] *qui est au pouvoir et qui n'y est point.*

[36] *avec ceux qui mangent au premier, et ceux qui boivent au rez-de-chaussée.*

[37] 'between the occupation of receiving . . . , and that of amusing.'

[38] Leave these two words out.

[39] 'I give myself much movement.'

[40] 'cup,' *liqueur.*—'my old,' &c.—'an argument in your cup, better;' see T u r k i s h T a l e, note [26].

[41] *que tous ceux du palais de Westminster.*

[42] 'that, and;' *et avec cela.* [43] *A votre santé.*

[44] *Je vais vous conter cela.* [45] Supply the ellipsis of the verb.

[46] 'Yes, sir, yes, the supper!'

[47] *me sentir de l'appétit;* or, *me sentir en appétit:*—The pronoun *me,* in the second phrase, is in the accusative, whereas in the first it is not, and means 'within myself.'

[48] *une fière brèche.* [49] *à.*

[50] *Vit-on jamais un gaillard* (or, *un jeune homme*) *plus effronté!*

[51] 'Why, really,' *Ma foi.* [52] 'well tell,' *trop vous dire.*

[53] *Entièrement, dites-vous?* [54] *Et par parenthèse.*

[55] 'It's my habit.' [56] *Vous excusez, monsieur?*

[57] 'I excuse you, certainly.'

[58] *Néanmoins, je ne sais trop; mais notre Brigitte.*

[59] See H a r e & T o r t o i s e, n. [7]. [60] *le menu du souper.*

[61] *la carte.* This word, *carte,* was also used, till lately, in the sense of 'bill,' 'account,'—of eating-houses (*restaurants*) and inns; but now the term *addition* has prevailed in the latter sense.

[62] 'my,' emphatically.   [63] Leave this word out.

[64] *la note des plats.* Mr. Hardcastle does not use '*carte*,' for his house—and *he* knows it—is not a *restaurant.*

[65] *Le voilà sur ses grands chevaux.*

[66] 'the.'   [67] 'who was a judge.'

[68] *Diantre!*—a vulgar, but milder word for another exclamation of the same kind.

[69] *la corporation des menuisiers, ou celle.*

[70] *un petit cochon avec de la compote de pruneaux.*

[71] *Au diable* (vulg.); and leave out 'I say,' as well as 'say I' in the next line.

[72] 'a delicious dish.'   [73] Use the future.

[74] *avec des.*   [75] *un pouding et une crè . . . crè . . . une crème.*

[76] *La peste* (or, *Peste—Peste soit*) *de vos.*   [77] *aussi embarrassé.*

[78] Simply, 'as at the table of the ambassador of France.'

[79] *Comment donc.*   [80] *Voilà l'affaire du souper réglée.*

[81] *il s'agit maintenant de.*   [82] *me laisser m'en occuper seul.*

[83] *Moi vous laisser ce soin! Monsieur, trouvez bon que je vous dise que cet article-là est de ceux auxquels je veille toujours moi-même.*

[84] *Non; je prétends que vous soyez parfaitement.* The verb *prétendre*, in the sense of *vouloir*, governs the subjunctive.

[85] *C'est un parti pris, voyez-vous.*

[86] *mais elle ne ressemble pas mal à l'impudence d'autrefois.*

A HIGHLAND REVENGE.

[1] *Une vengeance dans les hautes terres* (or, *les Highlands*) *de l'Ecosse.*

[2] *les forces des Mac-Gregor.*   [3] Use *faire.*   [4] 'the.'

[5] *éloigné de ses yeux.*   [6] *quoi qu'il en soit, cette.*

[7] *pâles et défigurés.*   [8] 'with as much . . . as.'

[9] 'He threw himself at the feet of the chief's wife.'

[10] *les pans* (literally, 'the skirts') *de son plaid* (manteau écossais).

[11] *avec autant de désespoir.*

[12] 'Fear acted on his mind with such strength.'

[13] *comme cela arrive.*   [14] 'covered with *(de)* a deadly paleness.'

[15] *se tordant les mains.*   [16] 'the most solemn.'

[17] 'with *(de)* all his soul.' The idiomatic expression, *aimer quelqu'un comme ses yeux* (or, *comme la prunelle de ses yeux*) would be too familiar for elevated style, like this.

[18] *Par une inconséquence, suite du désordre de son esprit.*

[19] *au.*

[20] 'he asked,' &c. ; simply translate, 'were he to breathe no longer *(plus)* any *(de)* other air than that of.'

[21] 'the scorn,' &c. ; simply, *l'air de mépris et de dégoût.*

[22] *Je t'accorderais la vie.*

[23] 'to enjoy oneself,' here, *se trouver heureux.*

[24] *tandis que des gens sans naissance et sans courage foulent aux pieds des hommes illustrés par leur bravoure et par une longue suite d'aïeux.*   Put a full stop here.

[25] 'you could,' &c. ; *Au milieu du carnage général, tu serais aussi heureux que le chien du boucher, qui lèche le sang des bestiaux qu'on égorge.*

[26] *lâche chien.*   [27] *ce.*   [28] *qui superplombait le lac.*

[29] Simply, 'I may say.'—'I may,' *je puis*, which is more quaint than *je peux*.

[30] Turn, 'for during some *(quelques)* years I often started up out of my sleep *(je m'éveillai souvent en sursaut)*.

[31] Use the future of *vouloir*.

[32] 'although I expected at every instant to share.

[33] Simply, *une grosse pierre.*   [34] *se partageaient ses vêtements.*

[35] *pour voir si ;* and make the rest of the sentence fit, according to this alteration here.

[36] 'without resistance.'

[37] 'settled,' &c. ; *se refermerènt sur lui en reprenant leur calme accoutumé, et la vie qu'il avait demandée avec tant d'instance, s'éteignit à jamais dans cet abîme.*—'for ever,' is, in French, *à jamais*, and *pour jamais* ; the former expression is stronger than the latter : *"un homme est perdu* à jamais."—when it is absolutely impossible for him to rise from his abjectness ; *il est perdu* pour jamais, if it is only believed that he will not rise again.

THE WIDOW AND HER SON.

[1] 'the produce.'   [2] *l'appui et l'orgueil de leur vieillesse.*

[3] *un si digne garçon, si aimable, si doux avec tout le monde, si respectueux.*

[4] *On éprouvait un plaisir délicieux en le voyant le.*

[5] *celui de son mari.*   [6] *femme.*

[7] *de se louer et de travailler sur un* (or, simply, *de se mettre aux gages d'un*) *des petits bâtiments qui desservaient une rivière voisine.*

[8] *pris par la presse* (enrôlement forcé, levée de matelots en Angleterre), *en entraîné loin de son village pour servir sur mer.*

[9] *languissant*, in this sense.

[10] 'to sink,' here, *descendre.*—'his :' use the definite article.

[11] *tomba à la charge de ;* or, *se fit inscrire sur les registres des pauvres de.*

[12] Turn, 'Everybody liked her in the village, and they *(on)* showed towards her *(lui,*—literally, to her).'

[13] Turn, 'The cottage . . . &c., not letting (use *se louer,* the reflective voice).'

[14] See **Mahomet's Miracles,** note [12].

[15] See **Hearers and Doers,** note [69].—'now and then,' *de temps à autre,* or, *de temps en temps.*

[16] *légumes,* in this sense; and *végétal,* only in the more general sense of 'a plant,' 'a tree :' *végétal* is also an adjective, as in *le règne* (not *royaume,* there) *végétal,* 'the vegetable kingdom.'

[17] See **Travelling Incident,** note [9].

[18] *se présenta : il avait l'air effaré* (wild) *et empressé* (eager).

[19] 'and seemed to be worn out.'

[20] 'O my mother, my dear mother.'

[21] 'your son,' &c. ; simply, 'your *(ton)* poor George.'—'to know,' in the sense of 'to recognise,' is *reconnaître,* not *connaître.*

[22] 'foreign,' *à l'étranger,* and after the noun.

[23] *aurait suffi pour l'anéantir.*

[24] 'When the villagers had heard.'

[25] *était de retour ;* and use 'they' before 'crowded.'

[26] 'allowed them to give him.'

[27] See **Hare and Tortoise,** note [7].

[28] 'to break down,' *abaisser.*—'manhood,' here, *l'homme.*

[29] *lit de douleur.*

[30] *faisait mollement reposer sa tête sur le duvet.*

[31] *son.*   [32] *ne saurait être ni.*

[33] *par ces infortunes mêmes ;* and leave out 'the,' before 'dearer.'

[34] *une tache flétrit.*   [35] Leave out these last five words.

[36] *elle lui tiendra lieu de l'univers.*—This expression, *tenir lieu de,* means, 'to be as much as,' 'to be equivalent to :' as in this well-known line of Racine,—

    "Un bienfait reproché tint toujours lieu d'offense."

[37] See **Sophia's Little Bird,** note [33].

[38] See **Pope to Wycherley,** note [14].

[39] *Il ne laissait pas sa mère s'éloigner de lui.*

[40] See **Hearers and Doers,** note [69].

[41] 'to start' (from sleep), *se réveiller en sursaut.*

[42] *alors.*   [43] 'It is thus that.'

[44] *histoire simple, mais déchirante.*

[45] In such a case, 'how' is not expressed in French, and no preposition is used between *savoir* and the next verb.

[46] 'to take a kind of ;' and leave out 'for her son.'

[47] 'or something similar.'

[48] 'to manifest by outward signs one of those griefs that cannot be expressed outwardly *(au dehors)*.'

[49] *ces tombeaux gravés d'inscriptions.*

[50] 'those pompous marbles which a cold sorrow has raised to departed pride *(l'orgueil qui n'est plus)*.'

[51] 'and when from there I carried my looks upon.'

[52] *encens ;* in the singular.

[53] *était bien au-dessus de tous ces vains mausolées.*

[54] 'but they only spread a few *(quelques)* flowers on the little *(le peu de)* way which remained to her to make towards.' The adverb *peu* is often thus used substantively, in the sense of 'the small quantity,' just as *le trop* (literally 'the too much') means 'the excess;' but we do not say *le beaucoup.*

[55] 'There elapsed one or two Sundays without her appearing at church at her usual place.'—'usual,' here, *accoutumée.*

[56] See **Muly Moluc**, note [7].　　　[57] 'a kind.'

[58] *rendu le dernier soupir.*

POOR RICHARD.

[1] This admirable production of Dr. Franklin is known in France under the title of *La science du bonhomme Richard.*

[2] *J'ai ouï dire.* The verb *ouïr* ('to hear') is old and defective; it is only used now in the infinitive and the compound tenses (as here, in the compound of the present indicative).

[3] 'at a place where.'

[4] Simply, *pour une vente à l'enchère.*　　　[5] *de la dureté.*

[6] *s'adressant à un bon vieillard en cheveux blancs et assez bien mis, lui dit.*

[7] *de ce temps-ci.*　　　[8] *en peu de mots ;* or, *en raccourci.*

[9] *'Le sage entend à demi-mot.'* This form of the Proverb is little used ; the following are the current sayings : *'A bon entendeur, demi-mot* (or, *salut,* or, again, *peu de paroles).'*

[10] *et souvent on emploie 'bien des mots pour ne pas dire grand'chose'* (Proverbial).

[11] See **A Turkish Tale**, note [13].—'Poor Richard,' *le bonhomme Richard.*

[12] *s'expliquer ;* or, *dire sa façon de penser.*

[13] 'to gather around,' *faire cercle autour de.*—'gathering . . . he ;' alter this construction, which is not grammatical.

[14] *Nous sommes cotés pour le double.*

[15] 'three,' &c., *pour le triple.*—'four,' &c., *pour le quadruple.*

[16] *et, pour ces impôts-là, le percepteur ne peut nous obtenir ni diminution ni délai.*

[17] *'Aide-toi, le Ciel t'aidera'* (Proverb).

[18] *exigerait de ses sujets la dixième partie.*

[19] *est bien plus exigeante chez la plupart d'entre nous.*

[20] *use plus que le travail ; la clef est claire tant que l'on s'en sert.*

[21] See D e r v i s, note [12].

[22] *'Renard qui dort la matinée n'a pas la gueule emplumée'*(Proverb).

[23] *nous aurons le temps de dormir dans la bière.*

[24] *des biens ;* and invert this phrase, thus, 'the most precious of,' &c.

[25] *'Le temps perdu ne se répare* (or, *recouvre) point'* (Proverb).

[26] Simply, 'time enough is always,too short.'

[27] *Debout donc et à la besogne,—à la besogne, dans un but utile.*

[28] *et attrape à peine le bout de son ouvrage à la nuit.*—'while ;' *et, d'autre part.*—The French proverbs on this subject are, "Qui dort grasse matinée ('lies in bed till late in the morning,' 'sleeps it out') trotte toute la journée ;" and, "Qui dort jusqu'au soleil levant, vit en misère jusqu'au couchant ;" and, also, "Trop dormir cause mal vêtir."

[29] *l'a bientôt attrapée.*   [30] 'give health, wealth, and wisdom.'

[31] *Activité n'a que faire de souhaits.*   [32] 'of hunger.'

[33] *'Nul bien sans peine'* (proverbial)·

[34] *il faut m'aider de mes mains, faute de.*

[35] Supply the ellipsis.   [36] *écrasées d'impôts.*

[37] *un métier est* (or, *vaut) un fonds de terre.* The nearest French Proverb to this, is, "Il n'y a point de si petit métier qui ne nourrisse son maître."

> "Travaillez, prenez de la peine :
> C'est le fonds qui manque le moins."

[38] 'which combines *(réunit)* honor with *(et)* profit.'—'office,' *emploi.*

[39] *sans quoi,* or, *autrement.*   [40] *laborieux.*

[41] *La faim regarde à la porte du travailleur ; mais elle n'ose pas y entrer.*

[42] *commissaire.*   [43] *découragement.*

[44] *Il n'est que faire que vous trouviez un trésor ni qu'il vous arrive un riche héritage.*

[45] *pendant que c'est.*

[46] *'Un bon* aujourd'hui *vaut mieux que deux* demain' (Proverb).

[47] *Ne remets jamais à demain* (or, *au lendemain) ce qu tu peux faire* aujourd'hui (or, *le jour même).*

[48] Turn, 'If you were in the *(au)* service of a good master, would you . . . ,' &c.—'that he should,' &c. ; *qu'il vous surprît les bras croisés* (figurative, and much used, for *à ne rien faire,* 'doing nothing,' 'idle').

[49] 'But you are.'

[50] Use a synonymous expression here, in French, (and there *is* one,) to avoid the unnecessary repetition of the same.—Likewise, translate here 'idle' by, *à ne rien faire.*

[51] 'in gloves,' *ganté* (just as we say *botté*, 'in boots'); but translate here, '*Jamais chat emmitouflé* ('muffled') *ne prit souris*' (Proverb).

[52] *à la longue 'les gouttes d'eau savent la pierre*' (Proverb).

[53] *coupe.*

[54] *font tomber.* The French have the following proverb, which presents this idea inverted: "On n'abat pas un chêne au premier coup."

[55] The construction, in French, must be, either, 'The diligent man will obtain this leisure,' or, more forcibly, 'This leisure, the diligent man will obtain *it ;*' but the English construction is not allowed.

[56] Simply, 'are two.'

[57] *Bien des gens voudraient vivre uniquement d'industrie, sans travailler.* There is no fear of any ambiguity, here, as *vivre d'industrie* is always used in a bad sense.

[58] *échouent.*　　　　　[59] *le travail au contraire.*

[60] 'they'll run after you.'　　　[61] 'is not in want of shifts.'

[62] *me donne le bonjour.*

[63]　　　　"Arbres ni gens ne s'accommodent guère,
　　　　　　D'un constant changement :
　　　　. Oui, croyez-moi, plus souvent l'on prospère
　　　　　　Sans déménagement."

[64] '*Trois déménagements valent un incendie*' (Proverb).

[65] *Puis ailleurs.*　　　　　[66] *Et ailleurs encore.*

[67] The French have, upon this, the following proverb: "On ne trouve jamais de meilleur messager que soi-même."

[68] *Le Bonhomme dit aussi.*

[69]　　　　"Par la charrue entends-tu t'enrichir ?
　　　　　Il faut alors de ta main la tenir."

[70] The French proverb in common use is, "Il n'y a rien de tel que l'œil du maître."

[71] Turn, 'In the things of this world, it is not faith which saves, but doubt.'

[72] The French have the following proverb: "Nul ne fait si bien la besogne que celui à qui elle est."

[73] *Faute d'un clou, le fer du cheval se perd.*

[74] 'for want of a shoe, one loses the horse.'—'rider was lost ;' turn, . . . 'is lost.'

[75] *le tout.*

[76] The French proverb used here would be, "Pour un point Martin perdit son âne."

[77] *Voila pour.*　　　　　[78] *à mesure que.*

[79] *et mourra sans le sou.*

[80] '*Grande chère et petit testament*' (Proverb).

[81] "Adieu fonds, quand la femme, au thé qui trop s'adonne,
　　　　Laisse là rouet et tricot ;
　　Et que son homme aussi, pour le punch abandonne
　　　　Scie ou rabot."

[82] *l'Amérique n'a pas enrichi l'Espagne, parce que ses dépenses ont toujours dépassé ses recettes.*

[83] *Renoncez donc à ;* or, simply, *Laissez là.*

[84] *et des charges du ménage.*

[85] Turn, 'one vice costs more to nourish than.'

[86] *par-ci par-là* (familiar), to avoid repeating unnecessarily the same expression for 'now and then,' a little above.

[87] *ne tirent pas à conséquence.*

[88] '*Les petits ruisseaux font les grandes rivières*' (Proverb).

[89] Turn, 'It only requires (use *falloir*) a small leak *(fente),*' &c.

[90] *Les gens friands seront mendiants.*

[91] '*Les fous font les fêtes, les sages en ont le plaisir*' (Proverb).

[92] *et peut-être seront-ils en effet vendus au-dessous du prix coûtant* ('cost price'),—or, *prix courant* ('current price').

[93] *n'en avez que faire.*

[94] '*Qui achète ce qu'il ne peut, vend après ce qu'il ne veut*' (Proverb).

[95] *Réfléchis bien avant de profiter du bon marché.*

[96] 'or that the purchase, by the strait which it brings.'

[97] *Les bons marchés ont ruiné nombre de gens.* The proverb is, "Les bons marchés ruinent," 'Good bargains are ruinous'—or, 'empty the purse,' or, 'A good bargain is a pick-purse.'

[98] *ont fait jeûner leur ventre.*—'Many a one,' *Bien des gens ;* or, simply, in the interrogative form, *Combien.*

[99] 'Far from being,'   [100] Supply the ellipsis.

[101] *brillent à la vue, combien de gens s'en font un besoin !*

[102] *les gens du bel air.* This expression is always used in a bad sense,—ironically.

[103] Simply, 'have maintained themselves by industry and frugality.'

[104] 'in which case,' &c.; turn, simply, by 'which proves that.'

[105] *sur ses pieds est plus grand.*

[106] *gentilhomme,* here.   [107] 'had.'

[108] 'without knowing how this fortune had been acquired.'

[109] 'It is day, they thought;' see V i c a r of W a k e f i e l d, n. [81].

[110] 'what does so paltry an expense make on such a sum ?'

[111] Turn, 'But by dint *(à force)* of taking out of *(puiser à)* the meal-tub, without putting anything in it, we find the bottom of it.'

[112] 'as says poor Dick; and it is then, it is when the well is dry *(à sec,* here) that they *(on).*

[113] 'followed.'   [114] '*Argent emprunté porte tristesse*' (Prov.).

[115] *et, de fait, non seulement à l'emprunteur, mais au prêteur même, lorsqu'il a affaire à certaines gens.*

[116] *il veut rentrer dans ses fonds.*

[117]   "L'orgueil de la parure, abominable vice,
       Nous vole notre bourse en flattant un caprice."

[118] 'a beggar that cries as loud.'

[119] 'and with a great deal more sauciness.'

[120] *pour que vos anciennes et vos nouvelles acquisitions ne jurent pas entre elles.*

[121] *réprimer.*   [122] Add, 'in size.'

[123]   "Le grand vaisseau peut risquer davantage ;
          Mais toi, petit bateau, tiens-toi près du rivage."

[124] *de.*   [125] Put this verb and the next two in the present.

[126] *envie du paraître.*   [127] *éveille la jalousie.*   [128] *s'endetter.*

[129] Turn, 'because, not having any money to lay out *(débourser)*, we hope to dress *(nous parer*, in this sense, not *nous habiller)* gratuitously.'

[130] *au terme fixé.*

[131] Simply, *vous inventerez de pitoyables excuses.*

[132] We cannot dispense with *en*, here, if we use *venir* (as *venir à* means 'to happen to'), *en* is not, after all, strictly necessary with *arriver*, which we may very well use, instead of *venir*, in the sense of the text.

[133] *dans les mensonges les plus tortueux et les plus vils.*

[134] Turn, 'Lying is but the second vice ;' but leave the construction of the rest of the sentence as it is.

[135] 'Debt carries lying upon its back, says he again on *(à)* this subject.' We must obviously use a different turn from the English, as 'to ride' is *montrer à cheval* (or, *à âne*, &c.), or, elliptically, *monter*, when the rest is well understood : the former expression, of course, could not do, and the latter would decidedly be ambiguous and obscure *(monte la dette* would certainly be understood to mean, though it would make no sense with what precedes, 'raises—increases the debt,' and *monte sur le dos*, &c., to signify merely, '*gets* upon the back, &c.).

[136] *courage*, here.   [137] 'a ;' and likewise, just after.

[138] *sus ;* followed by no article.   [139] 'are.'

[140] *est un attentat formel à ;* leave out 'and,' after 'please.'

[141] 'and that such . . . &c., is.'   [142] *pour briller.*

[143] Turn, 'is authorized to *(à)* deprive you, at his pleasure *(selon son bon plaisir).*'

[144] 'for a slave' (see Cæsar's Career, &c., n. [25]).

[145] 'if you are not.'   [146] 'have made.'

[147] Use the singular, and without any article.

[148] *forment une secte superstitieuse, observatrice des jours.*

[149] *Le jour de l'échéance.*

[150] *à mesure que*, in this sense,—indicating a progress, succession, or proportion.

[151] '*Fais une dette payable à Pâques, et tu trouveras le carême court*' (Proverb).

[152] 'and able to.' The English construction is not allowed in

French, on account of the want of symmetry it exhibits in those two parts of the attributes which are separated by 'and.'

153   "Gardez pour vos besoins, pour l'âge de retour:
       Le soleil du matin n'est pas pour tout le jour."

Or, in four lines :—

     "Gardez pour les besoins et l'âge de retour,
       Gardez pour la soif une poire,
       Si vous voulez reboire:
       Le soleil du matin n'est pas pour tout le jour."

This idiomatic expression, *garder une poire pour la soif*, corresponds to 'to lay something by for a rainy day.'

154 'than to keep one warm.'

155 '*Il vaut mieux se coucher sans souper que de se lever avec des dettes*' (Proverb).

156   "Gagne autant que tu peux ; du gain fais un trésor:
       C'est la pierre qui change argent et cuivre en or."

157 *cette pierre philosophale.*

158 *l'impôt.*

159 'is that of.'

160 Supply the ellipsis.

161 'they would be quite useless to you.'

162 See Pope to Wycherley, note 14.

163 'a school that costs dear ;' or, 'a school where lessons are dear.' Do not confound *cher*, adverb, with *cher*, adjective: the adverb, of course, is always invariable.

164 'and yet they do not learn much *(grand'chose)* in it.'

165 Use *savoir* in preference to *vouloir.*

166 'do not listen to.'

167 'she will not fail to rap your knuckles *(de vous donner sur les doigts).*'

168 Use *faire.*

169 *et chacun enchérit.*—'auction ;' simply *vente*, here, instead of *vente à l'enchère*, as, by using the latter expression at the beginning of this extract, we thus stated, once for all, what kind of sale it was.

170 'to find,' in this sense, *voir*, or *s'apercevoir.*

171 *brave homme.*   172 'had said.'

173 'The frequent quotations which he made must have tired *(avaient dû fatiguer).*'

174 *bon sens*, here.   175 *Quoi qu'il en soit.*

176 *de mettre cet écho à profit pour moi-même.*

177 'stuff for,' *de quoi me faire.*

178 'to make the old one (leave this last word out) last.'

179 *si tu peux en faire autant, tu y gagneras autant que moi.*

180 'thine,' &c. ; turn, 'at thy service.'

Dr. JOHNSON to the EARL OF CHESTERFIELD.

[1] *articles.* [2] See Hearers and Doers, n. [19].

[3] Never separate thus, in French, the subject from the verb (see Cowper to S. Rose, n. [25], and Sir Roger de Coverley, n. [2]).

[4] *abord.*—'your Lordship;' turn, 'you, my Lord;' (*son abord*, here, would sound awkward.)

[5] See Muly Moluc, note [7]. [6] *et étranger au grand monde.*

[7] *de voir dédaigner ce qui, si peu que ce soit, est tout pour lui.*

[8] 'seven years, during which.' [9] *moment.*

[10] Invert. [11] *finit par connaître.*

[12] 'The attention which you have deigned to give (to grant) to.'

[13] 'would have been kind if it had come sooner.'

[14] *jusqu'à présent que.* [15] *il n'y a pas de.*

[16] *à ne point reconnaître* (or, *voir*).

[17] *de ;* or you may leave it out. [18] *jusqu'ici.*

[19] See The Rivals, note [74].

[20] *je me disais* (styled myself) *autrefois avec une si vive joie mêlée d'orgueil.*

[21] *de votre Seigneurie ;* and, in such cases as this, observe, in French, exceptionally, the same construction as in English : not only is it more civil to put first the title of the person whom you address, but, besides, this construction is more regular, as your own name will then follow immediately, as it ought, 'humble obedient servant,' or whatever else you may think proper to style yourself.

THE NATIVE VILLAGE.

[1] *des manches de lignes ;* or, *des gaules.* [2] 'like a child.'

[3] 'as though,' *que.*—'were to ;' use *aller.*

[4] When *excepté* follows the noun, it agrees with it both in gender and number ; when preceding the noun, it remains invariable.

[5] *non-réalité* (coined for the purpose).

[6] 'I wandered . . . into,' *Après avoir erré.*

[7] 'it is to have joined (use *se joindre*) to an old maiden aunt of mine (*une vieille fille de tant à moi*).

[8] *Il me semble que je les vois encore se balancer en rasant le sol.*

[9] *et aussi.*—'cooings :' use the singular, that the ellipsis (of 'was there,' already expressed, rather than of 'were there,' not expressed before) may be correct.

[10] 'My father and my mother.' Translate so on account of 'both,' which follows : for the same reason that we do not use *parent* in the

singular, in this sense, we cannot say either *deux parents* in the same sense,—*deux parents* simply means 'two relatives.'

[11] *car on eût dit que,*—to avoid too frequent repetitions.

[12] *J'aurais bien voulu revêtir toutes les formes, tous les attributs d'un enfant.*

[13] 'by an exaggeration of the fancy.'

[14] 'I asked.'   [15] See Tit for Tat, note [20].

[16] 'and it was only after that, that I dared to go.'

[17] *sur.*   [18] *Je continuai ma route;* or, *Je passai outre.*

[19] Remember that this construction is not French.

[20] 'upôn it,' *dessus.*   [21] 'not unfrequently,' *assez souvent.*

[22] *On n'y faisait mention que de.*

[23] *Où enterre-t-on donc toutes les mauvaises gens?* (Pope to Wycherley, n. [6].) When the adjective *tout* precedes *gens*, it sometimes forms, by being put in the masculine, an exception to the rule just mentioned (the present case, however, is within the rule). The above-mentioned exception with regard to *tout*, takes place :—1st, when *tout* is the only adjective which precedes, as *tous* (masc.) *les gens ;* and, 2nd, when *tout*, though not being the only adjective preceding, is coupled with another adjective which has the same termination for both genders, as *tous* (masc.) *les habiles gens, tous* (masc.) *les jeunes gens ;*—but we must say, as above, *toutes* (fem.) *les mauvaises gens*, as the adjective *mauvais* (masc.) has a different termination *(mauvaise)* in the feminine.

[24] *orne*, or *pare*, or *décore.*

[25] 'when dead;' see Cowper to S. Rose, note [10].

[26] *C'est un des traits de la nature humaine qui font que je l'aime* (or, *qui me font l'aimer*).

ON FORMING A TASTE FOR SIMPLE PLEASURES.

[1] 'On the formation of the taste of.'   [2] Use *revêtir.*

[3] 'All that, will exclaim . . . . , is but.'

[4] 'the truth of these reflections.'

[5] 'he is deaf—*i. e.,* dead, insensible—*(sourd)* to the melody ... &c.'

[6] Turn, 'and leaves to be inhaled *(à,* and the infinitive active) by *(à)* his menial rustics that,' &c.

[7] *par une négation ;* or, *négativement ;* or, *par la négative.*

[8] *prendre part à ;* or, *participer à.* Observe that *participer* followed by *de* means 'to participate,' in the sense of 'to be of the same nature ;' whereas, when followed by *à,* it means 'to partake of,' 'to participate,' in the sense of 'to share (in).'

[9] *s'empêcher de,*—with the infinitive, in this sense.

[10] *en quelque sorte.*   [11] *qui en font un véritable paradis.*

[12] *profusion d'agréments.*

[13] *Les roues de sa voiture résonnent sur le pavé* (or, *par les rues*).
[14] 'where he pursues.' [15] *parfums.*

SCENE FROM THE PLAY OF "MONEY."

[1] 'neice,' &c.; simply, 'his sister's daughter.'

[2] 'not taller than that.' [3] Simply, *la sienne* ('his).

[4] *après avoir mangé, pour lui faire plaisir, d'un de ses maudits pilaux au curry?*

[5] 'finest.'

[6] *car il était glorieux* (or, *fier*) *comme un paon, le cher oncle.*

[7] *Et laid! . . . . . . ne m'en parlez pas;* or, more concisely, *Et d'une laideur . . .*

[8] 'Poor (see Sophia's Little Bird, note [33]) dear man! Alas, yes, indeed.'

[9] *A merveille.*

[10] *Comme elle est fine, cette petite fille-là!* or, simply, *Comme elle est fine!*

[11] 'Not in the least,'—as rendered several times before.

[12] *blague* (very familiar) *que tout cela, enfant, blague d'un bout à l'autre* (or, *depuis A jusqu'à Z*).

[13] *A la faveur* (or, *Par le moyen—Sur la foi*) *de;* or, simply, *Sur.*

[14] *par an.*

[15] 'I obtained credit enough to be able to spend 800*l.* (*en dépenser huit cents*).

[16] *le père Liardeur;* or, *le père Lalésine.*—'Dicky Gossip,' *Jean Ducancan.*

[17] *un corps électoral.* [18] *aussi bien posé.*

[19] *La blague, ma chère enfant, il n'y a rien comme la blague.*

[20] *foi.* [21] *te donner du relief;* or, *faire florès* (fam.).

[22] *tu te présentes bien dans un salon;* or, simply, *tu te présentes bien.*

[23] *j'avais jeté les yeux sur.* [24] *chercher à trouver.*

[25] *faire* is often quaintly used, with such a construction, instead of *être,* in relation to a person's appearance or qualities.

[26] *original.* [27] *il n'a pas un écu vaillant.*

[28] *je veux être pendu.*

[29] We say, *tenir à distance,* without any article, in this sense: the literal translation, therefore, will not do here, and you must change the construction a little.

[30] *C'est ce qui te trompe;* or, *C'est en quoi tu te trompes.*

[31] *à.*

[32] *traitement;* or, *appointements;* or, *honoraires;*—*salaire* and *gages* mean 'wages,' the former, of workmen, and the latter, of servants,

[33] 'produces a good effect;' or, 'looks well *(fait bien).*'

[34] Use *m'en débarrasser* (or, *déliverer*, or, *défaire*).

[35] Supply the ellipsis, which is not French.

LORD CHATHAM'S SPEECH.

[1] 'your.'

[2] Simply, *mais j'affirme.*

[3] *en répondre.*

[4] *Cette mesure fera voir.*

[5] *leur enlever;* or, *les priver de.*

[6] 'there will remain still to them.'

[7] *Qu' importe que* (with the pres. subj.); or, *Quand même* (with the conditional): or, simply, *Quand* (with the conditional).

[8] *voyage*(or,, better, *marche) à travers.*

[9] *d'après.*

[10] *dons gratuits.*

[11] *l'impôt sur les navires* (impôt qu'on levait pour la construction des navires).

[12] *sympathique.*

[13] Leave out 'an,' here; but if there was a comparison established (ex., 'he fought as a lion'), 'a,' or 'an,' should be translated.

[14] *subtilités.*—'attempting,' *tendant.* Notice that present participles are essentially invariable, in French, except when used adjectively.

[15] 'the great senates;' or, 'the first senates.'

[16] *pas de.*

[17] *réclamer la préférence sur;* or, *vouloir être mis au-dessus de.*

[18] 'a national union founded on a principle.'

[19] 'on,' &c., *en allant aux voix.*

[20] 'to hide themselves;' or, 'to show themselves no more.'

[21] 'such or such.'

[22] *je vous en suis* (or, *je m'en porte) garant;* and leave out 'that.'

[23] *J'y engage ma réputation.*

[24] *sentiment;* or, *disposition.*

[25] 'whatever they may be.'

[26] Once more, avoid this kind of construction (Turkish Tale, n.[26]).

THE DEFEAT OF THE SPANISH ARMADA.

[1] Use *aligner*, here (a naval term), not *ranger* (a military term).

[2] 'in a length of some seven miles from one horn to the other.'—'some,' *environ*, or, *quelque.*

[3] 'The vast vessels sailed slowly on, having the wind behind them *(ayant le vent en poupe)* which blew from the southwest.' We say, likewise, in the same sense, *avoir* (and also *filer*—'to sail on') *vent*

arrière (i. e., lit., 'to have—to sail on with—the wind right aft—astern').

⁴ *par derrière.* ⁵ *Un combat en chasse.*

⁶ 'a still greater number.'

⁷ 'to close with,' *joindre ;* or, *en venir aux prises (aux mains,* as well, if speaking of men) *avec.*

⁸ *à virer de bord ;* or, *à louvoyer.*

⁹ 'relatively but few losses.' ¹⁰ *avec raison,* in this sense.

¹¹ *de.* ¹² Use the singular.

¹³ *doit savoir choisir ses vaisseaux* (or, *ses bâtiments de guerre)*; *qu'il soit bien persuadé qu'un combat naval exige quelque chose de plus que de l'audace.*—Some persons still use *vaisseau de guerre,* but this expression forms now a kind of pleonasm, as *vaisseau* alone implies a *war*-ship, whilst *navire* is said of any other ship (merchant vessel or &c.); *bâtiment* is the general term for all kinds of ships.

¹⁴ *se battre à distance, et en venir à l'abordage.*

¹⁵ 'To clap together *(mettre ensemble)* ships.'—'in a swift;' turn, 'of a swift ship.'

¹⁶ *est* (or *c'est) le fait* (followed by *de,* not by *à*— 'to').

¹⁷ 'to lie off,' *être* (or, *se trouver) devant* (or, *à la hauteur de).*

¹⁸ *prirent le large.*

¹⁹ This was the name of an ancient Venetian kind of galley.

²⁰ *aborda par accident.*

²¹ *et échoua sur la côte* (or, simply, *échoua) ;* or, *et fit côte.*

²² *côte de Flandre.* Always use the name of the country, instead of the adjective, in such a case as this.

²³ 'the day appeared.'

²⁴ 'they obeyed,' &c. ; turn, 'she (i. e., *la flotte*—fem.) obeyed,' &c. 'Now was,' &c. &c. ; turn, 'It was for the English a precious opportunity of coming seriously to action, and of preventing for ever the Spaniards from letting loose *(lâcher)* the fleet of the Duke—the prince —of Parma *(Parme)* against England ; and that opportunity was admirably used *(mise à profit).*

²⁵ *à former et à serrer leur ligne* (a naval term).—The military term is, *serrer les files.*

²⁶ *Dunkerque.*

²⁷ 'the' should not be repeated, as both adjectives qualify the same noun.

²⁸ Simply, *Mais laissons parler un écrivain contemporain, H—.*

²⁹ 'affray' *(échauffourée)* would now be the word, here.

³⁰ 'having put itself again *(de nouveau)* in order of battle.'

³¹ 'There ;' put 'within sight of Gravelines' last, and put a full stop after 'Gravelines.'

³² 'to get the wind of,' *gagner le vent* (or, *le dessus du vent) sur* (or, *à).*

³³ *rade,* in this sense ; and turn, 'the road of C—.'

[34] 'rather than change *(de,* besides *que,* before the verb).'

[35] We should say, now-a-days, 'and standing only upon the defensive.'

[36] 'although.'

[37] 'warlike,' in this case, *bien armées en guerre.*

[38] *en grandeur.*   [39] Simply, *agilité.*

[40] Obsolete, for 'wished,' 'liked.'   [41] Use *presser vivement.*

[42] *à force de leur lâcher* (or, *tirer*) *des bordées coup sur coup.* There is a misconception to be guarded against, here: *coup* is not used exactly for *coup de canon* (firing of a gun), though it might be said to mean that, indirectly, in this particular case; the idiomatic expression *coup sur coup* ('one after another') may be said of almost anything, as, *e. g.,* "Après maints quolibets (low jokes) renvoyés *coup sur coup.*"

[43] *une grêle de boulets* (or, *de fer*) *et de plomb.*

[44] *projectiles* (missiles).—'failed,' after 'until.'

[45] Give to the whole of this old English style a modern French construction.

[46] 'to join with,' *rallier* (a naval term.'

[47] *percés d'outre en outre* (or, *de part en part*)—or, *traversées des deux bords* (naval)—*par les boulets.*

[48] *firent également force décharges d'artillerie; force,* used thus adverbially, means 'plenty of.'

[49] *Il revient peu d'honneur au gouvernement anglais, du fait.*

[50] 'so deficiently . . . as to be unable;' turn, 'too deficiently . . . to be allowed (or, enabled).

[51] simply, *dans cette journée* (in this battle).

[52] Use *remmener.*

[53] 'to combats that promised more glory.'

[54] 'to chase,' as a naval term, *donner chasse* (or, *la chasse*) *à.*

[55] *vincible;* a new (French) word, little used as yet.

[56] *s'éloigner.*   [57] *en se dirigeant vers la Norwége.*

LITTLE EPPIE'S MISCHIEF.

[1] *pour lui permettre de grimper dans des endroits dangereux.*

[2] *à monter une nouvelle pièce d'étoffe.*

[3] *elle en avait tiré cette conséquence philosophique, que.*

[4] *sur une tablette.*   [5] *bien plus sage qu'à l'ordinaire.*

[6] *Ce ne fut que lorsqu'il eut besoin de.*

[7] *interrogeant d'un regard effrayé.*

[8] *Une sueur froide couvrait son front.*

9 *Il restait une espérance, c'était que.*
10 *il n'y avait rien qui pût la faire distinguer.*
11 *Croyant d'abord, dans son trouble, voir.*
12 *dont l'été diminuait la profondeur en laissant une large bordure.*
13 *et qu'il pourrait lui arriver du mal.*
14 *Que cela ferait une impression suffisante.*
15 *lui offrait la perspective d'un nouvel amusement.*
16 *en venir aux extrémités.*
17 *en tremblant d'avoir.*
18 *L'emploi du trou à charbon ayant ainsi manqué complètement son effet, la confiance de Silas dans l'efficacité de cette punition se trouva fort ébranlée.*

THE MONKEY AND THE TWO CATS.

1 *à soumettre le cas à un singe.*
2 *Notre arbitre accepta avec empressement.*
3 *prenant une balance.*
4 *ce morceau est plus lourd que l'autre.*
5 *il enleva d'un coup de dent.*
6 *pour rétablir l'équilibre.*
7 See § 14.
8 *il leva l'audience.*

THE YOUNG PHILOSOPHER.

1 See § 46, 1.
2 *mettant pied à terre.*
3 *s'échappa.*
4 *voyant ce qui se passait.*
5 *courut à travers champs.*
6 *faisait un coude.*
7 *ses belles couleurs et son air enjoué.*
8 *tu as ratrappé.*
9 See § 3.
10 *Vraiment?*
11 See § 17.
12 *dis-moi.*
13 *Oui, beaucoup, par ce beau temps.*
14 *Mais n'aimerais-tu pas mieux jouer?*
15 *agréable.*
16 See § 2, 3.
17 See § 46, 14.
18 *Depuis quand avez-vous été?*

[19] *See § 27, 12.*   [20] *See § 46, 42.*

[21] *Si.*   [22] *Qu'est-ce que cela ?*

[23] *Par exemple des balles.*   [24] *mon frère Tom.*

[25] *des ballons qu'on lance à coups de pied.*

[26] *pour faire des commissions.*

[27] *voyez-vous.*   [28] *je n'y tiens pas beaucoup.*

[29] *See § 17.*   [30] *See § 46, 43.*

[31] *Cela m'est bien égal.*

[32] *J'aimerais autant n'en pas avoir du tout.*

[33] *See § 30, 2.*   [34] *tu es un vrai philosophe.*

[35] *Ce n'est rien de mal j'espère.*

[36] *M. L. (riant) Non, certainement.*

[37] *un A B C.*   [38] *Dis-le à ton papa.*

[39] *et ajoute que c'est.*   [40] *J'y vais.*

THE BROKEN FLOWER-POT.

[1] *en faïence de Delft.*

[2] *s'éparpillèrent aux pieds de mon père.*

[3] *Transporté dans une autre sphère par ses études.*

[4] *Miséricorde !*

[5] *répondit à cet appel.*   [6] *communicatif.*

[7] *des gens silencieux et réservés.*

[8] *et vous saviez combien j'y tenais.*

[9] *Ne dis donc pas de menteries* (childish and familiar expression, instead of *mensonges*).

[10] *hardi comme un page.*

[11] *qui s'était décidé à retirer son chapeau.*

[12] *tout grands ouverts.*

[13] *il était là tout à côté.*

[14] *et il ne l'a pas fait exprès.*

[15] *ajouta-t-elle tout bas.*   [16] *en s'approchant.*

[17] *pour voir quelle figure vous feriez.*

[18] *à la première histoire pareille que vous essaierez de.*   See also § 37.

[19] *d'un air suppliant.*

[20] *dont vous lisez les histoires.*   [21] *les larmes aux yeux.*

[22] *aphorisme (phrase sentencieuse).*

[23] *See § 46, 1.*   [24] *par la même occasion.*

[25] *à quelqu'un de cet endroit.*

²⁶ *Je courus à la maison chercher la boîte.*

²⁷ *chemin faisant.*

²⁸ *Pourquoi cette question, mon enfant?*

²⁹ *C'est que comment alors ma boîte de dominos peut-elle se changer en.*

³⁰ *celui qui veut sérieusement devenir bon.*

³¹ See § 36.   ³² See § 37.

³³ *la joie qui vint affluer à mon cœur, faillit m'étouffer.*

³⁴ See § 34.   ³⁵ *marchands d'articles de fantaisie.*

³⁶ *toutes sortes de jouets et de jolis riens.*

³⁷ *à propos.*

³⁸ *cherchait le compte dans ses livres.*

³⁹ *mon petit garçon que voici.*

⁴⁰ *cette boîte à ouvrage qui fut mise en loterie l'hiver dernier et dont vous avez engagé Mrs. Caxton à prendre quelques billets.*

⁴¹ *n'épargna pas ses éloges.*

⁴² *dût-elle nous coûter le double.*

⁴³ *ne détruisez pas les effets que cette leçon doit produire jusqu'à l'heure de sa mort.*

SYDNEY SMITH BUILDS HIS HOUSE.

¹ *mon bénéfice.*   ² *Fraîchement arrivé de Londres.*

³ *de prendre à ferme.*   ⁴ *un presbytère.*

⁵ See § 34.   ⁶ *on lui avait dit.*

⁷ *en vint à un tel degré de confiance.*

⁸ *il découvrit un beau jour que.*   ⁹ *il se mit à rire au point que.*

¹⁰ *Je me mis sérieusement à l'œuvre.*   ¹¹ See § 46, 9.

¹² *et je m'enfonçai dans mon grand fauteuil.*

¹³ *argile.*   ¹⁴ *tombaient en syncope.*

¹⁵ *me retarda de six semaines.*

¹⁶ *murs tout ruisselants d'humidité.*

¹⁷ *je remplis à la lettre la promesse que j'avais faite à.*

¹⁸ *ce qui, si l'on tient compte de mon ignorance, demandait une certaine dose d'énergie.*

¹⁹ *je la baptisai du nom de Fagot.*

²⁰ *dans le fonds de magasin.*

²¹ *cette voiture étant en assez mauvais état.*

²² *les enfants du village criaient après, et les chiens aboyaient.*

INDEX.

S. R. URBINO'S CATALOGUE

OF

STANDARD EDUCATIONAL WORKS

For the Study of Foreign Languages.

Readers will confer a favor on the Publisher by notifying him of any errors
that may be found in any of his works.

FRENCH.

Otto's French Conversation Grammar. Thoroughly revised by FER-
DINAND BÔCHER, Professor of Modern Languages at the Massachusetts
Institute of Technology. Twenty-ninth edition. 12mo. Cloth $1.75

French Reader to the above. By Prof. F. BOCHER. With Notes and Vo-
cabulary 1.50

L'Instructeur. A practical Introductory French Grammar. By L. BONCŒUR.
12mo. Boards 0.75

Lucy: Familiar Conversations in French and English. 12mo.
Cloth 0.75

Hamilton, Smith, and Legros' French and English and English
and French Dictionary. 2 vols. bound in one. Half binding 9.50

Contes. Par Mme. CARRAUD and others. 1.00

Le Petit Robinson de Paris. Par E. FOA. Avec Vocabulaire. 12mo.
Paper, 60 cents; cloth 0.90

Contes Biographiques. Par E. FOA. Avec Vocabulaire. 12mo. Paper,
75 cents; cloth 1.00

Pour une Epingle. Par J. T. DE ST. GERMAIN. Avec Vocabulaire. Paper,
50 cents; cloth 0.75

Le Clos-Pommier, par A. ACHARD; and Les Prisonniers du Caucase.
12mo. Paper, 60 cents; cloth 0.75

Le Robinson Suisse (Illust.) 1.75

Le Roman d'un Jeune Homme Pauvre. Par O. FEUILLET. 12mo.
Paper, 75 cents; cloth 1.25

Le Conscrit de 1813. Par ERCKMANN-CHATRAIN. With Notes by
Professor FERDINAND BÔCHER. Paper, 75 cents; cloth 1.25

La Petite Fadette. Par G. SAND. With Notes by Professor FERDINAND
BÔCHER. Paper, 75 cents; cloth 1.25

Les Nouvelles Genevoises. Par TOPFFER. 12mo. Paper. 1.12

Cinq - Mars; ou, Une Conjuration sous Louis XIII. Par A. DE
VIGNY. 12mo. Paper. 1.25

De l'Allemagne. Par MADAME DE STAEL. Paper 1.85

Fables de Lafontaine (Illust.) 75

Theatre Classique. Cloth 1.75

La Tulipe Noire. Par A. Dumas 50

Ancient History for Translation into French. By L. FLEURY 90

The Translator. English into French, With Notes. Cloth 1.25

Les Princes de l'Art: Biographies des Peintres, &c. 1.50

MODERN FRENCH COMEDIES.

La Cagnotte. Par MM. E. LABICHE et A. DELACOUR $0.3C
Le Village. Par O. FEUILLET 0.25
Les Femmes qui Pleurent. Par MM. SIRAUDIN et THIBOUST 0.25
Les Petites Miseres de la Vie Humaine. Par M. CLAIRVILLE . . . 0.25
La Niaise de Saint Flour. Par BAYARD et LEMOINE 0.25

WITH VOCABULARIES.

Trois Proverbes. Par TH. LECLERQ 0.30
Valerie. Par SCRIBE. 0.30
Le Collier de Perles. Par MAZERES 0.30

PLAYS FOR CHILDREN, WITH VOCABULARIES.

La Petite Maman; par Mme. de M. Le Bracelet. 12mo. Paper . . 0.25
La Vieille Cousine; par E. SOUVESTRE. Les Ricochets. Paper . . . 0.25
Le Testament de Madame Patural; par E. SOUVESTRE. La
Demoiselle de St. Cyr; par LA COMTESSE DROHOYOWSKA. Paper . 0.25
La Loterie de Francofort; par SOUVESTRE. La Jeune Savante; par
Mme. CURO. Paper. 0.25

COLLEGE SERIES OF MODERN FRENCH PLAYS,

WITH ENGLISH NOTES, BY PROFESSOR FERDINAND BÔCHER.

12mo. Paper.

I. La Joie Fait Peur. Par Madame de GIRARDIN 0.30
II. La Bataille de Dames. Par SCRIBE et LEGOUVÉ 0.40
III. Le Maison de Penarvan. Par JULES SANDEAU 0.40
IV. La Poudre aux Yeux. Par MM. LABICHE et MARTIN 0.40
V. Les Petits Oiseaux. Par MM. LABICHE et DELACOUR 0 40
VI. Mademoiselle de la Seigliere. Par J. SANDEAU 0.40
VII. Le Roman d'un Jeune Homme Pauvre. Par O. FEUILLET . 0.40
VIII. Les Doigts de Fee. Par E. SCRIBE 0.40
IX. Jean Baudry. Par A. VACQUERIE 0.40

Vol. I. (I. to IV.), bound in cloth $1.50
Vol II (V. to VIII.), ,, ,, ,, ... 1.75

In Preparation,

COLLEGE SERIES OF FRENCH CLASSIC PLAYS.

TESTIMONIALS.

I use "Otto's French and German Grammar" at our College
and the Collegiate School, and can confidently recommend it to all
similar institutions.

OCTOBER, 1864.　　　　　　　H. STIEFELHAGEN,
Professor Modern Languages at King's College, Windsor, Nova Scotia.

I have examined many works designed for pupils studying the
French Language, and among them consider "Otto's French Conversation Grammar," revised by Bôcher, superior to any other.
I use it in my classes, and take pleasure in recommending it as
admirably adapted for the purpose.

A. WERTHEIM,
Professor of Modern Languages at the University, Louisville, Kentucky.

Among many works designed for pupils studying the German
language, I consider "Otto's German Conversation Grammar"
superior to any other. I use it in my classes, and take great
pleasure in recommending it as the best work which has yet been
published for the use of schools.

A. WERTHEIM,
Professor of Modern Languages, Louisville, Ky.

BOSTON, March, 1865.

Mr. URBINO, Boston.

MY DEAR SIR, — "Otto's French Grammar" revised by Prof.
F. Bôcher, is the best Instructor ever published; at present, it sur-
passes Fasquelle and the Ollendorf System, by its simplicity. It
has the advantage of telling, in one page, what the others require
three or four to express. The rules for the pronunciation do honor
to the reviser; besides, the lessons are so well placed, and so progressive, that they bring the student into the difficulties of our
language with very little exertion. At last, permit me to thank
you for taking, by this publication, the most tedious part of our
labor as teacher. It is so clear, that any one could teach the
French Language without difficulty.

I remain, Sir, yours,

P. J. BORIS,
Professor of French Language,
18, Boylston Place, Boston.

MARLBORO', Mass., April 9, 1866

S. R. URBINO, Esq.

DEAR SIR,—I used Otto's Grammar in two classes at Edgartown High School,—one class quite advanced. The testimonial of Mr. Hunt and others expresses my sentiments, and you may use my name if you choose.

Yours truly,

A. H. WENZEL,
Principal of Marlboro' High School, late Principal of Edgartown High School.

WOBURN, April 12, 1866.

Mr. URBINO.

DEAR SIR,—The opinion of Messrs. Hunt and others with respect to the merits of Otto's French Grammar, I indorse in full.

Yours truly,

THOMAS EMERSON.
Master of Woburn High School.

S. R. URBINO, Esq.

MY DEAR SIR,—I am now using Otto's French Grammar, revised by Prof. Bôcher; and, so far as we have advanced, I am better pleased with it than with any other work of the kind which I have previously used.

Yours truly,

GEORGE N. BIGELOW.
Principal.

STATE NORMAL SCHOOL, FRAMINGHAM,
April 16, 1866.

BOSTON, April 16.

Mr. URBINO.

DEAR SIR,—I have used Otto's French Grammar for several years in all my schools, and find it much superior to all those which I have as yet seen, for the simplicity and clearness with which the rules are explained.

I am happy to say, also, that your series of French Comedies and your other French books can be highly recommended for school and private reading: they are well selected.

Yours truly,

O. BESSAU.

NEW HAVEN, CONN., April, 1866.

S. R. URBINO, Esq.

DEAR SIR,—I thank you for the specimens of your French and German series, which you have been kind enough to send me from time to time. You are doing, as it appears to me, a real service to the study of these two languages, especially of the German, in our country, by putting at reasonable prices so excellent editions of classical and unexceptionable texts within the easy reach of teachers and scholars. I have used several of them in my classes, and can heartily recommend them to instructors of pupils of every grade.

I am, sir, very respectfully,

Your obedient servant,
WILLIAM D. WHITNEY,
Prof. of Sanscrit and Instructor in Modern Languages at Yale College.

OTTO'S FRENCH CONVERSATION GRAMMAR. Revised by Ferdinand Bôcher. Boston: S. R. Urbino.

It is with great pleasure that we direct the attention of all lovers of the French language to this publication. . . . It is particularly fit for a text-book in our schools, for the following reasons : 1, It is short, without being superficial. 2, It is logically arranged. 3, Its course of instruction is a progress, in a natural gradation, from the easy to the difficult. 4, Theory and practice go hand in hand. 5, Its outside appearance does credit to the publishers.—*Michigan Teacher*, May, 1866.

BATES COLLEGE, June 9, 1866.

S. R. URBINO, Esq.

DEAR SIR,—Will you allow me to thank you for calling my attention to Otto's French Grammar, edited by Prof. Bôcher? We have used it thus far this year with entire satisfaction. It will be but simple justice to award it the first place as a text-book for mature students, at least among all with which I am acquainted, whether published in this country or in Europe. Its chapter on Pronunciation is surpassingly complete and practical.

Gratefully yours,
B. F. HAYES.

TRINITY COLLEGE, December, 1864.

Mr. S. R. URBINO, Boston.

I have used "Otto's German Grammar" since you issued the first edition, and like the method better than any other. We use it in all the Institutions in Hartford where the German is taught, and the pupils learn with rapidity, and like their Instruction book.

I have also used the French and Italian Grammars based on the same method, your "College Series of Modern French Plays," and your other French publications, and recommend their use in Colleges and Schools.

Respectfully yours,

L. SIMONSON.

I have used "Otto's French Grammar" revised by Prof. Bôcher, ever since it was published. To say that it is superior to Ollendorf's Method, and Fasquelle's, it is not to say much. But I think it is better than most Grammars introduced into this country, though coming to us with far less claims and pretensions than them all.

BOSTON, March 28.   J. B. TORRICELLI.

STATE NORMAL SCHOOL,
FRAMINGHAM, Mass., March 25, 1865.

S. R. URBINO, Esq.

MY DEAR SIR, — I have used "Otto's German Grammar," and prefer it to any other book of the kind with which I am acquainted.

Yours truly,

GEO. N. BIGELOW.

ST. LOUIS, May 15, 1865.

Mr. S. R. URBINO, Boston.

I take pleasure in recommending "Otto-Bôcher French Conversation Grammar." It combines the practical with the theoretic, and is so arranged as to make the acquisition of the French language easy and pleasant to the student. Its adoption in my classes has given entire satisfaction.

M. GIBERT,
Instructor in French at the Mary Institute

English High School,
Boston, March 31, 1866.

Mr. Urbino.

Dear Sir,—After a six months' trial, we conclude that Otto's French Grammar, revised by Bôcher, is superior in all respects to any other of which we have knowledge.

Very respectfully yours,

E. HUNT,
WILLIAM NICHOLS, Jr.,
ROBERT EDWARD BABSON,
THOMAS SHERWIN, Jr.,
Teachers in English High School.

I fully and emphatically indorse the above opinion respecting Otto's French Grammar.

JOHN D. PHILBRICK,
Superintendent of Public Schools

State Normal School.
Salem, Mass, April 8, 1866.

S. R. Urbino, Esq.

My Dear Sir,—We are using in our school several of your publications with much satisfaction. This is especially the case with Otto's French Grammar. As a class text-book, this grammar is, in my opinion, the best in the market.

For the excellence of your school-books, both as to matter and typographical beauty, you richly merit the gratitude of teachers and pupils.

Yours truly,

D. B. HAGAR.

Cambridge, April 6, 1866.

Mr. S. R. Urbino.

Dear Sir,—*Otto's French Grammar*, revised by Bôcher, which we have been trying with a class in our "shorter course of study," has been adopted for all our French classes, in place of Fasquelle's book. We can heartily indorse the testimonial from the teachers in the Boston High School.

Yours truly,

W. J. ROLFE,
Master of Cambridge High School.

Dictation Exercises. By E. M. Sewell, auther of "Amy Herbert," and by L. B. Urbino. Boston: S. R. Urbino.

"We are already deeply indebted to Miss Sewell, and this little book adds one item more to the list of valuable books which she has furnished to us and our children. This is emphatically a school-book with a soul in it, and we think nothing can exceed the skill and ingenuity with which these exercises are drawn up. No teacher can glance at it without at once perceiving its importance to him: and in our opinion, in the teaching and spelling, it has not its equal.— *Transcript.*

Dictation Exercises. By E. M. Sewell and L. B. Urbino. (pp. 174.) Boston: S. R. Urbino.

"Bad spelling is so common, in spite of all our schools. that it is worth the while even of an accomplished writer like the author of 'Amy Herbert' to prepare a good spelling-book; for such is the volume before us.

"It is arranged, however, on a plan so novel, in English, as to deserve special attention. The words are arranged in continuous, though rather comical, sentences, which are to be written down, from dictation, by the learner. The lessons are progressive, and cannot fail to interest more than the old columns of disconnected words. It is well printed by Mr. Urbino."— *Commonwealth*

If a child of average capacity, that has been drilled in an ordinary spelling-book, and then subjected to a course of lessons in this book of Dictation Exercises, cannot spell correctly the words of the language, it would prove, what I do not believe, that correct spelling *cannot* be attained by *all* pupils, by seasonable *study* and *drill.* I believe that every public and private school in America would be greatly benefited by using this valuable treatise.

Very truly yours,

WILLIAM E. SHELDON.

VASSAR FEMALE COLLEGE,
POUGHKEEPSIE, N.Y., April 19, 1866.

Mr. URBINO.

DEAR SIR,—I am now using many of your publications in this college, of which I am particularly pleased with the German and Italian Grammars, and with Bôcher's College Series of French Plays. Otto's German Grammar, I regard as a model of scholarly thoroughness and practical utility; and the other works of your list, as far as I have examined them, recommend themselves, not only by the beauty of their mechanical execution, but also by the intrinsic merit of their redaction.

Very truly yours,

W. I. KNAPP,
Professor of Ancient and Modern Languages and Literature.

STATE UNIVERSITY OF MICHIGAN,
April 20, 1866.

I HAVE adopted Otto's German Conversation Grammar as a text-book in this University, and have no hesitation in recommending it as by far the best grammar of the German language published in this country. No other work with which I am acquainted presents such a happy combination of what are called the Analytic and Synthetic methods of instruction. The statement of principles is clear and philosophical; and the examples which illustrate the niceties of their application are all that could be desired. The French Grammar, by the same author, is similar in plan, and possesses equal excellences.

I have examined the standard educational works for the study of foreign languages, published by S. R. Urbino, and take pleasure in recommending them to all students of the languages and literatures of Europe. They are well selected, amply elucidated by English notes, and, in convenience of form and excellence of typography, are all that could be desired.

E. P. EVANS,
Professor of Modern Languages and Literature.

S. R. URBINO, PUBLISHER,
14 Bromfield Street, Boston.